ADVERSE EFFECTS
Women and the Pharmaceutical Industry

ADVERSE EFFECTS

Women and the Pharmaceutical Industry

Edited by

KATHLEEN McDONNELL

The
Women's
Press

CANADIAN CATALOGUING IN PUBLICATION DATA

Main entry under title:
Adverse effects: women and the pharmaceutical industry

Co-published by International Organization for Consumers Unions.
Bibliography: p.
ISBN 0-88961-108-4

1. Women–Drug use. 2. Drug trade. 3. Women's health services. I. McDonnell,
Kathleen, 1947- II. International Organization of Consumers Unions.

HD9665.5.A49 1986   338.4.761383   C86-094869-2

Cover drawing by Heather Walters
for the *Side Effects* project. *Side Effects,* a play on women and
pharmaceuticals, was originally developed and produced by INTER-PARES
and the Great Canadian Theatre Company for Women's Health
Interaction (WHI)
Cover and book design by Liz Martin
Photo credits: p. 9 by FDA Consumer,
p. 87 by ILO and p. 173 by AM/Keystone
Production by Susan Siew and Ellison Chung

The views expressed in the articles are those of the authors and do not necessarily
reflect those of IOCU and the Women's Educational Press

Published by Women's Educational Press
229 College Street, no. 204
Toronto, Ontario M5T 1R4

Printed and bound in Canada

CONTENTS

◂▸

ACKNOWLEDGEMENTS

IN OUR SEARCH for an editor for this book, we were looking for a woman with not only proven expertise in writing and editing and a background in health issues but also the competence to handle the complex co-ordination involved in an international anthology like this. We were fortunate to have found Kathleen McDonnell, who combined all these qualities and added to them care and thoroughness.

We are thankful to all the contributors to this anthology, most of whom are actively involved in advocacy activities for women's health. They made time to write for this book. Their contributions clearly reflect their experience, commitment and concern.

It was again a pleasure to work with Liz Martin of the Women's Press Collective in Toronto, Canada, who designed the cover and the book.

The final phase of this project was the team work of several people at the IOCU office in Penang. Thanks to Susan Siew and Ellison Chung for assembling the book and overseeing its production, to Penny Fernandez and Jerry Jambu who took on the arduous job of proof-reading and to Siva who made countless trips to the typesetters.

We also gratefully acknowledge the financial support from the Swedish International Development Authority which made this work possible in the first place.

◄►

FOREWORD

Anwar Fazal
Director, IOCU Regional Office for Asia and the Pacific

THE WORLD is littered with inappropriate, wasteful and even unsafe medical remedies aggressively promoted by those hungry for profits and careless of life. Women in particular, because of their own special health needs and their role in providing for the health care of others, are victims of violence and targets for manipulation by both the pharmaceutical industry and population control policy-makers.

It was against this backdrop that the idea for *Adverse Effects* was conceived. The book sets out to examine and expose, through a series of case studies, how women the world over are exploited and injured by drugs. It would be a dismal story if this was the only focus, but in country after country the case studies demonstrated that women are organising, and succeeding, in fighting the violence and manipulation.

The book is also exciting for two other significant processes.

Firstly, it is a manifestation of the growth of citizen's groups, whose efforts have been synergised in a variety of networks, formed co-operatively and able to respond globally to issues. IOCU is proud to have initiated one of them — Health Action International (HAI), which has an active women and drugs working group.

Secondly, this publication provided a platform for the interaction of a team of health activists, led by Kathleen McDonnell. They brought together different skills, various backgrounds, and both industrialized and Third World perspectives. With this diversity, also came a rare combination of commitment, courage, care and competence.

Behind every such venture there is usually a special person. This particular anthology was born out of the efforts of Foo Gaik Sim, Head of IOCU's Information and Research activities. It was Gaik who conceptualised the idea for such a book, raised the necessary funds, contacted the relevant people and co-ordinated the team of people who worked on this project.

The work of people like Gaik and Kathleen and a host of others is making a real difference in the way in which health needs for women are being perceived and met and most of all in enlarging the power of ordinary people to gain more control over their own lives.

This book will add to that effort.

9th October, 1986

◄►

Introduction: Finding a Common Ground

Kathleen McDonnell

IN 1984 THE MOST successful consumer boycott in world history came to an end. In October of that year, Nestle, the Swiss multinational, finally agreed to abide by the international code for the marketing of infant formula adopted by the World Health Assembly three years before. The code was intended to eliminate some of the company's most blatant marketing practices, such as the distribution by hospitals of free samples of baby formula, and placed restrictions on others. The adoption of the code was the result of over a decade of fierce campaigning by a global coalition of consumer, church, and human rights groups, which claimed that the shift from breast-feeding to bottle-feeding promoted by Nestle and other baby formula manufacturers was killing and maiming untold numbers of infants in the Third World. The success of the Nestle boycott was a watershed of the international consumer movement and sowed the seeds for action on many other fronts.

Chief among these new movements that are gaining prominence in the eighties is the consumer campaign against unsafe as well as unnecessary drugs. It has become increasingly clear in recent years that there are thousands of drugs on the world market that are dangerous, ineffective, overpriced, or some combination of these. Because of the tremendous variation in drug licensing pro-

(Thanks to Anita Hardon and Lenny Achthoven of WEMOS for their help in developing the ideas contained in this article.)

cedures in different countries, many drugs that cannot be sold in developed nations like the United States or that are available only by prescription in those countries are freely available over the counter in poorer nations. One of these drugs, chloramphenicol, is sold throughout Latin America, for example, and is given to infants and young children suffering from diarrhea, often in the form of chocolate-flavoured tablets popularly known as "sweeties for diarrhea." But this same drug has been linked to aplastic anaemia, a severe and often fatal blood disease, and in the United States its use is restricted to life-threatening conditions. Another anti-diarrheal drug, clioquinol, has been shown to cause blindness and paralysis in some users and was the subject of a successful $150 million liability suit against the manufacturer, Ciba-Geigy, in Japan in 1977. Yet surveys done in the early eighties showed that the drug was still widely available in a number of countries, where it was used routinely for the treatment of mild diarrhea.

Many of the most dangerous and inappropriately marketed drugs are aimed at children. Steroidal preparations sold as appetite and growth stimulants are widely available over the counter in many Third World countries. Stunted growth and loss of appetite are among the most common results of malnutrition; yet, spurred on by misleading advertising, many worried parents spend their money on these drugs instead of on badly needed food for their children, in the hope that they will bring about some magic cure. The real problem, of course, is not medical, but social and economic: despite the pharmaceutical companies' claims, poverty cannot be cured by taking a pill. Other steroid drugs are promoted just as inappropriately. Some preparations containing the male hormone testosterone are marketed throughout Africa as male "potency pills," which promise to "improve the quality and quantity of erections" and "give a man that something extra."

There have been some important attempts to curb the problem of unsafe, unnecessary, and overpriced pharmaceuticals. In 1977 the World Health Organization (WHO) launched its Action Program on Essential Drugs, which designated about two hundred drugs that were known to be safe, cheap, and of proven therapeutic value. In June 1982, the government of Bangladesh introduced its New Drug Policy, taking the unprecedented step of ordering off the market over 1,500 drugs considered hazardous or of questionable value. Since 1981 Health Action International (HAI), an informal network of consumer groups from over twenty-six countries, has been engaged in a variety of action and education projects on drugs, such as the development of "anti-advertisements" aimed at two dangerous anti-diarrheal drugs, Lomotil and clioquinol.

Recently women active in health and consumer movements have begun to ask, "Where do we fit into all this?" What has been missing is a specifically woman-centred perspective on drug issues. But is such a perspective really needed? Is it not enough to talk about unsafe drugs themselves? Why single out women's concerns in particular?

First, throughout the world women are the "pathway" for medicines within the family. It is women who are the health care providers — for their children, husbands, elderly parents, and relatives. It is women who decide what drugs to buy and who administer them. Yet this central role of women in health care has gone largely unnoted, perhaps precisely because it is so universal, so apparently "natural" for women to assume responsibility for the care and healing of others. Only very recently has this aspect of women's role in the home begun to be studied in any kind of serious way. In 1986 a Canadian study of 165 women found that nearly three-quarters of them shouldered the full responsibility for family health care, with no appreciable help from others. The authors of the study noted the "overwhelming importance of the numberless daily, routine, preventive, monitoring and promotional tasks which serve to maintain and build the health of the family."[1] So deeply entrenched is this aspect of the woman's role that women who worked outside the home were found to be shouldering just as much of the responsibility for keeping the family healthy as the women who did not.

The multinational pharmaceutical companies, however, are only too aware of this "guardian of health" function that women fulfill. As Milagros Querubin and Michael Tan point out in their article in this anthology, drug companies specifically direct their advertising to women, playing upon their desire to take care of their families in the best possible way. And increasingly, women themselves are worrying about the part they play in pharmaceutical consumption. At the 1984 International Conference of Women in Nairobi, many Third World women voiced concern about the safety of the drugs that women in their home countries routinely give their children, such as antibiotics and anti-diarrheals.

Another crucial reason to examine drug issues from the perspective of women is the fact that women themselves use drugs more than men do, most often in ways related to their reproductive capacity. A whole family of hormonally based drugs, including the contraceptive pill, estrogen used in replacement therapy, and would-be abortifacients such as EP drugs, are used almost exclusively by women. Some of these, such as diethylstilbestrol (DES) and EP drugs, are known to be dangerous, yet are still on the market in countries around the world, as several authors in this anthology attest to. Carla Marcelis and Mira Shiva document the stalled campaign to get EP drugs off the market in India. And Anita Direcks and Ellen 't Hoen argue persuasively that we still have not learned the real lessons of the DES debacle.

The hazards of many drugs used by women are still unknown or only suspected, and many others are used incorrectly or too liberally. In her article Ann Rochon Ford shows how the use of hormones is "getting out of hand" in North America and charges that important critical questions are not being asked about such therapies as estrogen replacement and the use of progesterone for premenstrual syndrome. And some questionable marketing practices of the pharmaceutical industry often play a large part in "creating demand" for these drugs. Estrogen is aggressively advertised for a wide range of menopausal symptoms, mainly in the developed countries, while EP drugs are widely but falsely advertised as hormonal pregnancy tests in many parts of the Third World.

The drugs and devices that women use specifically for family planning pose their own particular problems. This is because "family planning" itself is a two-edged sword. On the one hand, the availability of contraceptives gives women the possibility, for the first time in history, to control their own fertility and destiny. But contraceptives can also endanger the health of women. The Pill, for example, may increase the risk of heart disease, and IUDs may cause serious pelvic infection, as Ann Pappert's article discusses. Because contraceptives are used by healthy women rather than by women who need to be treated for an illness, they constitute an alteration of the usual risk/benefit ratio. In fact, the hormonal contraceptives actually create an abnormal state in the body

by preventing normal conception from taking place. Family planning experts sometimes obscure this fact by comparing the risks of
pregnancy and childbirth to the risks of using contraceptives. But
although pregnancy and birth are sometimes dangerous, neither is
an illness, but natural and necessary physiological functions.

So the notion of "informed consent" becomes particularly
crucial where family planning is concerned. Since the use of contraceptives entails some risks to their health, women must be informed of these risks and be allowed to make their own choices ac-
cordingly. And indeed, the notion of "choice" and the "cafeteria"
approach to contraception are universal watchwords in family
planning programs throughout the world.

But the true politics of family planning, especially in the Third
World, cannot be understood in isolation from the ideology of
population control. In most developing countries, large-scale family planning programs exist, not to increase women's control and
autonomy, but to allow governments to exert some degree of control over the size of their populations. Because the developed countries, particularly the United States, have such a stake in the
economics of the Third World, they also have a strong interest in
controlling the size and nature of the work force in these countries
through population-control measures. So the United States heavily
funds family planning programs that promote these aims. Cary
LaCheen's article in this anthology documents meticulously just
how the pharmaceutical industry itself is involved in promoting this
ideology and at the same time working to expand its own contraceptive markets in the Third World.

Because family planning programs are largely aimed at population control, particular kinds of contraceptives are being
developed and promoted in the Third World. These methods, such
as injectables, subdermal implants, and anti-pregnancy vaccines,
tend to minimize the control exerted by the individual woman. Of
these, the only ones in wide use are injectable contraceptives, chiefly Depo-Provera and Net-Oen. Both these drugs have been the
cause of intense controversy. In her article Vimal Balasubrahmanyan explains why health activists are working to keep injectables
out of India's family planning programs. She argues that these
methods cannot be used safely in India and other poor countries,
chiefly because of the lack of proper medical back-up. In another

article, Lynn Duggan examines the medical controversy surrounding Depo-Provera, and shows how this drug has been actively promoted in Thailand and elsewhere to foster the aims of population control rather than reproductive self-determination for women.

Women are the heaviest users of another class of drugs that have nothing to do with biological reproduction but everything to do with female socialization. From minor tranquillizers like Valium to sleeping medications to tricyclic anti-depressants, women are the major consumers of mood-modifying drugs. Studies from a number of countries consistently show that women are prescribed these drugs more often than men, and the reasons for this are inextricably tied up with notions of female passivity and helplessness. Many doctors prescribe mood-modifiers because they help women adapt more readily to an inherently oppressive role, and women turn to them because they help calm the anxieties. And as Jim Harding's article demonstrates, women's tendency to turn to mood-modifying drugs increases as they age, with the major difference that the variance between the sexes lessens as older men increase their consumption of these drugs. The latter could be interpreted as a sad indicator of the fact that only in old age do men, as a group, become as oppressed as women are all their lives.

Although the attention of the consumer movement on pharmaceuticals has concentrated mainly on drug abuses in the Third World, women's issues form a common ground on which the concerns of the First and Third Worlds meet. There are enormous differences in women's situations, of course, and there is no doubt that it is women in the developing countries who face far greater dangers from unsafe drugs, because of inadequate medical back-up and far less stringent controls on the marketing of drugs. North American women, for example, are not subjected to high-pressure advertising to give their children dangerous anti-diarrheal preparations. Nor are they offered incentives to allow themselves to be injected with long-acting contraceptives. On the other hand, women in the developed countries are greater targets for the overuse of tranquillizers and hormonal drugs such as estrogen. What is clear is that, wherever we live, our common position as women exposes us to the risk of unsafe or incorrectly used pharmaceuticals. We are up against a vast, multinational industry whose impact is global, and more and more women in both developed and developing countries are coming to realize that nothing less than a global response is called for. Sari Tudiver's article in this anthology bears testimony to the intense energy that has gone into the formation of women's organizations and networks concerned with pharmaceutical issues in the past few years.

But what influence can these efforts have in the face of a powerful multinational industry determined to hold on to its markets and its profits? Years of campaigning against even the most flagrant drug abuses has shown the daunting difficulties facing consumer groups, as evidenced by the time taken to get drugs like clioquinol off the shelves. Neither measures like the Bangladesh New Drug Policy and WHO's essential drugs program addresses women's concerns in particular. Yet the Bangladesh government has faced tremendous opposition from the international pharmaceutical industry since the new policy was introduced and few other countries have taken concrete steps toward developing lists of essential drugs along the lines proposed by WHO. If measures like these face such opposition, what chance do women's concerns have to be taken seriously and acted upon?

None, really, if the larger issue of health care and the way it is delivered is not addressed. For the problem of unsafe drugs is not simply one of a few "bad apples" that need to be disposed of, for the problem to be solved. Rather it goes hand-in-hand with a global health system with badly disordered priorities, one that is spiralling ever more out of control. This system emphasizes cure rather than prevention and views the body as something like a machine, consisting of discrete parts that can be treated in isolation from each other. It favours expensive drugs and high-tech treatments while systematically disparaging older folk healing traditions as "unscientific" and "quackery."

Drug companies and drugs are not themselves the problem. There is an important place in any effective health care system for the rational use of Western pharmaceuticals. But in many poor countries, it is precisely the most useful and necessary drugs that are in critically short supply, while thousands of questionable and outright dangerous products flood the local pharmacies and village dispensaries.

What is needed is a new philosophy, a new approach to health — one that is paradoxically old as well. This approach combines the rational use of modern pharmaceuticals with a real respect for traditional remedies and healing systems. In many parts of the world, this approach is already being implemented, though not without difficulties and obstacles. Primary health care programs in much of the Thrid World, for example, combine folk medicine and practical wisdom with the judicious use of modern drugs and therapeutics. As the limits of Western, high-tech medicine become clearer, particularly in Third World contexts, traditional methods of healing are being revived and accorded a renewed respect by peoples all over the world.

This trend is parallelled by the growing popularity of what is commonly known as the holistic health movement in many of the developed countries. A highly mixed bag of long-established systems such as homoeopathy and acupuncture holistic health practices have been the cause of controversy, partly because of their alleged lack of a scientific basis, but also because they tend to discourage drug treatments and pose a challenge to the "pill-for-every-ill" mentality that has brought the pharmaceutical industry such enormous profits.

Although at present the global medical system is dominated by men and "male" values, it is perhaps not surprising that women are in the forefront of the new health movements. As Milagros Querubin and Michael Tan explain, women are the key participants in innovative primary health care projects being developed in the Philippines and many other countries. Women's health activists all over the world are working to foster more holistic, less interventionist forms of health care, as well as reviving old and trusted practices such as midwifery and herbal medicine. Clearly, it is these efforts that will transform the global health system into one that truly promotes health rather than profits and disease. Just as clearly, this transformation cannot occur without the active participation and leadership of women throughout the world.

◄►

NOTES

1. Caitlin Kelly, "Care for health is left to women, study says," Toronto *Globe and Mail,* April 23, 1986, p. A5.

I: Women as Drug Consumers

In part I we look at some of the drugs used exclusively or particularly by women and at the problems associated with these drugs. In "EP Drugs: Unsafe by Any Name," Carla Marcelis and Mira Shiva examine high-dose estrogen-progesterone preparations, which are widely used in developing countries as hormonal pregnancy tests and to induce abortion, although they are not effective for either of these users and are believed to be harmful to the fetus. Anne Rochon Ford's article "Hormones: Getting Out of Hand" looks at the increasing use in North America of hormone treatments for such conditions as premenstrual syndrome and the menopause and examines some of the marketing factors involved in this trend. "DES: The Crime Continues," by Anita Direcks and Ellen 't Hoen expresses alarm at the continuing use of this harmful drug in the Third World and presents the case for a world wide ban on the use of DES. In "Mood-Modifiers and Elderly Women in Canada: The Medicalization of Poverty," Jim Harding shows how the trend toward the over-prescribing of mood-modifying drugs to women, first recognized in the early seventies, persists into the mid-eighties, and how these drugs are inappropriately used as medical solutions to social problems, particularly where the elderly are concerned.

EP DRUGS: UNSAFE BY ANY NAME

Carla Marcelis and Mira Shiva

IN MOST DEVELOPING COUNTRIES, poor regulation, the dependence of doctors on drug companies for information about drugs, and people's unquestioning belief in Western medicine make it possible for the pharmaceutical industry to wield virtually uncontrollable power. One consequence is that the industry can continue to sell unsafe products that were long ago taken off Western markets in developing countries. This article examines one of these products, a group of hormonal preparations known as EP drugs.

The history of EP drugs shows that the pharmaceutical companies are in no hurry to correct a dangerous situation when profits are involved and that governments do not always have the ability to do so. This is especially true of drugs used only by women, as in the case of EP drugs.

EP DRUGS: ONE WOMAN'S STORY

When Mercy, a Filipino woman, saw that her period was late, she went to her doctor to find out if she was pregnant. He gave her an injection of Gynaecosid, an EP drug. He did not ask her whether she would want to terminate her pregnancy if she was found to be pregnant. Nor did he say anything about the side-effects or possible risks of the drug he had given her. Three months later her period had still not returned. Mercy went back to her doctor three times, and every time he gave her the same injection, without any examination and again without telling about side-effects and possible risks. After the third visit, the doctor confirmed Mercy's pregnancy. She later gave birth to a boy with a club foot. According to Mercy, the use of EP drugs is very common in the Philippines. Women know of the existence of these drugs and many buy them (if they have the money) every time their periods are late. Doctors who are ignorant that EP drugs are no longer recommended for pregnancy testing still prescribe them for this purpose. Mercy was shocked and angry to hear that these drugs are ineffective and have long been taken off the market in most European countries because they can cause birth defects.

EP DRUGS: THE FACTS

High-dose estrogen-progesterone combination drugs (EP drugs) contain the same female sex hormones as the Pill but at much higher levels. EP drugs have been around for a long time and have been sold under many different brand names. In the 1950s they were brought into the market as a treatment for missed periods since they were thought to start menstruation in women whose periods were delayed and who were not pregnant.

A woman whose period did not start after taking EP drugs was presumed to be pregnant, and so EP drugs also began to be seen as a simple pregnancy test. But because the drug could apparently bring on menstruation, women all over the world have taken and are continuing to take EP drugs to induce abortion. The women hope that a drug that can start menstruation in non-pregnant women may also do so in pregnant women, something that EP drugs do *not* do. Although no pharmaceutical company has ever claimed that these drugs will induce an abortion, doctors in many countries nevertheless prescribe them for this purpose, and the drug can be easily bought over the counter.

The next part of the history of EP drugs is not so new or exceptional. Other hormonal drugs brought into the market for use by women, synthetic estrogen, for example, or the birth control pill, have a similar history of initial use without sufficient research, and a later change in indication and/or dosage. About twenty years after EP drugs came on the market, research began to uncover

Table 1

The most common EP drugs and countries where they have been reported from. This list is far from complete, there are many more EP drugs. Countries are only the ones that have reacted to the HAI research.

Name of Product O/I*	Content	(Dosage)**	Manu-facturer (Countries)***
1. Cumorit Oral O	10	mg norethisterone acetate 0.02 mg ethinylestradiol (2x)	Schering (Th, K, Ph, D.R., Par.)
2. Cumorit Forte I	50 3	mg progesterone mg estradiol benzoate (2x)	Schering (Th, K, Ph, D.R., Par.)
3. Cristerona FP Forte I	10 2	mg progesterone mg estradiol (1x)	Gramon Grador (Par)
4. Cyclogesterin I	10 1 0.05	mg progesterone mg estrogen mg NNdimethy-lacetamide	Upjohn (Peru)
5. Corpubenzon F I	50 3	mg progesterone mg estradiol benzoate	Scanpharm (Th)
6. Amenorone Forte O	50 0.05	mg ethisterone mg ethinytloestra-diol (3x)	Roussel (Th)
7. Disecron Forte I	50 25	mg progesterone mg oestradiol benzoate	Nicholas (I)
8. Degonon F O	100 0.05 0.1	mg ethisterone mg ethinyloestra-diol mg cyanocobala-mine	Cox lab./Ang Nguan Heng (Th)
9. Di-Pro-Oleoso I	12.5 2.5	mg progesterone mg oestradiol benzoate (2-5x)	Organon (Th, Mex)
10. Duoluton O	0.5 0.05	mg norgestrel mg ethinyloestradiol	Schering (I, Mex, K, G)
11. Duosterone I	50 5	mg progesterone mg oestradiol benzoate (2x2)	Roussel (Arg)

Name of Product	O/I*	Content	(Dosage)**	Manufacturer (Countries)***
12. Dosdias	I	12.5 2.5	mg progesterone mg oestradiol benzoate (2x)	Lab. ELEA (Arg)
13. E.P. Forte	O	30 0.06	mg hydroxyproges- terone acetate mg ethinyl estradiol (3x)	Unichem (I, Th)
14. Gestex	O	6 0.1	mg norethindrone mg mestranol (1x)	Medichem (Ph)
15. Gynaecosid = Ginecosid	O	5 0.3	mg methyl estrenolone mg methyl estradiol (2x)	Boehringer Mannheim (D.M., K, Ph. Mal)
16. Gynaecosid = Ginecosid	I	50 3	mg progesterone mg estradiol butinil acetate	Boehringer Mannheim (D.M., K, Ph. Mal)
17. Lut-estron Forte	I	25 3	mg progesterone mg estradioldi- propionate (1x)	MAC (I)
18. Lutoginestryl- F	I	50 5	mg progesterone estradiol benzoate (1x)	Roussel (Mex, D.R., Peru)
19. Menstrogen Oral	O	10 0.01	mg ethisterone mg ethinyles- tradiol (4x4)	Organon (I, Mal)
20. Menstrogen	I	12.5 0.02	mg progesterone mg ethinyl estradiol	Organon (I, Mal)
21. Menstrogen Forte = Metrigen Fuerte	I	50 5	mg progesterone mg estradiol benzoate (1x)	Organon (I, Mal, Mex)
22. Osterone	I	25 2.5	mg progesterone mg estradiol benzoate	Lyka (I)
23. Orasecron Forte	O	60 0.05	mg ethisterone mg ethinyl estradiol (3x)	Nicholas (I)

Name of Product	O/I*	Content	(Dosage)**	Manu-facturer (Countries)***
24. Orgalutin	I	2.5 mg Lynestrenol 0.05 mg ethinyl oestradiol (20x)		Organon (I)
25. Protadol	I	20 mg progesterone 2 mg oestradiol benzoate (2x)		Philalab (Th)
26. Pregnone Forte	O	50 mg progesterone 0.15 mg ethinyl oestratriene 0.1 mg cyanocobala-mine		L.B.S. Lab Ltd. (TH)
27. Progyluton	O	2 mg estradiol valerate (11x) 2 mg estradiol valerate (10x) 0.5 mg norgestrel		Schering (D.R., Mex)
28. Progestradiol	I	12.5 mg progesterone 2.5 mg estradiol benzoate		Lasca (Par)
29. Pregnatest	O	100 mg hydroxy progesterone acetate 0.08 mg mestranol (2x)		Gador (Arg)
30. Synergon	I	10 mg progesterone 1 mg folliculine		Ozimex (D.R.)

Note: By way of comparison, the oral contraceptive Microgynon, made by Organon of the Netherlands, contains 0.15 mg levonorgestrel and 0.03 mg ethinylestradiol.

*   O: Oral.   I: Injectable

**   Number of dosages admitted in consecutive days, e.g. 2x means one dose per day given on two days (= one dose two times).
4x4 means four doses given on four consecutive days (= four doses four times).

*** Countries where use of the drug has been reported.

Countries:
I	= India	Par	= Paraguay
Th	= Thailand	Mex	= Mexico
K	= Kenya	Mal	= Malaysia
Ph	= Philippines	Arg	= Argentina
D.R.	= Dominican Republic	G	= West Germany

evidence that they were unreliable as pregnancy tests and ineffective as a treatment for missed periods. Of even greater concern was the indication that EP drugs might cause birth defects in babies whose mothers took them early in pregnancy. Since the most common use of EP drugs at that time (the 1970s) was for hormonal pregnancy testing, women who took the drug for this purpose but who later turned out to be pregnant unknowingly exposed their unborn babies to the possibility of birth defects. Women who now take EP drugs to induce abortion run the same risk. Even worse since we now know they are ineffective as abortifacients.

One Indian study that was reported in the *International Journal of Gynaecology and Obstetrics* in 1976 compared two groups of 150 women who had no other signs of pregnancy than a delay of fourteen days or less in the onset of their periods. One group was given an EP injection (50 mg of progesterone and 3 mg of estrogen benzoate in oil); the other group was given no EP drug. There was no difference in the number of women starting their menstruation within seven days, demonstrating that EP drugs are ineffective in inducing menstruation. In fact, the women who had not received an EP drug started their periods within one to three days, while the women who had taken an EP drug were more likely to start theirs in four to six days; thus the treatment even appeared to *delay* the onset of menstruation. The women who were given EP treatment complained significantly more often of vomiting and headaches than those who were not.

Of the women treated with the EP drug who did have their periods within seven days, nearly 20 per cent turned out *not* to be pregnant, indicating that EP drugs are also unreliable as pregnancy tests.[1] The Royal College of General Practitioners' survey into the outcome of pregnancy found a 10 per cent abortion rate after the administration of Primodos, an EP drug manufactured by Schering. Two other researchers, Brotherton and Graft, reported an incidence of 7.6 per cent spontaneous abortion following the use of hormonal pregnancy tests.[2] The spontaneous miscarriage rate (i.e., without drugs) is 10 per cent. It is clear then, that EP drugs are also ineffective as abortifacients.

In 1974 the *British Medical Journal* reported that synthetic sex hormones, such as EP drugs, may damage the fetus and that the association between the taking of such hormones during pregnancy and congenital birth defects, including defects of the heart, circulatory system, central nervous system and limbs, had been reported.[3]

In 1981 the World Health Organization recommended that hormonal pregnancy tests no longer be used. On the use of EP drugs as a treatment for missed periods, the report says: "Women who are not pregnant will have their menses further delayed if hormones are administered."[4]

In the mid-seventies such respected medical journals as the *Lancet* and the *British Medical Journal* carried editorials advising doctors against using EP drugs as hormonal pregnancy tests.[5] A number of Western countries then began to withdraw these drugs from the market — among them Australia in 1975, the United States in 1975, the United Kingdom in 1977, Belgium and Austria in 1978, and Germany in 1980. Others required that warnings on the use of EP drugs during pregnancy be included on the package inserts and disallowed their use for pregnancy testing. But although the growing body of evidence about the dangers of EP drugs was sufficient to bring about a market change in Australia, the United States, and most European countries, hardly anything was done in developing countries. When Australia withdrew EP drugs from the market for pregnancy testing in 1975, WHO informed all other governments of this action and the reasons for it. But developing countries did not withdraw EP drugs from sale in their countries nor adopted measures that would have ensured their safe use.

THE MARKETING OF DRUGS IN DEVELOPING COUNTRIES

In most developing countries, the poor and particularly the women, do not have adequate health care. A 1979 WHO report estimates that in many developing countries up to 70 per cent of the people receive no organized health care at all.[6] Although drugs are not necessarily the best solution in an environment where poverty, hunger, and a lack of clean water and safe housing are the real causes of ill health, they can sometimes save lives. But where there is no efficient system of basic health services, it is almost impossible to distribute drugs safely and effectively. Absurd situation occur. For example, while essential drugs like penicillin are often out of stock, vast numbers of inessential and sometimes harmful drugs are freely available from street stores, even in the smallest towns. Drug regulatory agencies are supposed to carefully weigh the possible benefits of a drug against the risks before allowing it to be sold and subsequently to monitor its use. Underfunded, in the Third World, they cannot carry out even the most basic inspections and controls, and have to rely totally on the pharmaceutical companies for information on drugs.

Pharmaceutical companies are only too ready to take advantage of this situation. Like any other industry, the pharmaceutical industry is in business to make profits. It makes good business sense, if the industry can get away with it, to play down the side-effects, to give more indications for the use of the drug than proven, or to omit contra-indications for the use of the drug. The consequence is that inessential and potentially harmful drugs can more readily be available in developing countries and that drugs withdrawn from sale in developed countries can continue to be sold in the Third World. Furthermore, many essential, life-saving drugs are often out of stock because they are less profitable for the pharmaceutical companies. In her book *Bitter Pills* (1982), Dianna Melrose clearly documents all the complex factors involved in drug marketing and regulation in the developing world. She shows, for example, how the poor in the Third World have an array of questionable products such as vitamin tonics, cough and cold remedies, and anti-diarrheals to spend their money on. Strongly influenced by aggressive advertising, consumers are led to believe that these products are cure-alls and that it is better to spend money on drugs than on food. When one child in a family is sick, the mother pays for an expensive drug because she believes it will cure her child faster. As a result it may well mean the whole family goes without food for a day or two.[7]

In 1983 the disciplinary board of NEFARMA (the Dutch member of the IFPMA — the International Federation of Pharmaceutical Manufacturers Associations) stated in a ruling against the Dutch pharmaceutical company Organon that "pharmaceutical companies have more responsibilities and have to be more careful when marketing drugs in countries where the infrastructure provides less guarantee for a responsible use of those drugs."[8] In other words, the drug industry has even greater responsibility to provide truthful and complete information on their products and be scrupulously ethical in their promotional and advertising practices in Third World countries. If this were so, then EP drugs and other useless and harmful drugs would not still be on the shelves of drugstores in the Third World. But the campaign in India since 1982 for a ban on EP drugs, shows public-interest groups have to fight the pharmaceutical industry all the way.

EP Drugs: The Campaign in India

In the seventies, high-dose estrogen-progesterone combinations became popular in India for pregnancy testing and a variety of gynaecological problems, including menstrual irregularities, dysfunctional uterine bleeding, dysmenorrhea (menstrual pain), premenstrual tension, endometriosis, and post-menopausal syndrome. By 1982 an estimated 180,000 pregnant women in India were using high-dose EP drugs each year. Most of them were unaware of the dangers of these drugs.

The above conditions and a long list of others constituted the "medically accepted" indications for which the drugs were being advertised and used. Gradually, however, these drugs came to be used primarily for inducing abortions and for hormonal pregnancy testing. Anxious women with secondary amenorrhea, terrified at having become pregnant, were often administered an EP drug. The withdrawal bleeding that occurs was often taken as evidence that their pregnancy had been terminated, and is still called "medical" termination of pregnancy as opposed to "surgical" termination of pregnancy (abortion). Many of the women were not pregnant at all but were not having their periods for other reasons. EP drugs were initially popularised among doctors and chemists by medical representatives of the companies producing these drugs. Later, women themselves were buying them freely over the counter and taking them in total ignorance of their possible harmful effects on the fetus.

In 1975, when Australia withdrew EP drugs from the market, the Indian Director General for Health Services (DGHS) decided to allow the products to be marketed but curtailed their use in pregnancy testing and issued the following warning:

There is some evidence to show that hormonal preparation when used during pregnancy may lead to fetal abnormalities and as such
these *should not be used during pregnancy or for pregnancy
diagnosis unless a decision has been taken to terminate the pregnancy
after its confirmation.*

Later, in February 1979, Dr. Palaniappan, a professor of obstetrics
and gynaecology at Kilpauk Medical College in Madras, published
a study in the *Journal of the Indian Medical Association,* showing
that 31 per cent of fifty-two mothers who took hormonal preparations in early pregnancy gave birth to malformed babies. But it was
not until January 1982, at a workshop in Pune organized by the
Voluntary Health Association of India (VHAI) that the problem of
EP drugs was seen as a very serious one. It was the first time that individuals, groups involved in health and consumer issues, journalists, academicians, and members of people's science movements
had been brought together specifically to study drug issues in India
and to discuss co-ordinated action. The decision to launch the first
national campaign on EP drugs was made at this historic meeting.
Later, on March 8, International Women's Day, the campaign was
officially launched. The campaign was based on a number of con-
siderations. The dangers of EP drugs echo those of thalidomide in
their possible effect on unborn babies, and it would not be difficult
for the public to understand and support a campaign to ban the
drug. Moreover a campaign against the use of dangerous drugs by
women, especially in pregnancy, would draw in women's groups as
well as human rights groups and other social action groups, apart
from consumer and health groups.

Health personnel and consumers were largely ignorant of the
dangers of the drug. In fact, it was found that most doctors and patients had not heard of the warnings issued by WHO and the Director General of Health Services in 1975 — seven years earlier —
against the use of EP drugs for pregnancy testing: it was obvious
that there was no effective dissemination of information, even of
the government's own directives. In addition, the continued recommendation for "pregnancy testing" on the package inserts and in
the Monthly Index of Medical Specialities (MIMS) clearly showed
that these warnings were being flouted. The campaign on EP drugs
would be to demonstrate the need for monitoring the drug information being given out by the companies.

The EP campaign was launched under the banner of a network of groups called "Health Action India," a name that was later changed to the All India Drug Action Network (AIDAN). The first part of the campaign consisted of obtaining, screening, compiling, and disseminating information, including a list of the various brand names of EP drugs sold in India.

In the period that followed, network members reviewed the medical literature on EP drugs; screened newspapers, and magazines, the pharmaceutical indexes; and then compiled and disseminated information. During this laying down of the ground-work for the campaign it became clear that the ignorance of health personnel and consumers was colossal and that the use of EP drugs to induce abortion much wider than had been imagined.

Table 2

Brand Names of Estrogen-Progesterone Combination Drugs Available on the Market in India

1. Lut-Estron Forte (Mac)
2. E.P. Formo (Unichem)
3. Gaestaplon (Khandelwal)
4. Seorodyl (Allenburys)
5. Cyclenorm (MPI)
6. Iymoral (Organon)
7. Duoluton (German Remedies/Schering)
8. Oestrone (Lyka)
9. Disecron Forte (Nicholas)
10. Menstrogen (Organon)
11. Norlestrin (Parke-Davis)
12. Orasecron Forte (Nicholas)
13. Orgaluten (Organon)
14. Primolut-N (German Remedies/Schering)
15. Voldys 21 (Glaxo)

The campaign soon began to have impact. On March 18, 1982, EP drugs was again a subject of the authorities' attention. A directive was issued that the following warning was to be added: "*Not to be used for pregnancy test and in suspected cases of pregnancy.*" This warning, printed in indelible ink was to be displayed prominently on cartons of injectables and the tablet packages. The warnings also added that these products were indicated only for secondary amenorrhea (absence of periods not due to pregnancy).

This action was a positive step, but AIDAN continued to apply pressure on the government through a variety of measures, including petition and letter-writing campaigns and the distribution of information handouts about the dangers of EP drugs. Many popular magazines carried features on the dangers of EP drugs. Socially conscious doctors, journalists, feminists, and health activists pooled their knowledge, skill, and efforts. New allies, like Mrs. Bhanumathy of Madras, were made. She had been single-handedly fighting against the use of EP drugs since 1979 and had been writing extensively in newspapers and magazines and to health authorities.

In the face of such intense public pressure, the authorities sought the views of its own medical experts, who concluded that there was no reason for any continued use of high-dose EP drugs. So in June 1982 the Drug Controller of India banned EP drugs on the following grounds: (1) that many other countries in the world had banned them, (2) that the drugs had been widely misused, and (3) that there were safer substitute drugs available in India.

Although the ban order was issued on June 26, 1982, the ban on production was to be effective only from December 31, 1982, and the ban on sales from June 30, 1983. AIDAN strongly criticized this aspect of the ban order. Why, members asked, was a drug designated as hazardous by the Drug Control Authorities allowed to be sold for another six months to a year, just to allow the stocks to be finished? Why were the drug industry's profits being given priority over the health of women and unborn babies? Nevertheless, campaign members felt victorious at having brought about the ban of a dangerous drug. This was the first co-ordinated campaign to lead to the banning of a drug in India.

And true to form, the drug industry gathered its forces almost immediately to contest the ban. A flood of newspaper articles followed, carrying headlines like "Dispute over ban on drugs," "Uproar over drug ban," and "Ban on estrogen-progesterone drugs hastily conceived?" In July the pharmaceutical company Unichem informed the Drug Controller of India that high-dose EP drugs were essential and that they were required for treatment of gynaecological disorders, and in August the Organization of Pharmaceutical Producers of India (OPPI) also made representations to the government against the ban. OPPI maintained that to its knowledge there were no non-hormonal substitutes available in India for the treatment of a host of menstrual disorders such as dysfunctional uterine bleeding, endometriosis, polymenorrhea, oligomenorrhea, amenorrhea and post-menopausal syndrome. The drug companies claimed that if EP drugs were being misused, the problem should be dealt with through education, not by a ban. The industry's views were widely reported in the media and managed to cast some doubt in the mind of the public.

In July 1982 Unichem Laboratories, producers of EP Forte, and another company, Nicholas, filed a writ petition against the ban in the Bombay High Court. Later Organon, a Dutch pharmaceutical company, did the same in the Calcutta High Court. Consumer groups responded to these actions with their own writ petition in early 1983 against continued sales of banned drugs, including EP drugs. In their petitions, the drug companies denied that EP drugs were dangerous, pointing to the government's own decision to continue to allow the sales of drugs for a period of time as evidence that the government did not believe them to be so either. The companies also produced affidavits from prominent doctors and organizations like the Federation of Obstetricians and Gynaecologists of India protesting the ban. Many of these affidavits were similarly worded. The notation "c.c.: Organon" appearing at the bottom on some of the affidavits was evidence that the affidavits were duplicates of a master copy prepared by Organon.

Shocking to say, the drug authorities succumbed to this pressure and in Janury 1983, a stay order against the ban and a two-year extension of the production licence were granted by the court. Despite the fact that only three companies went to court to obtain the stay order — all other brands of EP drugs by other companies were allowed to remain on the market as well. A campaign built on the blood, sweat, and tears of numerous groups and socially conscious individuals all over the country was suddenly checkmated. Moreover, a health problem was being dealt with in the courts, where a wealthy and powerful industry was able to exploit legal loopholes. The stay order was a bitter setback.

AIDAN attempted to keep up the campaign and approached leading doctors, pharmacologists, and experts from WHO and drug regulatory bodies in other countries for their views. Questions about the continued sale of EP drugs were asked in Parliament. But Dr. Gathoskar, the Drug Controller of India, and other government officials pleaded helplessness as the case was in the courts. *To date no effort has been made from any official quarter to get the stay order vacated.*

Faced with our failure to get the ban implemented and a complex legal situation, VHAI made an effort to mount its own legal action, which proved difficult, especially in regard to obtaining evidence and affidavits from women and doctors. Even though many doctors are fully aware of the dangers of EP drugs, they are reluctant to get involved in court actions.

EP DRUGS IN INDIA TODAY

Even though EP drugs are still being sold, there is much greater knowledge of their dangers. VHAI has tried to popularize the use of the Nancy Kit, based on the immune assay of human chorionic gonadotrophin (HCG) in the urine, among women's groups for safe pregnancy testing. One of the reasons women bought EP drugs over the counter was that they did not want to visit doctors as this involved travel, waiting, and added expense in consultation fees. They found it easier and cheaper to buy EP drugs from a neighbouring chemist shop.

Traditional attitudes towards menstruation also have a bearing on the EP issue. A delay or absence of periods is considered unhealthy, as it is associated with the retention of "bad" blood in the body. Many diseases are supposedly associated with this condition. Having periods thus has a cultural importance to women. In certain communities a menstruating woman is considered unclean and is not even allowed to enter the kitchen. Among better-educated middle-class women, lack of periods may cause concern, giving rise to a feeling of lack of femininity and womanliness.

It should be noted that women in the traditional Indian society depended on signs and symptoms of pregnancy for confirmation of pregnancy. Trained "dais" and birth attendants diagnosed pregnancy at eight to twelve weeks. But just as increased medicalization of birth control has taken place, so also has unnecessary chemical tampering of women's and unborn children's bodies with EP drugs. When safe urine tests can confirm pregnancy, the continued availability of such dangerous drugs can only be viewed as callous profiteering.

Looking back on the EP campaign, we feel that its most important achievement was that it brought a large number of concerned groups and individuals from different backgrounds together, to work in solidarity. It taught us ways of seeking, using and disseminating information. It gave us courage to challenge irrational statements even when they were made by so-called "prestigious" authorities. The campaign also taught us that such activities require consistent and concerted effort. They can be totally unpredictable and we need to be constantly alert and have reserved capacities to respond to surprises.

At present, the government is in the process of formulating a new drug policy for India, and activists in the EP campaign have had to turn their attention to other drug issues — shortages of essential and life-saving drugs, the continued sale of dangerous drugs, and the need for a rational overall drug policy. In the developing countries, where survival is the main issue, where natural and industrial calamities, and political violence demand urgent attention, and where dangerous drugs and pesticides are sold by the dozen, it is very difficult to give one's undivided attention to one product like EP drugs.

Furthermore, the fact that vested interests could twist the government's arm so easily in a large country like India, which has many technical and scientific resources, gives an indication of the powerful forces that such campaigns have to face.

As of January 1986 the stay order against the EP drug ban remains unchallenged. We had expected that the Drug Controller and government authorities, with the help of the copious evidence provided by groups like VHAI and AIDAN, would reject the drug companies' arguments. But they have not done so. So the EP campaign continues, in India and internationally, and it promises to be an uphill battle, despite the fact that there is no reason for keeping EP drugs on the market.

◄►

NOTES

1. D. Vengada Salam *et al., International Journal of Gynaecology and Obstetrics,* 14 (1976); 348 — 52.

2. Isabel Gal, ''Risks and benefits for the use of hormonal pregnancy tablets,'' *Nature,* Nov. 24, 1972.

3. ''Synthetic Sex Hormones and Infants,'' *British Medical Journal,* editorial, Nov. 30, 1974.

4. ''WHO Scientific Group on the Effects of Female Sex Hormones on Fetal Development and Infant Health,'' WHP Technical Report Series 657, 1981.

5. ''Are Sex Hormones Teratogenic?'' the *Lancet,* editorial, Dec. 21, 1974.

6. ''WHO Drug Policies Including Traditional Medicines in the Context of Primary Health Care,'' Report and Background Documentation, New Delhi, 1979.

7. Dianna Melrose, ''Bitter Pills, Medicines and the Third World Poor'' (OXFAM, 1982).

8. ''Ruling of the Disciplinary Court of NEFARMA on complaint against Organon International's Marketing Practices re anabolic steroids,'' The Netherlands, Dec, 1983.

HORMONES: GETTING OUT OF HAND

Anne Rochon Ford

IN THE MATERNITY WARD of a large hospital in down-
town Toronto, Stephanie lies awake at night, worrying. Two
days ago, while only in the fifth month of her first pregnancy, she
was admitted to the hospital by her obstetrician because her cervix
has begun dilating prematurely. The reason? While Stephanie's
mother was pregnant with her twenty-eight years ago, she was given
a drug that her doctor believed would help her to maintain the
pregnancy, a powerful synthetic hormone called stilbestrol, or DES.
Today, Stephanie's cervic is misshapen because her mother was
given DES at a crucial point in the development of Stephanie's
reproductive organs. When she was admitted to the hospital two
days ago, she was told that she would be given two drugs —
Vasodilan, to arrest the contractions, and Celestone, to help the
baby's lungs develop faster in case it is born prematurely. Since she
was sixteen, Stephanie has known she is a "DES daughter" and has
been watched closely by a physician who is knowledgeable about
DES. She never anticipated, however, that she would have to make
a decision about taking drugs while she was pregnant, a similar
decision to the one her mother faced twenty-eight years ago. The
product of one medical mistake, Stephanie is wondering how safe
these drugs are that the doctors are now giving her. Could her unborn child become the victim of yet another medical mistake?

At the age of thirty-three, Janice is very worried that she still is
not pregnant after two years of "trying." After months of fertility

tests, she is tired of being told to relax. She wants to see some results after all the money she and her husband have spent on specialists. She visits a new specialist who tells her of a drug that has helped women get pregnant in the past. She is suspicious about drugs since her mother told her a few years ago that she had taken DES when she was pregnant. Janice has wondered all along whether the reason she can't get pregnant is that her mother took DES. She discusses it with her husband and decides to take the drug the doctor has suggested. From the day she takes the first pill until one month later, when she manages to conceive, she worries constantly about her decision. She stops taking the drug but continues to worry. Within six weeks, she miscarries. After this painful experience, she is left with the difficult decision of whether or not to go back on the drug. Her doctor reassures her that this drug has "a terrific track record." Wanting to believe him, Janice decides to take the drug again.

In spite of the legacies of DES, thalidomide, and the Dalkon Shield, many of us want to believe that drugs and devices for women are safer today than they were twenty-five years ago. Testing and regulations are much more stringent today than in the days of DES, doctors reassure us, and in the hope of relieving pain, getting pregnant, or carrying a pregnancy to term, women take scores of drugs whose long-term effects are still unknown. Raised in an era when we have come to expect quick solutions to problems, many of us leave our doctors' offices with a prescription in hand.

But the "pill-for-every-ill" mentality is not the only reason that women of our generation are still so willing to take drugs. Concurrent with the development of that mentality has been the trend in modern medicine towards "pathologizing" what in the past were seen as normal processes. From menstruation to menopause, women now have drugs for every aspect and every phase of their reproductive lives and beyond. In spite of the questionable record of synthetic hormones like DES and Provera, and of how little is known about their action on all systems of the body, new uses are being found for this category of drugs all the time. Bloating and mood swings before our period now have a label — premenstrual syndrome — and a drug solution, progesterone. Whereas in the past, women reached menopause, got through it, and went on to a life without menstrual periods, we now have increasing numbers of women being given two hormones, estrogen and progesterone, to keep them menstruating indefinitely.

So myopic, at times, is the vision of modern medicine and so profit-oriented are the drug companies that when the two put their heads together, the best they seem to be able to come up with are drug solutions for drug-induced problems, as in the cases of Janice and Stephanie above. To the objective observer, the era of wonder drugs would appear to be in its heyday, and profits made from synthetic hormones have never looked better.

In the beginning, women had periods. Sometimes they were painful, and so they took herbal concoctions to help relieve the pain. Women (most of them) got pregnant and bore babies. Sometimes they lost their babies in childbirth, or died giving birth. If a woman could not get pregnant, she had to bear the stigma of being called "barren." Sometimes, she accepted this and did other things with her life, but in many cultures she was a virtual outcast. If a woman lived long enough, she eventually stopped having periods. The transition was not always smooth, but she usually got through it. Admittedly, the era before modern Western medicine was no golden age. Women suffered, and they knew that many things simply had to be endured and that many problems had no solution.

Today, for the first time in history, the entire span of the female reproductive years can be controlled with synthetic hormones. Let's consider a hypothetical, though plausible, situation. A girl might begin taking birth control pills (the most widely used form of synthetic hormones) in her teens. Her doctor will probably tell her, "It's safer now than it's ever been," but not explain that the pill alters a normal bodily function — the menstrual cycle — and "tricks" the body into thinking that it is having periods. Nor is the doctor likely to mention that the drug's effect on future fertility is not completely known.

Having been on the pill for ten or fifteen years, she goes off it in her late twenties with the hope of starting a family. It may take her five months to regain her normal periods, and when she does, she suffers from terrible menstrual cramps. Her doctor prescribes an anti-prostaglandin drug (such as Ponstan or Motrin), which is similar to hormones in substance and which can have serious side effects on the gastro-intestinal tract.

Off the pill for about a year and still not pregnant, she may begin to wonder if something is wrong and so she consults a fertility specialist. He recommends clomiphene citrate, or Clomid, a synthetic hormone used to induce ovulation. It works for her and she becomes pregnant. When she passes the supposed due date, her labour is induced with oxytocin, another synthetic hormone. After a difficult labour and a caesarean delivery, she has difficulty breast-feeding and decides to abandon it after a few days. To prevent her breast from becoming engorged, the hospital staff gives her more synthetic hormones.

She goes back on the pill after the birth of her child. By her late thirties, she begins to notice that her mood swings have become accentuated around the time before her periods. Her doctor tells her this is premenstrual syndrome (PMS). In the hope of finding a solution, she goes to a PMS clinic, where she is prescribed natural progesterone, which, it is believed, will help relieve her symptoms. She is told that this is still an experimental use of progesterone, but she is not sure whether she should be worried since she was not given much information about it beyond that. She takes the progesterone and finds that it helps her.

Because she finds it difficult to give up smoking, her doctor recommends that she go off the birth control pill in her late thirties. After doing so, she soon begins to have irregular periods. By the age of forty-seven, she begins to experience hot flushes. Her doctor tells her this is a slightly premature menopause and prescribes estrogen and progesterone. He reassures her that they are safe and will also help to prevent brittle bones as she gets older. The combination of estrogen and progesterone causes her to have a monthly blood-like discharge similar to a period. While she finds this a nuisance, she decides that it's probably not as bad as hot flushes and brittle bones. When she askes her doctor how long she will have to stay on this medication, he says "indefinitely." Although few women will experience all the above interventions in their lifetime, it is a rare woman who will not have been prescribed at least one of the above treatments in the course of her reproductive years.

To the pharmaceutical industry, to large segments of the medical profession, and even to many women, the situation described above is considered progress. But if this is progress, what is the price? What personal control will women have left over their own reproductive lives if this dependency on pharmaceutical fixes persists? Because this is the first time in history that women's reproductive cycles can be so extensively controlled by synthetic hormones, it is imperative that we begin asking some of these questions now. As women are collectively gaining control over other aspects of our lives, are we in fact *losing* control in this area? I will attempt to explore some of these questions by looking at a few of the problems associated with some of the hormone drugs in current use in North America.

In any discussion of hormone drugs, we must begin with an understanding that relatively little is known about their action on all systems of the body. As one American biologist has said, " ... the gynecologist/obstetrician is probably more of a medical empiricist than any other specialist; that is, the gynecologist administers hormones as a treatment because they work and not because there is a clearly-defined understanding of their action in the body."[1] For example, the original use of DES was to prevent miscarriage; it was later found that not only was it ineffective for this purpose, but that altering dosages could actually bring on a miscarriage — hence its use as a post-coital contraceptive. The very popular fertility drug Clomid (clomiphene citrate) was originally used to prevent ovulation but is now used to induce ovulation in women. The controversial drug Depo-Provera (medroxyprogesterone acetate) can cause very heavy bleeding in some women and a total cessation of periods in others. In a 1985 issue of the *New England Journal of Medicine,* two separate studies looking at the link between estrogen and increased risk of heart disease came up with completely contradictory results.[2] The jury is still out on many questions about the safety of hormone drugs, and yet doctors continue to prescribe them in great numbers, often telling their patients little about the risks.

An interesting case in point is estrogen replacement therapy for menopausal women. When the female hormone estrogen was first synthesized in the laboratory in the late 1930s, many uses were found for this new "wonder drug." It was not until the 1960s that the drug began to be marketed more heavily for menopausal symptoms, following the publication of a book entitled *Feminine Forever* by Robert Wilson. Wilson's research for the book was funded by Ayerst Laboratories, the company that manufactures Premarin, the most popular form of synthetic estrogen used in replacement therapy. In his book, Wilson warned of the ravages of aging and for the first time spoke of menopause as a "deficiency state." The best solution for such a deficiency, claimed Wilson, was to replace what was lost, that is, estrogen. Wilson's book was widely read by women and doctors alike, and the sales for estrogen tripled in North America between 1965 and 1975.

By 1975, studies were released showing the link between estrogen replacement therapy and cancer of the endometrium (the lining of the uterus). Sales of the drug dropped. The Food and Drug Administration (FDA) in the United States prepared package inserts for patients receiving estrogen and replacement therapy that carried the following warning: "You may have heard that taking estrogen for long periods (years) after the menopause will keep your skin soft and supple and keep you feeling young. There is no evidence that this is so however, and such long-term treatment carries important risks." Following the proposal for inserts, pharmaceutical companies manufacturing estrogen for replacement therapy petitioned the FDA and sued in federal court to block the estrogen regulation. The American Medical Association and the American College of Obstetrics and Gynecology joined in the suit, claiming that the information was "in no way pertinent to the proper concerns of the patient" and "wholly unsuitable for lay persons without medical or scientific training." Nevertheless, the regulation to use package inserts was eventually made law in the United States.

After a temporary drop in estrogen sales following the announcement of the link to endometrial cancer, the sale of this drug rose again in the early 1980s for two reasons. One was that the practice of combining estrogen with progesterone for replacement therapy was found to diminish the ill-effects of the estrogen on the endometrium. One of the strongest proponents of this combined cyclic therapy is Dr. Penny Wise Budoff, who makes a strong argument for the addition of progesterone in her popular and influential book *No More Menstrual Cramps and Other Good News* (1980). The addition of progesterone has helped renew the popularity of estrogen replacement therapy in recent years. But many of the questions regarding safety are still unanswered, and the proponents of the combined therapy fail to recognize the absurdity of using one synthetic hormone, progesterone, to combat the ill-effects of another synthetic hormone, estrogen. Nor have they addressed the implications of the fact that women continue to have periods well beyond their menopausal years when they receive the combined therapy.

Another reason that sales for estrogen replacement therapy have risen in the past few years is that the main companies manufacturing it have begun to advertise the need for estrogen in the prevention of osteoporosis. The influence that the drug industry has had on the public's concern about osteoporosis has been enormous. Until very recently, for example, advertisements for Premarin concentrated on the menopausal symptoms that it could alleviate, specifically hot flushes and vaginal dryness. More recently, however, Ayerst has chosen to advertise Premarin as much for the treatment of osteoporosis as for menopausal symptoms. Doctors are therefore receiving the message that this is an appropriate and recommended use for the drug. Pharmaceutical companies usually confine advertising for prescription drugs to medical journals but, in what may be an unprecedented move, Ayerst is simultaneously conducting a public education campaign about osteoporosis through popular women's magazines such as *Redbook* and *Women's Day*. Advertisements prepared by Ayerst's public relations firm show old women hunched over, looking pathetically at the camera. The message — that osteoporosis is a horrible and frightening disease — is loud and clear. The text of the advertisements tells women that this disease can be avoided with proper exercise and calcium, but repeatedly warns women that they should talk to their doctors about it. So when a woman asks her doctor about this crippling disease, is the doctor more likely to talk to her about diet and exercise, or to write out a prescription for estrogen?

This example is for a few reasons. The condition of osteoporosis, a loss of calcium in the bones that causes them to become porous and brittle, was discussed in the medical literature as early as the 1930s. During the 1940s, studies showed that there was a link between estrogen and bone loss. Ayerst Laboratories did not invent this idea. Women have been suffering from osteoporosis since time immemorial. What Ayerst did do was help to make osteoporosis a household word and to inject a healthy amount of fear into North American women about this disease, thereby helping to create an enormous market for their product: well-intentioned but gullible doctors serving fearful women.

The osteoporosis-estrogen replacement therapy issue serves as a good example of how large pharmaceutical companies can legitimate certain diseases or syndromes by advertising their "cure" for that disease or syndrome. Women must be made aware that the treatment a doctor prescribes can be greatly influenced by the pharmaceutical industry. Doctors are wined and dined by the drug companies at conferences, and given endless perks, gifts and free samples. In his book *The Real Pushers: A Critical Analysis of the Canadian Drug Industry,* a Toronto doctor, Joel Lexchin, discusses this practice:

> Some companies donate a supply of calling cards. In one case, a Canadian doctor was given an all-expense-paid trip to a U.S. drug factory. The trip included expensive entertainment and X-rated films. Doctors who become drinking buddies with detail men often get free supplies of drugs for their families, with the cocktails thrown in for good measure. There are always rulers, paper weights, note pads, paintings, photographs, books and a variety of other little trinkets available to doctors free for the asking. At medical conventions and conferences, the companies often have hospitality suites where free liquor is supplied ... At one, jelly beans were given away to promote tranquilizers. ...[3]

Doctors receive regularly, free of charge, medical journals that are highly subsidized by the pharmaceutical industry and that are heavily weighted with advertisements from the industry. Even the most well-intentioned doctor cannot escape this ever-present influence. The industry's aim is to persuade doctors to use their product, and in that same line of thinking, women are seen by the industry as "the market." At one symposium on menopause in Toronto sponsored by Ayerst, a representative from the industry commented to one of the organizers that the percentage of women taking Premarin was notably lower in Canada than in the United States. He added, "There's a huge untapped market out there!" That market is an unsuspecting female public.

To begin to understand the extent to which hormone drugs are given in North America (and the Third World, although that is not my emphasis here), we must look at the larger question of how menstruation, menopause, and every phase of a woman's life cycle in between, have come to be seen by modern medicine as potentially pathological. When the traditional view of the human body (which is essentially a mechanistic notion) is applied to the female life cycle, the result is a confused meeting of logic and reasoning on one hand, and variation and unpredictability on the other. Modern obstetrics and gynaecology have been developed by men, who can study and try to understand the patterns of the female body but can never *know* them. Male body patterns, while characterized by some fluctuation are, for the most part, homeostatic. The varied and rhythmic nature of female body patterns is a concept that is somewhat alien to the male experience. Thus we have seen a male "norm" applied to the female system. And so the cyclic and fluctuating nature of women's bodies has come to be considered in some way in need of correction. Changes in mood that flow with our menstrual cycles (today called "premenstrual tension") could be seen as normal, but instead, have come to be regarded as "sick" and needing to be fixed. Labels of "out-of-control" and "raging hormones" have become a millstone around the necks of women. There is no room for the idea that all these fluctuations and changes might be desirable. Women, for the most part, have accepted the "sick" label, and seek cures for their "ailments."

There are, of course, some conditions of the female cycle that *are* pathological. Cervical dysplasia, cancer of any of the reproductive organs, endometriosis, pelvic inflammatory disease, blocked fallopian tubes, and other such structural problems are worthy of attention, medical or otherwise. But there is also a host of "female disorders" that may not really be disorders at all, but the natural way in which our bodies were meant to function. Pain in childbirth, for example, is a necessary part of easing a baby out of the birth canal. Painful menstruation may mean that that particular woman's uterus needs to contract more than some others in order to release the uterine lining each month. Knowing this may not make the pain any easier to bear, but it helps us understand our bodies better. Yet the predominantly male-run profession of medicine (especially obstetrics and gynaecology) chooses to prescribe drugs to harness and control these natural bodily functions, rather than encourage women to seek out alternative, non-drug approaches.

It would be simplistic to say that women's reproductive processes are managed with drugs because a male medical profession does not understand the female body. While this is an important factor, it is not the only reason that hormone drugs are so widely prescribed today. The role of the pharmaceutical industry cannot be ignored. Although doctors in the 1930s may have synthesized estrogen with all the best of intentions, the impact that their discovery has had has been far from benign. When a profit-oriented industry enters the picture, it becomes hard to measure what are good intentions and what is purely the profit motive. Pharmaceutical companies manufacturing synthetic estrogen have profited immensely from this discovery. In the United States alone, $80 million worth of estrogen is dispensed annually in replacement therapy. With such a money-maker, it has been in the best interests of the pharmaceutical industry to find other uses for its products. Medical researchers are encouraged with money from drug companies to carry out research to find such uses. In the name of progress, these uses are found, tested on "that untapped market out there," and eventually marketed, once approval is granted — in Canada by the Department of Health and Welfare. Doctors are the medium through which these drugs are dispensed, and as indicated above, no expense is spared in marketing these products to doctors. As Lexchin notes, "Companies spend about $2900 per doctor per year in their efforts to convince or confuse. As one observer put it: 'No other group in the country is so insistently sought after, chased, wooed, pressured and downright importuned as this small group of doctors who are the de facto wholesalers of the ethical drug industry.' "[4]

Because the pharmaceutical industry has the corner on the market of information about drugs, doctors have few sources of information about drugs other than the industry. Why shouldn't a doctor believe, for example, that estrogen replacement therapy is the very best solution for hot flushes, when most of the literature he or she is reading says just that?

An article published recently in a prominent Canadian medical journal illustrates the extent to which the use of synthetic estrogen is being encouraged today to control every aspect of the female reproductive cycle.[5] The author leads the reader through the female life cycle, showing every point at which estrogen can be used effectively. Under the heading "Use of Estrogens in Childhood," he notes that "though it is rarely needed, ... In the baby girl with labial adhesions, after deft separation, some estrogen cream may be applied twice weekly for a month to prevent readhesion." He notes that prolonged use will cause "premature feminization." He continues through puberty, adolescence, and the childbearing years and concludes with menopause. With respect to the use of estrogen cream for vaginal atrophy (thinning of the vaginal walls that can cause dryness), he says:

> Absorption is uncontrolled, and the estrogen is conjugated by the liver only after it has been circulated to the end organs. The dose is therefore, possibly excessive — and certainly not under good control. It is useful for those patients whose compliance is improved if therapy is perceived as local; however their physician must appreciate that the hormone has generalized systemic effect, even though the patient believes she is being treated locally.

The implication seems to be that the doctor should not *tell* the woman that the estrogen will have an effect on her entire system, even though she is applying it locally as a cream. The reason for not telling her seems to be that it might "interfere with compliance."

One of the interesting things about this article is that it was considered by a few doctors I had discussed it with informally as very moderate and reasonable, even cautious, with respect to the question of when to use estrogen. So prevalent in modern medicine is the tendency to prescribe drugs rather than seek other solutions, that someone who advocates a modicum of restraint is seen as moderate. More than anything, this points up just how deeply ingrained in the medical mind is the notion that prescribing hormones for many conditions is perfectly acceptable. As a woman, I read that article and feel despair for our sex and a certain sense of violation at the extent to which questionable hormones can be fed to us. But what is most important, and what we must look at more critically, is the assumption about women that are behind the decisions to prescribe hormones so freely.

In Canada in 1985, Upjohn Canada, the manufacturers of Depo-Provera, applied to the federal Department of Health and Welfare for approval of the controversial drug as an injectable contraceptive. Despite widespread doubts about the safety of this drug, the Department of Health and Welfare gave strong indications that it would approve it for use in Canada, with one spokesman noting that "It is now culturally acceptable to say that menstruation is a nuisance." The same official went on to say that women taking the drug would need to be taught "that it is not unhealthy for their genitals to be in a dormant state. Their genitals [were] just like they were when they were nine or ten years old."[6]

If the drug referred to were to be used to treat a fatal disease, in rare circumstances, these remarks might be easier to understand. However, Depo-Provera is a drug that will be used on *healthy* women to prevent conception. These remarks illustrate well the attitudes of some doctors about the female reproductive system: reducing menstruation to "a nuisance" and encouraging the use of a drug on healthy women that forces their reproductive organs into a "dormant," immature state.

Comments like those of the doctor above are not just the product of a society that paradoxically loathes and adores women and their reproductive powers. They are also the product of medical training that parcels the body off into discrete, mechanical parts rather than viewing it as an indivisible whole and of pharmaceutical advertising that reinforces such views. One advertisement for Premarin tells doctors that menopause is a time "when women outlive their ovaries." An historical look at how women's bodies have been viewed over the centuries may shed some light on how the female reproductive cycle has come to be considered in need of control by hormone treatments.

It was only very recently in history that the functioning of the female reproductive organs was first understood. From the Aristotelian theory of menstruation as "an overabundance of nutrients from the abdomen which caused an excess of blood" to the Victorian belief that too much mental activity would "compromise uterine function,"[7] the female reproductive cycle has been misunderstood and shrouded in mystery for over two thousand years. During the late nineteenth century, a significant period in the development of modern medicine doctors believed that undue stress on a woman's mental functions would inevitably impair her reproductive functions and that a wide variety of physical disorders in women (including headaches, backaches, and nervousness) were the result of a poorly functioning reproductive system. Many believed that two vital organs such as the uterus and the brain could not develop well simultaneously, and this argument was used for years to deny higher education to young girls and women. Doctors of that era saw women as both "the product and the prisoners of their reproductive systems.[8] What made women special could also be what made them weak and vulnerable. And if a woman denied her biological destiny by not bearing children, it was felt that she would be punished with a host of illnesses for the rest of her years.

It oftens takes generations before attitudes catch up with scientific knowledge, and the case of medical understanding of the reproductive system may well be an example. While the scientific theory today might *say* that menstruation, childbirth, and menopause are not illnesses, they are nonetheless treated as illnesses, with powerful and often dangerous hormone drugs.

What is perhaps most insidious about the current state of affairs, which finds increasing numbers of hormones on the market each year, is that many women have come to believe that these drugs are their salvation. Indeed, one of the main premises of a book by the historian Edward Shorter, *A History of Women's Bodies,* is that women have modern medicine to thank for liberating them from their biological destinies with such advances as caesarean sections and birth control pills. If we examine Shorter's theory a little more closely, what we find is a distinct loathing of female physiology. He notes in his Introduction, "Even once all these other changes had occurred, if women had still been dragging about with 'fallen wombs' and such, feminism would probably not have happened."[9]

In many cases, of course, women *have* been helped by hormone drugs. But it is incumbent upon us to examine at what cost these medical advances have been made. In out lifetime, we have seen birth deformities from thalidomide, vaginal cancer from DES and infertility from the Dalkon Shield IUD. How many more discoveries like these will it take before the parties involved — the pharmaceutical industry, doctors, and patients — realize that they are part of a continuum? The factors which perpetuate that continuum are many and complex, and there are no simple solutions.

At the very least we must embark on a dialogue about hormone drugs and we must challenge the claim that they are always for our own good.

◄►

NOTES

1. Ethel Sloane, *Biology of Women,* (New York: John Wiley, 1980).

2. Peter Wilson *et. al.,* "Postmenopausal estrogen use, cigarette smoking and cardiovascular morbidity in women over 50: The Framingham study", *New England Journal of Medicine,* vol. 313, no. 17 (Oct. 24, 1985), pp.1038 — 43; M.J. Stampfer *et. al.,* "A prospective study of postmenopausal estrogen therapy and coronary heart disease," *New England Journal of Medicine,* vol. 313, no. 17 (Oct. 24, 1985), pp.1044 — 9.

3. Joel Lexchin, *The Real Pushers,* (Vancouver: New Star Books, 1985), p.105.

4. *Ibid,* p.112.

5. R.J. Sollars, "The use of estrogens," *Canadian Family Physician,* 31, (April 1985), pp.807 — 10.

6. Ann Pappert, "Disputed drug may be approved as contraceptive," the *Globe and Mail,* Nov. 22, 1985, quoting Dr. Ian Henderson of the Department of Health and Welfare Canada.

7. R.O. Valdiserri, "Menstruation and medical theory: an historical overview," *Journal of the American Medical Women's Association,* 38, no. 3 (May/June 1983), pp.67 — 8.

8. C. Smith-Rosenberg and C. Rosenberg, "The female animal: Medical and biological views of woman and her role in nineteenth-century America," in J.W. Leavitt, ed., *Women and Health in America* (Madison, Wisc.: University of Wisconsin Press, 1984), p.13.

9. Edward Shorter, *A History of Women's Bodies,* (New York: Basic Books, 1982), p.xii.

DES: The Crime Continues

Anita Direcks and Ellen 't Hoen

IN THE LONG ROSTER of harmful drugs used on women, diethylstilbestrol (DES) needs no introduction. Given to millions of pregnant women in the forties, fifties, and sixties to prevent miscarriages, this synthetic hormone was later found to cause a rare form of cancer in some of the daughters of these women, as well as a host of other abnormalities in both male and female offspring. Along with thalidomide, a tranquillizer that also caused severe birth defects, DES has become an international symbol of the harmful consequences of inadequate drug testing and the "pill-for-every-ill" mentality.

Yet though thalidomide was withdrawn from the market as soon as its harmful effects were clearly established in the sixties, DES is still available throughout the world and is used for a wide variety of indications, including lactation suppression after childbirth, menopausal complaints, post-coital contraception, and in the treatment of breast and prostatic cancers. The 1985 World Conference of the UN Decade for Women held in Nairobi confirmed the worst suspicions of DES activists that the drug is still being given to pregnant women to prevent miscarriage in many Third World countries. A Kenyan doctor at the conference listed several brand names of DES that were still being prescribed to pregnant women at her hospital, and said she had not known that the drug was dangerous. From Mexico came a report that DES is available to pregnant women (and anyone else) over the counter. Representatives from a number of other countries including Brazil, Costa Rica, Rwanda, Peru, and Zaire made similar reports about the continued use of DES for complications of pregnancy, despite the fact that its use during pregnancy is prohibited in most Western countries. Because of this state of affairs, DES activists and consumer health activists from many nations are now calling for a world-wide ban on the production and marketing of the drug, a decision that will be examined more thoroughly later in this article. But for the present, the crime of DES continues against the health of women and their children.

THE DES STORY

DES is a synthetic form of the female hormone estrogen. It was discovered in 1938 by the English biochemist Sir Charles Dodds. The discovery of DES was remarkable, since it made possible for the first time the manufacture of a synthetic substance having estrogenic effects. Furthermore, DES was cheap to produce and could be administered orally, unlike natural estrogens that were (and still are) expensive and had to be injected.

According to Stephen Fenichell and Lawrence S. Charfoos, authors of *Daughters at Risk,* the U.S. Food and Drug Administration (FDA) played a key role in the launching of DES.[1] Despite evidence that estrogens could cause cancer in mice,[2] and a warning that DES was much more powerful than natural estrogens, the FDA had received more than ten requests from pharmaceutical companies by the end of 1940 to register DES and sell it for post-menopausal complaints. Indeed, Dodds had not taken out a patent on his discovery, so that any manufacturer could test it and bring it onto the market. The FDA had to be convinced that the various stilbestrols were of the same quality, and then determine whether stilbestrol was safer. Since the data supplied by the pharmaceutical companies were not sufficient for the FDA to approve DES, the manufacturers withdrew their individual applications and set up a joint study group. By May 1941, the FDA had received reports from the study group of over 5,300 safe and successful DES treatments of patients. How two doctors at the FDA and their assistants were able to work through this mountain of data in forty-five days will remain a bureaucratic mystery forever. But by mid-June the FDA was "convinced" by the evidence. On September 12, 1941, it informed the companies that their applications would be granted. Theodore Klumpp, an FDA official responsible for the approval of DES, later became president of Winthrop Chemical Company, one of the first manufacturers of DES.

During this same period, the husband-and-wife team of George and Olive Smith, medical doctor and biochemist, respectively, were investigating the role of hormones in pregnancy. In 1938 they published an article describing the relationship between progesterone and estrogen. They found that a drop in estrogen usually preceded complications such as miscarriages and premature births. A drop in the amount of estrogen meant also that the production of progesterone had declined. The Smiths concluded that progesterone deficiency was responsible for so-called "complications during pregnancy." On that basis, the two researchers believed they had found an indication for DES. They discovered that it was possible to act on the regulating function of the pituitary gland, which controls the balance between the production of estrogen and progesterone, by administering DES. While natural estrogens were not able to do so, DES *could* stimulate the pituitary to continually produce progesterone, regardless of the existing level of progesterone in the body. In fact, what they had discovered is that DES could upset the balancing mechanism of the pituitary.

In 1948 the Smiths published an article on the administration of DES during pregnancy in the influential *American Journal of Obstetrics and Gynaecology*.[3] The article was based on interviews with 632 pregnant women and 117 birth attendants. There was no control group for this research, and the 117 birth attendants had not been given standardized criteria for their surveys. Through the efforts of the pharmaceutical industry, which took care of reproducing and distributing the article, Smiths' findings were widely disseminated in the medical community. It was on the basis of a doubtful hypothesis and poorly conducted research that DES began to be used widely to prevent miscarriages. DES was also used preventively for possible complications in late pregnancy. In one advertisement, the manufacturer even claimed that DES was "recommended by routine prophylaxis in ALL pregnancies."

Popularizing DES

In the following years more uses for DES were found, including as a post-coital contraceptive, to stop the production of breast milk after delivery, and in the treatment of breast cancer in women and prostate cancer in men. In the Netherlands, DES was even included in a hair-growth tonic (Stilbepan) and in so-called sex pills and was used as a growth stimulator in cattle feed. Incredible success stories circulated about DES, without any scientific basis for the claims. On the contrary, in 1953 an American researcher, W.E. Dieckmann, demonstrated that DES had no effect whatsoever on the maintenance of a pregnancy.[4] According to his research, miscarriages were even *more* frequent among DES users than in a control group. Dieckmann's research was thorough: unlike the Smiths, his study was double-blind and had a control group. Yet the promotion of DES by the pharmaceutical industry continued unabated. The Smiths went so far as to claim that DES created a "better maternal environment" for the fetus.[5] The manufacturers advertised with slogans such as "For bigger and stronger babies too" and "Makes normal pregnancies more normal."

In the Netherlands, Professor W.P. Plate was one of the main promoters of DES. He publicized the Smiths' regimen in a clinical lecture reproduced in the Dutch *Journal for Medical Science*.[6] Next to the results of the Smiths' research, he announced those of his own study carried out on fifteen women treated with DES. Of the fifteen pregnancies, five babies were born at term, one was premature, the therapy was unsuccessful on four women, and another five were still pregnant when Plate published his results. Plate was henceforth frequently quoted in advertisements and in product instruction leaflets for various brands of DES, and from then on DES began to be prescribed on a large scale to pregnant women in Holland. Even the thalidomide affair, which punctured the myth that the placenta protects the fetus from harmful substances, had little influence on the prescribing habits of doctors when treating pregnant women. The outcome of all this aggressive promotion was that DES was prescribed to millions of pregnant women in countries all over the world, including the United States, Australia, Canada, France, Britain, Belgium, Czechoslovakia, the Ivory Coast, and Mexico.[7]

The Turnabout

In 1971 the American gynaecologist Dr. A.L. Herbst established the connection between DES and a rare type of vaginal cancer occurring among daughters of women who had taken the drug during pregnancy. Herbst and his colleagues noted that in a short three-year period, eight young women in the Boston area had developed this type of cancer, known as clear-cell adenocarcinoma, despite the fact that only three cases had been previously reported as occurring in young women in the international medical literature. A number of causes for the unusual occurrence were explored and ruled out, and it was a hunch on the part of one of the mothers, who remembered being given a drug during her pregnancy, that led to the identification of DES as the culprit. Herbst sounded the alarm. American doctors were warned later that year not to use the drug during pregnancy.

In the Netherlands the Ministry of Public Health informed the pharmaceutical industry in 1972 that the use of DES during pregnancy was henceforth forbidden. Yet the indication "for use in cases of risk of miscarriage" still appeared on the package inserts until 1975. Only a repetition of the original directive brought an end to this indication. In France it was only in 1977 that DES was banned for use during pregnancy.

Though cancer was the most dramatic and tragic outcome of the DES saga, other adverse effects were also found in DES daughters. They were frequently found to have vaginal adenosis, a benign but abnormal condition in which glandular tissue normally found inside the cervix and uterus is found lining the outside of these organs. Other deformations of the uterus, vagina, and fallopian tubes were discovered in DES daughters, resulting in a range of reproductive problems, including increased rates of spontaneous abortion, ectopic pregnancy, and premature births. Higher rates of cervical dysplasia and *carcinoma-in-situ* have also been found among DES daughters.

Later in the seventies, problems in DES sons began to crop up. They were shown to have a higher incidence of genital abnormalities such as epidedymal cysts and undescended testes, and fertility problems, such as low sperm count and motility. In the early eighties, still more disturbing effects of DES were uncovered, this time in the mothers themselves. Women who took DES during pregnancy were found to have a statistically significant increased risk of developing breast cancer. Given the frightening emergence of these effects, one by one, and the fact that others, still unknown, may yet surface in the future, it is small wonder that DES has come to be known as the "time bomb drug."

DES: LIFTING THE VEIL OF SILENCE

Initially none of the authorities in the countries where DES was used took any measures to warn people who had been exposed to DES of the hazards they faced. Neither did the pharmaceutical industry nor the medical profession. So in 1975, many DES mothers and daughters came together and formed DES Action in various American cities with the aim of seeking out and helping people who had been exposed to DES and informing the public about the dangers of the drug. The movement spread to other countries where DES had been used, including Canada, Australia, and the Netherlands in 1981. DES Action groups provide help and information to those who suspect that their mothers may have been given the drug during pregnancy, a fact that can be enormously difficult to verify given the passage of time and the vast array of brand names under which DES was sold. The groups also provide emotional support to the children of women who took DES and are extensively involved in political advocacy and public education. In July 1985, DES Action International was created at the World Conference of the UN Decade for Women in Nairobi to tackle the issue on an international level.

THE LESSONS OF DES

The sorry history of DES reveals many mistakes and considerable carelessness in the making of important decisions. Warnings published in 1938 about the carcinogenic properties of DES were ignored. There were hardly any experiments using DES on animals, particularly pregnant animals. Almost from the beginning, the experimentation was on women. When DES was approved in 1947 as a drug for preventing miscarriages, the manufacturers were not required to prove that the substance was safe for that purpose. DES had already been approved for other uses, and this application was for a new use of an already existing, approved drug.

DES causes a disturbance in the regulating function of the pituitary. This should have been seen as a warning, but instead it was considered a great potential. The Smiths' theory that DES helped to prevent miscarriages was refuted by the thorough research done later by Dieckmann. But this research was ignored, as were other studies with negative results. On the other hand, the Smiths' publications, supported by the pharmaceutical industry, had great influence in medical circles. Furthermore, the real causes of miscarriages were not properly investigated. It was assumed that they were caused by hormonal disturbances, but later research showed that the majority of all miscarriages were caused by abnormalities in the fetus. Yet DES was prescribed to millions of women around the world and was also given as a preventive measure to healthy women with normal pregnancies. These women were not told that there were questions about the drug's effectiveness. On the contrary, the promotion played on their strong desire to do everything possible to maintain their pregnancies. Finally, the thalidomide affair in the sixties showed that drugs could harm the fetus and that the placenta did not protect it from harmful substances, as had been previously believed. Yet throughout the sixties, critical questions were not being asked about DES.

Ban DES

At present the use of DES is restricted in Western countries. In the United States it is authorized for use in estrogen replacement therapy and in the treatment of cancer of the prostate gland and advanced breast cancer.[8] In Britain it is authorized exclusively in the treatment of prostate cancer and menopausal breast cancer.[9] In France and the Netherlands DES is indicated only for the treatment of prostate cancer.[10] The use of DES as a morning-after pill, as a lactation suppressant, or as a drug to prevent miscarriage is no longer approved in Western countries. But as we have seen, it is precisely on these indications that DES is still being used in several Third World countries. In most countries the prescribing of drugs is at the discretion of doctors, and there are no mechanisms for continual monitoring of their prescribing practices. As recently as 1984, a doctor at a student health facility in Toronto, Canada, was discovered to be prescribing DES as a morning-after pill. Despite the publicity, the doctor received no punishment.

At its founding meeting in July 1985, DES Action International called for a complete world-wide ban on DES, arguing that it is not an essential drug and that there are alternatives for the conditions for which it is still authorized. For instance, recent studies have shown that androgen treatment for prostate cancer has fewer side-effects than DES. Experience has shown that as long as DES is available, it will continue to be misused. Its ready availability in the Third World and the ease with which it can be used for unapproved purposes in both developed and developing countries justify the call for a complete ban. DES Action International is now in touch with women in several countries who are willing to take up the issue, and international co-operation will make it possible to find out where and to what extent DES is still being used. Steps must be taken now to stop the production and distribution of this drug. DES has already claimed enough victims.

◄►

NOTES

1. Stephen Fenichell and Lawrence S. Charfoos, *Daughters at risk, A personal D.E.S. history,* (New York: Doubleday, 1981), chap. 4.

2. In 1932 the French scientist Lacassagne carried out various studies on the influence of sexual hormones on the development of cancer. Lacassagne was able to induce breast cancer in male mice. He thus proved that estrogen was a potential carcinogen, at least in mice. His findings were published in 1938, in "Apparition d'adénocarcinomes mammaires chez des souris males traites par une substance oestrogene synthetique," *Comptes rendus biol.* (Paris), 129 (1938), p.641.
   At Yale estrogens were used to induce all kinds of cancer in male and female mice, rabbits, monkeys, and rats.

3. O.W. Smith, "Diethylstilbestrol in the prevention and treatment of complications of pregnancy", *American Journal of Obstetrics and Gynaecology,* (1948), p.821.

4. W.E. Dieckmann, M.E. Davind, S.M. Rijnkicwicz, *et. al.,* "Does the administration of diethylstilbestrol during pregnancy have therapeutic value?" *American Journal of Obstetrics and Gynaecology,* 66 (1953), p.247.

5. Quoted in Fenichell and Charfoos, *op. cit.,* p.45.

6. W.P. Plate, "Clinical Lecture," *Nederlands Tijdschrift voor Geneeskunde,* 96 (1952), p.1922.

7. Herbst and Bern, *Development effects of diethylstilbestrol* (DES) *in pregnancy* (New York: Thieme Stratton, 1981), p.65.
   These countries reported to the Herbst registry cases of clear-cell carcinoma of the vagina or cervix in so-called DES daughters. The figures quoted here by Herbst are, of course, by now very much out of date. From the Netherlands only one case was reported, whereas by 1985 there were thirty-eight known cases. DES may also have been used in other countries that have not reported to the Herbst registry.

8. Physician's Desk Reference (PDR), 1985.

9. ABPI Data Sheet Compendium, 1985.

10. Pharmacotherapeutisch Kompas, 1984; Dictionnaire des Specialites VIDAL.

MOOD-MODIFIERS AND ELDERLY WOMEN IN CANADA: THE MEDICALIZATION OF POVERTY

Jim Harding

MOOD-MODIFIERS have been called the second great revolution in pharmaceutical technology. However, they have never succeeded in winning the public's acceptance as did the "first revolution," the life-saving antibiotics.

It is probably more accurate to call mood-modifiers a revolution in artificial demand. With the growing public awareness of the primacy of market forces over public health — partly catalyzed by the women's movement and alternative health care movements — even the antibiotics (which have also been found to be greatly over-prescribed) have begun to fall from their medical pinnacle.

The history of mood-modifiers should itself create scepticism about these drugs. Even the name given them by the industry — "tranquillizer" — is a misnomer for these depressant drugs. Furthermore, the image of the pure scientist working in a quaint laboratory to help humanity is more myth than fact, especially in the case of the main mood-modifiers, the minor tranquillizers.

The world's biggest line of minor tranquillizers, the benzodiazepines, were actually created during research, undertaken between 1957 and 1963 in the United States aimed at the development of an anti-infective drug. And although the "discovery" didn't kill germs it was found to work as a muscle relaxant. What was to become the product Librium (chlordiazepoxide) and was to usher in the era of mass tranquillizers, was first tested at a zoo on a Siberian tiger resentful of its captivity: "What was needed was a tranquillizer that would calm the beast yet keep it conscious and alert so people could look at it.[1]

The chemical apparently had the desired effect. And we can be sure that the company quickly saw the potential market in a society more interested in keeping people functioning, even though they might be suffering from exceptional stress, than in reducing the stress. It is significant that this drug was next tested on the mother-in-law of a company executive. This line of research ultimately led to Valium, or diazepam (to become the world's most prescribed drug), and a whole array of products often referred to in industry circles as "housewives' pills".

We have come a long way since these experiments in the United States. In 1973 a Canadian study reported that by 1971 diazepam had the most sales of all prescription drugs in the province of Alberta, and that three of the top sellers were mood-modifiers. It also reported that a sample of 400 medicine cabinets in households in the city of Edmonton showed that 175 contained diazepam. Furthermore, mood-altering medications were the prescription drugs found most often.[2]

Before the rate at which diazepam was prescribed began to decline owing to bad publicity, another Canadian study found that 19 per cent of all people sixty and over in the province of Saskatchewan had been prescribed this drug at least once during the first year and a half of the government Drug Plan. It accounted for 21 per cent of all central-nervous-system (CNS) drugs prescribed out of hospital in the province. What is most revealing is that 14 per cent of men aged 60 — 69, 26 per cent of women aged 60 — 69, and 15 per cent of men and 22 per cent of women 70 and over, had received (on average) over four diazepam prescriptions during this period.[3] Since the elderly also received an overproportion of in-hospital prescriptions and over-the-counter drugs, they were obviously in far greater danger from multiple drug use than younger people.

In this article I will examine the social roots of the high rate at which these and other mood-modifiers are prescribed for women, particularly elderly women. I will do this in four main sections. The first will review some of the major studies that indicate that mood-modifiers are being over-prescribed to women, especially elderly women. The second will look in detail at the findings on over-prescribing to women from research in the province of Saskatchewan, which at present has the best prescription database in Canada. The third section will look at the delivery system — particularly the drug store — through which women and the elderly receive these drugs. And the fourth will discuss the developmental issues — particularly the medicalization of problems of social and economic underdevelopment among the aging — that are involved in the over-prescribing of mood-modifiers to women.

I OVER-PRESCRIBING OF MOOD-MODIFIERS TO WOMEN

As early as 1969 the World Health Organization (WHO) was recommending comparative studies of prescription drugs. At present (1986) it is still not possible to compare directly the rate at which mood-modifiers (or any other drugs) are prescribed and used in Canada to the rate in other countries. While pharmaceutical sales have been systematically monitored in Canada for several years, neither prescribing nor utilization patterns for various groups are yet studied regularly.[4]

Though we still cannot make systematic comparisons with other countries, we now know a fair amount about prescribing trends in Canada. The results can help us develop a model of prescribing trends to women, particularly elderly women, which can be tested and compared in other countries. The first research undertaken on mood-modifying prescriptions in Canada was in the early 1970s. Because it relied on pharmacy store records it tended to concentrate more on the characteristics of the drugs than on the practices of the prescribers. Partly because of the shortage of information, and the wide acceptance of the authority of the medical profession, there was a real hesitation to interpret any differences found in prescribing rates to various groups in a way that reflected badly on doctors' prescribing habits.

The Toronto Pharmacy Study

In 1971, the late Ruth Cooperstock, a researcher at the Addiction Research Foundation (ARF) in Toronto reported that prescriptions for women constituted 69 per cent of all mood-modifying prescriptions filled by the drug stores and hospitals in Toronto, Ontario.[5] Furthermore, it was found that 8 per cent of all prescriptions and 33 per cent of mood-modifiers were tranquillizers. Noting an Ontario study showing that only 56 per cent of total visits to general practitioners were from women, Cooperstock rejected the view, widespread among prescribers and medical authorities, that this sex difference was mainly due to more female visits to physicians. She ended however, by saying that the differential "between the proportion of all drugs and mood-modifiers going to women remains something of a mystery..."[6]

Because of the records used, the age of the female consumers could not be studied. The only references to age (which turned out to be the greatest predictor of prescribing rates) was a comment that perhaps the finding that higher rates went to city than suburban residents was due to the "differing age distributions of city and suburbs."[7]

The findings of this research were very similar to those of a 1969 study in the United States which found that 67 per cent of psychoactive prescriptions went to women.[8] Moreover, research done in Europe at about the same time confirmed the same trend. For example, a study in nine European countries of tranquillizer and sedative prescriptions during the previous year found that "in every country but Italy and Germany approximately two-thirds of the users of anti-anxiety sedative drugs [were] women. In Germany the figure [was] closer to three-fourths and in Italy closer to three-fifths."[9] Larger proportions of women fifty-five and older were found to be using these drugs.

The Winnipeg Survey of Pharmacies and Women

The first study in Canada that systematically investigated the characteristics of the women being prescribed mood-modifiers was undertaken in 1975 in Winnipeg.[10] This study combined a random survey of pharmacies in greater Winnipeg with questionnaries from 1,700 randomly selected women from a part of the city with a population of over 100,000. The objective was not only "to assess the incidence of prescription psychotropic use [but] to gather information on the variables in the life situation of the psychotrope recipient in order to better describe patterns of use.''[11]

It was found that 22 per cent of the 7,400 new or refill prescriptions in the one-week period studied were mood-modifiers. The most common were minor tranquillizers (40 per cent of all mood-modifiers) and barbiturate hypnotic-sedatives or sleeping pills (28 per cent). Next came non-barbiturate sleeping pills (11 per cent), stimulants (8 per cent), anti-depressants (6.5 per cent), major tranquillizers (6 per cent) and combination drugs (2 per cent).

The existence of a large sex difference in psychotropic prescriptions was confirmed. A total of 1,030 women and 443 men received these psychotropics. These findings were put in relative, rather than absolute, terms to calculate per capita prescribing:

> Since women are prescribed so many more such drugs although they represent only slightly more than half of Winnipeg's population (52.27 per cent vs. 48.87 per cent), a separate rate can be calculated for each sex. According to the results of this study then, women average 1.6 such prescriptions and men .8 per person per year.[12]

The interpretation of the difference, however, was made in purely quantitative terms. For example, the authors wrote:

> Women do receive much more than their share of psychotropic drugs but this result may be primarily a reflection of the fact that they receive more than twice as many prescriptions of all kinds than do men ... By the same token, women could very well be prescribed twice as many antibiotics or twice as many analgesics.[13]

About 65 per cent of the sample of women returned questionnaires. About 20 per cent said they had used one or more psychotropic drugs in the previous two weeks. An analysis to see what factors most clearly distinguished the reported users from non-users found:

> ... in descending order of importance ... the incidence of counselling; age; respondent's rating of her general health; average number of visits to a physician per year; and a happiness rating.[14]

What this means is that a significantly higher percentage of those reporting the use of some psychotropics had had some counselling (40 per cent) than those not using these drugs (13 per cent). Furthermore, the highest reported use of these drugs (55 per cent) was among women over seventy-five. An increase in the use of sleeping pills with age was the most obvious trend. The highest percentage of reported users (58 per cent) was among women rating their health as poor, and the next highest percentage (44 per cent) was among those rating their health as only fair.

The highest percentage of those receiving the most psychotropic prescriptions were among those who had made the most visits to their doctor. Finally, the highest percentage of women reporting the use of psychotropics (38 per cent) were among those rating themselves as unhappy.

Religious affiliation or the lack of it, per se, was not found to be significantly related to psychotropic drug use. However, "the more important religion was to the respondent, the more likely she was to report using a mood-modifier."[15] The highest proportion of those reporting psychotropic drug use were at home full-time (25 per cent) rather than having a part-time job (19 per cent) or full-time job (11 per cent). Those women reporting the lowest activity level had the highest reported use of psychotropics (30 per cent).

Women with the most children (five or more) reported the highest incidence of use of psychotropics (26 per cent). However no direct relationship was found between more children being at home and a higher percentage of women reporting the use of tranquillizers. These drugs were used by only a slightly higher percentage of women with one or two children at home (21.5 per cent) than by women with no children (19 per cent). The percentage for those with five or more children at home (19 per cent) and three or four children at home (16 per cent) was lower than both these groupings.

This finding not only reflected the trend to smaller families but began to show just how vital age was in the study of psychotropic prescriptions. As the authors said: "larger families are more characteristic of the older women who are also most likely to use psychotropic drugs."[16] Further evidence for this was the finding that fewer psychotropics were used by the more educated but that this was because the most poorly educated are also the oldest.[17] Once age was factored out, it was also found that divorced, separated, and widowed women did not use psychotropic drugs more than single or married women.[18] Age was likely also a contributing factor to the findings about ratings of health, doctor visits, ratings of happiness, and home-boundedness.

This detailed research helped catalyze the issue of over-prescribing to women and showed the need to focus on living conditions, not only prescribing trends, particularly among the elderly. By 1977, in her summary of the research to date, Ruth Cooperstock was listing age (and then sex) as the vital factors in describing the patterns of use of psychotropic prescriptions:

> Examining tranquillizers alone, people in their middle years tend to receive the highest proportion of these drugs. It would appear, however, that because the elderly receive so many more prescriptions in total than those in their middle years, they receive absolutely more tranquillizer prescriptions as well as both absolutely and relatively more sedative/hypnotic drugs. For example, in 1975 those 65 and over in Saskatchewan represented 11 per cent of the population but purchased 25 per cent of all tranquillizers.[19]

A United States Interview of Seniors

Comprehensive studies elsewhere continued to confirm the same trend for more women, particularly elderly women than men, to be prescribed mood-modifying drugs. An American study in 1977 designed to research the drug use and social characteristics of non-institutionalized elderly people was particularly revealing. The researchers interviewed 950 of 5,600 senior citizens living in a section of Washington, D.C. The sample was taken so that age, sex, marital status, income, and ethnic background were accurately represented. Forty per cent of the men and 60 per cent of the women in the sample agreed to take part in the interviews.

Psychoactives (tranquillizers, sedatives, and anti-depressants) were found to be the second most frequently reported prescription drugs used. These accounted for 15 percent of the prescription drugs taken in the previous twenty-four hours. It was also found that:

> Persons who perceived their family relationships as satisfactory reported using psychotropic drugs less frequently and/or in smaller amounts, while those who described their family relationships as unsatisfactory reported using psychotropic drugs in larger dosages and/or more frequently than chance would have predicted.[20]

Almost all those reporting the use of these drugs received them from a physician. More of those using psychotropics than other prescription drugs (51 per cent compared to 39 per cent) reported they could not perform their daily activities without these drugs. Slightly fewer of those using the psychotropics (29 per cent to 34 per cent) said that health was the main reason for their use of drugs. The authors speculated that drug dependency among the elderly might be an explanation for these findings. They also noted that the elderly being precribed these mood-modifiers would be more likely than younger people to have problems from the combination of drugs.

A clear picture emerges of the elderly in the least satisfactory living conditions being prescribed more of the mood-modifiers:

> Those who reported use of psychotropic drugs also indicated greater reliance on themselves and less reliance on family members in making decisions ... those reporting psychotropic drug use scored significantly lower on life satisfaction than those reporting no use of psychotropic drugs, and looked upon the present as the worst time in their lives.[21]

Furthermore:

> Those who reported using psychotropic drugs also indicated a need for social services, such as counselling, homemaking, legal aid, etc. Their expressed needs included three major concerns: help with housecleaning chores; help with legal matters; and help in establishing and maintaining contacts with other human beings, "to make sure I'm all right."[22]

This study also found that two-thirds of the seniors used over-the-counter (OTC) drugs, half of them analgesics from drug stores. Again the social characteristics of those using OTC drugs were important. An overall trend was that elderly users of both ethical (prescription) and OTC drugs tended to be older, less healthy and less satisfied with life than those who reported no drug use.[23]

As in previous studies, the quality of the living conditions, and the human needs that related to the rate of prescribing were again found to be different for the two sexes:

> ... Women in the sample reported using legal drugs — both ethical drugs and over the counter drugs — 2.65 times more often than men in the sample (72.2 per cent for female respondents, compared to 27.7 per cent for male respondents). Since women in the sample tend-

ed more frequently to be living alone and to be unmarried, the relationship between psychotropic drug use and sex for several of the other psychosocial variables was confounded.[24]

Overall this study found that prescription drugs, including the mood-altering ones, were used most heavily by elderly women who are living alone and not married.[25] Such a finding, based on a very careful methodology, contradicted the simplistic but all too common explanation that psychoactives are prescribed primarily for medical problems.

II Prescribing Trends in the Saskatchewan Drug Plan

By 1977 enough good studies had been done to establish that mood-modifiers were being over-prescribed to women, and mostly to disadvantaged elderly women. The pharmaceutical industry, medical profession, and related government bodies, however, all vigorously (in public though not necessarily in private) denied this conclusion. All tended to blame someone else, such as the consumer. Part of this strategy of denial and diversion was to criticize the research findings as unrepresentative. It is true that the studies had been done in particular cities, were based on seemingly dated pharmacy records, or included only a section of the population; however, it was steadily confirmed that the findings could be generalized.

It was not until computer records had accumulated for pharmacy claims to the universal Drug Plan (introduced by the social democratic government in Saskatchewan in 1974) that the kind of definitive research on prescribing rates that could not be denied (though it still could be ignored) was feasible. In her 1977 review of research on psychotropics, Cooperstock concluded that "because of the universal nature of the Saskatchewan plan the data presented from the province can be expected to be the closest to national figures, if such were available."[26] The first organization to publish reports on prescribing trends based on the out-of-hospital population of about one million people covered by the Drug Plan was the Saskatchewan Alcoholism Commission (now Saskatchewan Alcohol and Drug Abuse Commission, or SADAC).

The SADAC research looked at all central nervous system (CNS) drugs, not only those prescribed as mood-modifiers. It was concerned with the actual prescriptions going to people and the potential accumulation and interaction of drugs for various groups in the population. This scope of research was considered particularly vital in the case of the elderly since problems resulting from accumulation and interaction are greater for them, because they receive a greater variety of drugs.

Overall Sex Differences

The first report, released in 1978, was on overall prescribing trends in the province.[27] Table 1 compares the percentages of males and females receiving any CNS prescription during the period of this study. On the basis of these aggregate results, it was abundantly clear that more females than males were receiving such prescriptions. This was also the case in all but the youngest age group. It is equally significant that the discrepancy between the sexes was greatest among those between 15 and 29 and, though the difference

Table 1

PERCENTAGE OF SASKATCHEWAN POPULATION
Receiving Central Nervous System Prescriptions,
September 1975 — March 1977

Age	Male	Female	Total
0 — 9	11.7	10.1	10.9
10 — 14	7.8	9.1	8.4
15 — 19	16.3	24.9	20.5
20 — 29	10.3	23.4	16.7
30 — 39	31.8	34.7	34.7
40 — 49	36.3	39.5	39.5
50 — 59	39.0	48.1	43.6
60 — 69	44.5	56.2	50.3
70 +	47.4	63.2	55.6

Source: J. Harding, N. Wolf, and G. Chan. *A Socio-Demographic Profile of People Prescribed Mood-Modifyers in Saskatchewan* (Regina, Sask.: Saskatchewan Alcoholism Commission, 1978).

persisted through the older age groups it decreased among the oldest.

The discrepancy in rates of prescribing to men and women was particularly large for those 20 — 29. Eight times as many women as men received anti-depressants, and four times as many women as men received tranquillizers or sedatives and hypnotics. It was also found that, among people receiving CNS drug, over three times as many of the women as men were married (44.5 per cent compared to 13.9 per cent).

These aggregate results were limited in that they did not show sex comparisons within specific therapeutic categories. Such comparisons of prescriptions per male and female person in the different age groups are shown in Table 2.

In seven of the eleven age groups, more tranquillizer prescriptions per person went to females than males. In six of the age groups this was the case for the sedatives and anti-depressants. In almost all cases of elderly people, the women received more mood-modifier prescriptions per person than men. The only exception was in the case of anti-depressants for men 70 and over. The finding that women got more mood-modifier prescriptions per person also applied to the age groups of 40 — 49 and 50 — 59.

Sex comparisons of the rates of prescribing of tranquillizers and sedatives, and the percentages of the population getting tranquillizers and sedatives were even more revealing (see Table 3). Overall, for all people 20 and older, nearly twice as many women as men received tranquillizers (1.8 times) and sedatives (1.7 times). The discrepancy for tranquillizers decreased slightly from 1.8 times to 1.5 times as many women as men for those 60 — 69 and 70 and over. The discrepancy for sedatives was 1.6 times as many women as men for those 60 — 69 and 70 and over.

Though these comparisons are important, it is necessary to remember the reality on which they are based. Nearly one in three women and one in five men aged 60 — 69 and 70 and over received tranquillizers. Also one in ten women 60 — 69 and one in seven women 70 and over, compared to one in sixteen men 60 — 69 and one in ten men 70 and over received sedative prescriptions. Finally, in both age groups, for both classes of mood-modifiers, the elderly women received more prescriptions per person than the elderly men.

Table 2
CENTRAL NERVOUS SYSTEM DRUG PRESCRIPTIONS PER PERSON, SASKATCHEWAN,
September 1, 1975, to March 31, 1977

Age	Analgesics		Anti-Convulsants		Anti-Depressants		Tranquilizers		Other Psychotropics		CNS Stimulants		Sedatives and Hypnotics	
	Male	Female	Male	Female	Male	Female	Male	Female	Male	Female	Male	Female	Male	Female
0 — 2	1.2*	1.3	4.2	7.0	1.0	1.5	1.4	1.8				2.3	1.2	1.3
3 — 5			2.4	3.8	2.4	1.8	2.1	1.7			5.5	13.0		
	(1.1)	(1.1)											(1.1)	(1.1)
6 — 9			9.9	9.5	2.2	2.7	2.4	1.7			11.5	3.0		
10 — 14	1.1	1.4	9.7	8.5	2.3	1.3	1.8	2.0			2.8	5.0	1.8	1.1
15 — 19	1.5	1.6	8.0	8.9	3.2	2.5	2.7	1.8	7.0	2	2.6	2.7	1.4	1.2
20 — 29	1.6	1.6	22.5	5.0	3.1	2.4	2.8	2.6	13	19	5.0	2.3	2.0	1.8
30 — 39			6.2	6.1	4.1	4.2	3.8	4.4	1.5	5.5	1.8	4.8		
	(2.1)	(2.7)											(2.7)	(2.9)
40 — 49			8.4	5.2	4.2	4.5	4.7	5.0	7.5	4.1	6.6	1.7		
50 — 59	2.8	3.9	6.9	5.9	5.0	5.1	4.9	5.1	8.2	1.0	3.0	8.0	3.1	3.8
60 — 69	3.4	4.1	8.3	6.4	4.1	6.2	4.7	5.3	7.0	17	2.0	1.5	2.8	4.3
70+	4.2	6.0	6.1	5.8	6.2	5.9	5.1	6.1	10	2.0	5.5	2.0	3.7	4.2

Note: Data for analgesics and sedatives and hypnotics for 3-5, 6-9, 30-39, 40-49 are not available due to coding error. They are presented for people 3-9 and 30-49.

*Read as: Boys (from 0-2 years) in the 5% sample took an average of 1.2 prescriptions per person for analgesics during the first 19 months of the Drug Plan.

Source: Based on 5 per cent of the SADAC sample.

Table 3

Women and Men Prescribed Tranquillizers in Saskatchewan
September 1, 1975, — March 31, 1977

Age	Percentage of Saskatchewan Population*		Prescriptions per Person	
	Women	Men	Women	Men
20 — 29	11.1	2.8	2.6	2.8
30 — 49	24.3	14.2	4.7	4.3
50 — 59	28.1	16.5	5.1	4.9
60 — 69	32.4	18.3	5.3	4.7
70 +	31.7	21.0	6.1	5.1
Total	23.6	12.9	4.9	4.6

Women and Men Prescribed Sedatives and Hypnotics in Saskatchewan
September 1, 1975, — March 31, 1977

Age	Percentage of Saskatchewan Population*		Prescriptions per Person	
	Women	Men	Women	Men
20 — 29	1.8	0.4	1.8	2.0
30 — 49	4.6	3.1	2.9	2.7
50 — 59	7.1	3.9	3.8	3.1
60 — 69	9.6	6.0	4.3	2.8
70 +	14.8	9.1	4.2	3.7
Total	6.2	3.6	3.4	2.9

Women and Men Prescribed Analgesics in Saskatchewan
September 1, 1975, — March 31, 1977

Age	Percentage of Saskatchewan Population*		Prescriptions per Person	
	Women	Men	Women	Men
20 — 29	15.1	8.5	1.6	1.6
30 — 49	24.8	22.8	2.7	2.1
50 — 59	29.3	27.4	3.9	2.8
60 — 69	35.8	30.9	4.1	3.4
70 +	42.9	32.5	6.0	4.2
Total	26.8	22.0	3.7	2.8

Source: Based on 5 per cent of the SADAC sample.
* These figures are extrapolated from 5 per cent CNS drug study sample.

It is instructive to contrast these large sex differences in tranquillizers and sedative-hypnotics to the analgesics (see Table 3). Even though the over-prescribing to women is often justified by bio-medical arguments (e.g., problems from reproduction, longevity, etc.), and pain killers are commonly used for such bio-medical problems, no major sex differences existed for these drugs. The major sex differences clearly involved the psychoactives.

In some cases both the percentage of elderly men and the prescriptions going to them were higher than for some younger women. For example, twice as many men 70 and over received sedative prescriptions as women 30 — 39. They also received 25 per cent more prescriptions than these younger women. And twice the men 70 and over received tranquillizers prescritions than women 20 — 29. They also received 50 per cent more prescriptions than these younger women.

Over-Prescribing to Elderly Women

This, once again, points out how age as well as sex must be analysed directly to comprehend prescribing. Perhaps the most striking finding in this 1978 report was that, while people over 60 made up only 16 per cent of the population, they received 43 per cent of all CNS drug prescriptions. Because of this finding, a second report focusing on the elderly was undertaken and finally released, after some stalling and changes, in 1981.[28] It is an understatement to say that there was substantial opposition from the medical establishment and the Saskatchewan government to the release of these reports. Part of the explanation seems to be that the bureaucrats' memory of the doctors' strike after the introduction of medicare in the province in 1962 was still strong. Senior Health Department officials clearly did not want to appear to be interfering in the doctors' domain through any criticisms of their prescribing habits.

Overall, this research found that 50 per cent of people 60 — 69 and 56 per cent of people 70 and over received CNS prescriptions. This compared to 28 per cent of all people of all ages. Equally important, it found that people 60 — 69 received an average of 6.7 CNS prescriptions, and those 70 and over received 8.6 prescriptions. This compared to 5.3 per recipient of all ages.[29]

These CNS drugs were also analysed by pharmacological category. Depressants made up 40.3 per cent of all CNS drugs going to the elderly. This included the benzodiazepines (28.9 per cent), barbiturates (8.6 per cent), and other sedative-hypnotics (2.8 per cent). Just one drug, diazepam, (e.g., Valium) accounted for 73 per cent of all benzodiazepines and 52 per cent of all depressants. The major tranquillizers, most of which were the phenothiazines, were 9.2 per cent of all CNS drugs. One phenothiazine, thioridazine, accounted for 28 per cent of all major tranquillizers going to the elderly. The stimulants were 8.8 per cent of all CNS drugs. Almost all of these (97 per cent) were tricyclic anti-depressants. One drug, amitriptylene, accounted for 52 per cent of all these anti-depressants going to the elderly. The analgesics or

Table 4

*Number of Prescriptions per 1,000 Persons
in the Saskatchewan Population for CNS Drug Groups*

Drug Group	Men		Women	
	60 — 69	70+ over	60 — 69	70+ over
Benzodiazepines	754	814	1,624	1,426
Barbiturates	204	233	326	619
Other sedatives and hypnotics	26	98	92	240
All CNS depressants	984	1,145	2,042	2,285
Tricyclic anti-depressants	157	260	432	528
All CNS stimulants	159	285	443	536
Major Tranquillizers	186	413	219	701
Anti-convulsants	127	73	47	96
Narcotic Analgesics	269	397	413	601
Non-narcotic analgesics	787	980	1,041	1,945
All analgesics	1,056	1,377	1,454	2,546

Source: See source to Table 1. Table is based on 1976 Saskatchewan Hospital Services Plan population and from prescriptions in a 5 per cent sample of all Saskatchewan Prescription Drug Plan claims, September 1975 to March 1977.

pain killers were 39.7 per cent of all CNS drugs. About 26 per cent of them were narcotic and 74 per cent were non-narcotic. Analgesics containing codeine were about 15 per cent of all analgesics, while the synthetic narcotic propoxyphene (Darvon) accounted for 9.5 per cent of all analgesics. Finally, 2.5 per cent of all CNS drugs going to the elderly were anti-convulsants.

In all cases but the anti-convulsants, the prescribing rate was higher for elderly women than men. And, except for the benzodiazepines for women and anti-convulsants for men, the prescribing rate steadily increased with age. Prescriptions were calculated per thousand population to allow detailed age and sex comparisons (see Table 4).

Higher Total Dosage to Women

Unlike any earlier studies, the SADAC study analysed the average total dose (mean total quantities, or MTQ in milligrams) for many of the most-prescribed mood-modifiers (see Table 5). Again important sex differences were found.

With the exception of diazepam, which had very similar MTQs for women and men, women tended to get a more accumulated dose of the benzodiazepine drugs than men. The highest MTQ for flurazepam (a sedative and hypnotic often known as Dalmane) was for women 70 and over (2.3 grams compared to 1.4 for men). This was also the case for chlordiazepoxide, a tranquillizer often known as Librium (2.4 grams compared to 1.2). Women 60 — 69 also had a higher MTQ of flurazepam (1.8 grams compared to 1.3 for men) but a lower MTQ of chlordiazepoxide (1.5 grams compared to 2.0 for men).

The highest MTQ of amtriptylene, the main tricyclic anti-depressant, often known as Elavil, was also for women 70 and over (5.0 grams). This compared to 4.3 for men 70 and over. Women 60 — 69 had a slightly higher MTQ (4.8) than men 60 — 69 (4.7).

The fact that women weigh less than men and that the older women who got more of these drugs would not metabolize them as easily as younger people made these findings of particular concern. Further research, on estimated daily doses of chains of similar acting drugs over time, found that elderly women were in fact in far greater danger from drug accumulation (i.e., dependency).[30]

Table 5

Elderly Sex Differences in Mean Total Quantities for Most-Prescribed Mood-Modifiers in One-Year Period, in Saskatchewan (1975 — 1977)*

Rank Among CNS Drugs (by number of pre-sciptions	Generic Drug (Drug Classi-fication)	Men		Mean Total Quantity (in Milligrams) Women	
		60 — 69	70 & over	60 — 60	70 & over
1	Diazepam (tranquillizer)	999	744	957	813
3	Amitriptyline (anti-depressant)	4,710	4,286	4,798	4,955
7	Chlordiaze-poxide (tranquillizer)	2,021	1,191	1,490	2,389
9	Flurazepam (sedative)	1,314	1,438	1,817	2,315
10	Codeine (with ASA) (analgesic)	563 to 2,251	1,098 to 4,392	869 to 3,475	1,239 to 4,957

*Mean total quantity was calculated by multiplying strength in milligrams by number of units.

Source: These figures are from prescriptions under the Saskatchewan Prescription Drug Plan from September 1, 1975, to March 31, 1977. They are, however, calculated at 12/19 of this 19-month period to give an annual rate for comparison with other countries and regions. This expedient is justified since no significant seasonal variations in prescribing were found in the research. Calculations for codeine are given in terms of the range because different preparations of this combination drug could not be separated for analysis.

Official Government Reports on "Utilization"

In 1978, before the revised report on prescribing to the elderly was even released, the Saskatchewan Department of Health established the Joint Committee on Drug Prescribing, which was later renamed (on the recommendation of the medically oriented committee) the Joint Committee on Drug Utilization (JCDU), because the department did not want such emphasis on the medical profession. This did not mean that the committee was going to broaden its analysis to the pharmaceutical industry but, as we shall see, to concentrate on the extent of high and extreme users.

This committee identified the utilization of mood-modifying drugs as a primary topic of concern.[31] The fact that six of its first nine reports dealt with mood-modifiers shows how problematic these drugs were considered. Clearly some people believed that the so-called problem was a misconception partly caused by the release of the SADAC reports) that would be solved by official (and some believed more credible) reports. The approach the JCDU took to its research, symbolized by the semantic change from "prescribing" to "utilization," was questionable, however, on both methodological and policy grounds.[32] In spite of such manoeuvring, the problems of prescribed mood-modifiers, especially for elderly women, kept reappearing.

This research, based on all prescriptions (not a sample as done by SADAC), found that 20 per cent of Drug Plan beneficiaries during 1977 received prescriptions for mood-modifiers:

> Minor tranquillizers were prescribed most frequently (309 per 1,000 beneficiaries), followed by analgesics (158 per thousand) and anti-depressants (105 per thousand).[33]

Overall 10 per cent of all eligible beneficiaries received minor tranquillizers and 9 per cent received mood-modifying analgesics. Almost half (48 per cent) of those receiving any mood-modifier received minor tranquillizers and 44 per cent received analgesics. The next-highest percentages were for anti-depressants (14 per cent) and sedatives and hypnotics (12.5 per cent).

Unfortunately the smallest category used to assess prescriptions per person was from one to five prescriptions. Since most prescriptions are for one month, this "smallest" category would include people receiving mood-modifiers for almost half (five months) of 1977. The fact that 80 per cent of those being prescribed mood-modifiers got from one to five prescriptions, could therefore (in spite of the report's attempt to downplay it) be cause for concern.

Rather than refuting the earlier Saskatchewan research, the official research confirmed that elderly women were the group most likely to receive mood-modifiers. Thirty-four per cent of all beneficiaries in the province between 65 and 74 years received mood-modifiers. The percentage was even higher (40 per cent) for those over 75. An astonishing 42 per cent of women between 65 and 74, and 47 per cent of women over 75 received mood-modifiers in 1977. This compared to 27 per cent of men 65 — 74 and 31 per cent of men over 75.

Prescriptions per thousand eligible beneficiaries told the same story. Over three thousand mood-modifying prescriptions were issued for every thousand women aged over 75 in the province in the year being studied. In actuality these were going to a little less than half (47 per cent) of the eligible beneficiaries. We can therefore conclude that, on average, about half of those 75 and older received about six mood-modifying prescriptions in 1977. For all ages, 22 per cent of all active beneficiaries received six or more mood-modifying prescriptions during this period.

A second report was issued in 1979 assessing aggregate dosages of the mood-modifying drugs prescribed during the first quarter of 1977.[34] Some very questionable methods were used, such as looking only at average doses over three months (instead of actual lengths of time prescribed as was done in the SADAC studies), and using the same definitions of the level of doses (i.e., low, high, extreme) for the elderly as for younger adults, even though younger adults, because their metabolisms are faster, do not usually have the same extent or degree of problems with drugs as the elderly.

Even with these limited methods, which would definitely underestimate the problems of prescription drugs, the same story of elderly women and mood-modifiers was told. This report indicated that the highest number of cases of high dosage was for sedative-hypnotics (1,905) and for minor tranquillizers (1,322). Together these accounted for 85 per cent of all high dosages. The highest number of cases of extreme dosage was for sedative-hypnotics

(328), and the second and third for anti-depressants (177) and minor tranquillizers (176). In total these three drug classes accounted for 87.5 per cent of all cases of extreme dosages prescribed.

The age and sex of the 778 people prescribed extreme dosages was what would have been predicted by earlier research:

> Two-thirds of these were female. The percentage of females ranged from 73 per cent in the anti-depressant category to 44 per cent in the stimulant category.[35]

The average age of those prescribed extreme dosages was 53 years. For those prescribed extreme dosages of sedative-hypnotics, the average age was 60 years. Remember these were averages, meaning the high dosages were primarily going to the elderly.

The blaming of the consumer victim for the high rate of prescribing of mood-modifiers was (and remains) quite common in medical and industrial circles. The allegation behind this view is that addicted consumers, not pharmaceutical and medical practices, are responsible for the abuse of prescription drugs. It was therefore of some significance that this official study found that only 12 per cent of those receiving extreme dosages were obtaining them from more than two physicians. It reported that 525 physicians, nearly half of those practising in the province, prescribed mood-modifiers to the "extreme users" in the study.[36]

The Meaning of Declining Prescriptions

One drug that was prescribed more often to elderly women and that was highlighted in the SADAC reports was the pain-killer propoxyphene (Darvon). Because of growing concern about coroners' reports linking this product to drug-related deaths in the province, the call for its total banning in the United States by the Health Research Group, and the adding of it to the Schedule of the Canadian Narcotic Control Act in 1983, the JCDU issued a special report on this mood-modifier.[37]

It examined prescribing rates from 1977 — 82 and found a marked decrease from nearly thirty thousand prescriptions in 1977 to below nine thousand in 1982. Its percentage of all analgesics was reduced from 16 to 4 over these six years. The total number of patients receiving this potent drug declined from 5,141 in 1978 to 1,112 in 1982. Furthermore, the number of physicians prescribing this drug declined from 717 in 1978 to 383 in 1982.

This dramatic reduction in prescribing one of the most potent mood-modifiers showed that with the growing public pressure and some positive intervention by the Drug Plan, such reductions are possible. It, however, confirmed that earlier prescribing rates, especially to elderly women, were indeed very high and irresponsible. Furthermore, it is noticeable that these reductions were accomplished by the release of public information and programs aimed at the prescribers, not "drug abuse" programs aimed at consumers.

A second report concentrating on the benzodiazepines was released in 1983.[38] It showed an astonishing 55 per cent decrease in prescriptions for diazepam (Valium), from 213,549 in 1977 to 96,372 in 1982. This again showed that mood-modifying prescriptions could be greatly reduced and suggested that past rates were artificially and irresponsibly high.

But this report showed that sedative-hypnotic prescriptions had more than doubled, from 39,619 in 1977 to 96,473 in 1982. This was mainly the result of the addition of one product, triazolam, to the market and formulary in 1979. And though the addition of this product seemed to decrease the prescribing of the other main sedative-hypnotic by about 5,000 from 1977 to 1982, it led to an absolute increase of sedative-hypnotic prescriptions by 55,000. Like diazepam before it, triazolam appeared to be single-handedly responsible for rising prescription rates.

In 1984 the JCDU released a report showing that in 1983, 5,898 women compared to 3,245 men received this drug. Women 65 and over received 33 per cent of all these prescriptions, while men 65 and over received 18 per cent. So, while the amount of one benzodiazepine going to the elderly (particularly women) was being reduced the amount of another was being increased. As the JCDU itself said:

> The apparent level of use of triazolam in Saskatchewan suggests triazolam use may not always be in accordance with the usual recommendations for hypnotic therapy ... the manufacturer of triazolam has recommended that the dose of triazolam not exceed 0.5 mg daily

... During 1982, over half of those whose apparent daily dose of triazolam exceeded 0.5 mg daily throughout were 65 years or older.[39]

And, according to its own figures, 31 per cent of the cases where this occurred were for women 65 and over and 20 per cent were for men 60 and over.

These aggregate results suggested serious over-prescribing, particularly to elderly women. Nevertheless, the JCDU qualified itself by saying:

The JCDU realizes that appropriateness of drug use can only be assessed by the individual practitioner with full knowledge of the patient's history.[40]

This was identical to the kind of defences of the rights (i.e., privileges) of the prescriber that the JCDU made when the high rates of diazepam were found in 1977.

This dramatic shift from a highly promoted and ultimately stigmatized tranquillizer to a highly promoted (though not yet stigmatized) sedative shows the influence of non-medical and non-pharmacological market forces on prescribing trends. The influence of cross-cultural factors on prescribing practices has been noted in studies from other countries. Such a study, about Denmark, noted:

Consumption pattern in a historical perspective has changed from barbiturates to pain killers — for headache or migraine — to tranquillizers — for weak nerves or anxiety. Nowadays tranquillizers and nerve pills are "infected," low status words in Denmark, but sleeping pills — for sleeplessness and stress — are accepted in most social settings. The situation differs between societies and cultures; e.g., in Czechoslovakia stress among women leads to headache and thus to use of analgesics. Tranquillizers are not accepted as a means to treat every-day problems. Obviously, the consumption of mood-modifying drugs is a societal product and a societal problem.[41]

Companies such as Upjohn, which patented the sedative-hypnotic triazolam (as Halcion), obviously assess and try to shape such normative influences on medical diagnosis and prescribing. We may be seeing a process in Saskatchewan and Canada whereby tranquillizers (and anxiety) are becoming "infected," but the pharmaceutical industry is attempting to expand its market further by medicalizing sleeping problems. This, of course, will do nothing to come to grips with the social reasons why elderly women are being

The JCDU has issued one other report on mood-modifiers. In 1984, a JCDU update reported that the overall prescribing of mood-modifiers in general in Saskatchewan declined 4 per cent from 1977 to 1983. The percentage of the eligible population receiving these drugs went from 20 to 18. The number dispensed to women declined nearly 7 per cent and to men rose by 1 per cent.

Though this average decrease to women was a positive sign, averages can be deceptive. This report said the overall prescription rate decreased for analgesics, minor tranquillizers, major tranquillizers, phenobarbital, and stimulants. It should be noted, however, that it increased for anti-depressants, sedative-hypnotics, and lithium carbonate. Furthermore, the overall prescription rate increased for those 75 years and over.

The comparison of doses during the first quarter of 1977 and 1983 showed that the number of cases of both high and extreme levels increased for anti-depressants and major tranquillizers, as did the number of cases of high levels of sedative-hypnotics. For other mood-modifiers the number of cases of high and extreme levels decreased.

The cases of high levels of sedative-hypnotics in 1983 (2,229) was 60 per cent of all cases. And even though the number of cases of high dosage of minor tranquillizers fell from 1,322 to 921 between 1979 and 1983, the 921 cases still presented the second-largest number, and 25 per cent of all cases.

The number of extreme dosage levels going to women increased for major tranquillizers and phenobarbitals and decreased for all other mood-modifiers. The number of cases of extreme dosage levels going to men increased for anti-depressants, major tranquillizers, and phenobarbitals and decreased for all other mood-modifiers.

Trend Persists into the Mid-1980s

This was the last detailed information on mood-modifiers released from Drug Plan files. The plan, which remains the best source of information on mood-modifiers in Canada, continues to show that the elderly, particularly women, are getting more of these drugs. The 1984 — 5 annual report of the drug plan shows that even though the percentage of all drugs which are central nervous system

(CNS) drugs has been declining slightly since 1983, these drugs still make up the greatest proportion (almost 24 per cent) of all drugs dispensed. It also shows that the percentage of all CNS drugs which were minor tranquillizers has decreased from 5 to 4 per cent from 1982 to 1985. The percentage of all CNS drugs, however, has risen for both anti-depressants and analgesics and is about the same for sedative-hypnotics and major tranquillizers. Though the annual report does not break these categories down by age or sex, the likelihood is that elderly women continue to be the main recipients of these drugs. As the report says:

> The 65 plus age group made up 12.5 per cent of the eligible population, represented 15.3 per cent of the active beneficiaries, and received 34.9 per cent of all prescriptions ... For all age groups beyond 14, females received more prescriptions per active beneficiary.[42]

Recent studies outside Saskatchewan continue to confirm that a disproportionately large number of the elderly is being prescribed these mood-modifiers. The 1978 — 9 Canadian Health Survey asked what drugs were taken in a two-day period. Fourteen per cent (14 per cent) of those sixty-five and older reported tranquillizer use, and 22 per cent reported the use of pain-killers. This compared to 6 per cent of the total adult population who reported taking tranquillizers, and 16 per cent who reported taking pain killers.[43] An Ontario survey of psychoactive drug use during 1984 found 13 per cent of persons over fifty reporting using tranquillizers and 13 per cent using sleeping pills. In comparison, 9 per cent of the total adult population reported taking tranquillizers and 7 per cent, sleeping pills.[44]

III. THE ROLE OF THE PRESCRIPTION DELIVERY SYSTEM

The main trade of physicians in industrial societies has, unfortunately, become prescribing. And with the increase in the number of Canadian physicians — a 50 per cent increase between 1968 and 1978, while the population grew only by 13 per cent[45] — there has been a proliferation of prescribing. The industry obviously stands ready to promote, produce for, and profit from this expanding market. While this has happened the other end of the delivery system — the drug store — has also been expanding.

The 1971 Toronto study of prescribing to non-institutionalized adults found that a full 92 per cent of prescriptions were dispensed by retail pharmacies; the rest were dispensed by hospitals. This and other similar findings suggest that an analysis of the drug store is long overdue. In addition to being the place where most elderly people fill their prescriptions, the drug store is where many elderly persons shop for all the array of OTC drugs as a means to treat their ailments themselves and alleviate their overwhelming living conditions. With this in mind let us look at the drug store business across Canada for further insight into the over-prescribing of mood-modifiers to elderly women.

The drug store is now a powerful segment of the Canadian economy. According to Statistics Canada, in 1982 Canadian drug stores reported sales of over $4 billion. By 1984 sales had grown to over $5 billion.[46] About 75 per cent of these sales were in independent drug stores, and the rest were in chain stores.[47] We are probably going to see accelerated integration of drug stores into retail chains in the coming years.

The above figures represent total sales for a business that is steadily diversifying its products to include such things as junk food and pornographic videos as well as a wide array of household products. However, the Canadian drug store is still primarily trading in drugs — including the growing, lucrative OTC drug market. According to the survey of community pharmacy operations, 44 per cent of the drug store sales 1981 were for prescription drugs and another 21 per cent were for OTC drugs. (Cosmetics accounted for 4 per cent and other products for 31 per cent.)[48] Drugs, then, accounted for two-thirds of total sales in Canadian drug stores.

The sale of proliferating drug products seems to become even more vital to the pharmacy business. Total sales increased 11 per cent from 1980 to 1981. However, sales of prescriptions increased 14 per cent and those for OTC drugs increased 17 per cent in this one year. The cost of all products during 1981 was two-thirds of the sales, and other expenses (including salaries to owners or managers) were 28 per cent. This meant there was a profit rate of 6 per cent (of total sales before taxes).[49] In 1984 the total profits in drug stores were, therefore, around $300 million.

There are other indications that the pharmacy business is in better health than the general population. The 1982 survey of prescriptions showed that almost half (49 per cent) of the sales volume was for the dispensing of drugs.[50] Furthermore, the average price of a prescription was $10.55, a 20 per cent increase over the previous year. A little less than half (45 per cent) of these prescriptions involved secured payment or co-payment through government third-party drug plans.

In 1983 these figures continued to grow. The volume of prescription drugs was up by over 8 per cent; the average price per prescription was over $12.00 (more than double the 1978 price); and third-party drug plans ensured payment or co-payment for over half (53 per cent) of the prescriptions filled.[51]

The Saskatchewan Drug Store

Since the most comprehensive information on prescribing to the elderly in Canada comes from the Saskatchewan Prescription Drug Plan (SPDP), it is important to look in more detail at the pharmacy delivery system that dispenses drugs to the elderly in this province. The comparisons with other provinces and with Canada as a whole will be helpful in placing the issue of over-prescribing to elderly women in its political and economic context.

In 1982 the total sales in independent drug stores in Saskatchewan was nearly $100 million. This compared to nearly $61 million in the chain stores in the province. This indicates that in Saskatchewan the chain stores controlled a greater proportion of the drug store market (61 per cent) than they did in Canada as a whole (25 per cent). The increase in the total sales in the independent drug stores over 1981 was 22 per cent, compared to 17 per cent for the chain stores. This is a reversal from the Canadian increases in total sales of 25 per cent in the chains and 15 per cent in the independent stores.

These Saskatchewan drug stores appear to be doing quite well. Total sales in the nearly four hundred drug stores in the province increased 28 per cent in January 1983 over January 1982, compared to 20 per cent for the country as a whole. This was the largest increase of any province, and was mostly accounted for by an increase in total sales of 32 per cent for the independent drug stores. (The increase was 21 per cent for the chains.)[52]

Without a more thorough analysis of drug store sales it is risky to speculate on these comparisons. However, the special role that the government Drug Plan plays in Saskatchewan cannot be ignored. For example, in 1982 Saskatchewan had the second-lowest average prescription cost of $9.45, the lowest being in Quebec at $8.69.[53] This compared to the national average of $10.55 and the highest price, in British Columbia, of $11.65. Also in 1982 Saskatchewan recorded the smallest increase in prices for prescriptions. During 1982 prescriptions in Saskatchewan drug stores were a very similar percentage of the total volume (44.5 per cent) of sales as for the country as a whole (49 per cent). However, because of the existence of the comprehensive Drug Plan, almost twice the percentage of prescriptions had secured co-payment by the government (88 per cent) as for the country as a whole (45 per cent).

One of the main goals of the Drug Plan was to keep costs down, and it appears to have initially met this objective. However, by 1983 the average price of a prescription in Saskatchewan had risen to $12.33, which was above the national average of $12.05. The Saskatchewan price was also higher than Quebec, Ontario, and Manitoba. And in 1983 the biggest price increase occurred in Saskatchewan. Also the percentage of prescriptions with secured co-payment by a third-party drug plan was down slightly (to 86 per cent).

The Drug Plan and the Welfare of the Elderly

It is tempting to relate such shifts as increasing price to the change from a social democratic to a conservative provincial government in April 1982. It is well known that the Conservative Party, which claims to speak for businessmen, was not favourably disposed to such direct government intervention in the economy as the Drug Plan. After taking power, the Conservative government quickly initiated a review of the Drug Plan. However, it is noteworthy that in its submission to the new government the association of pharmacists said they preferred the existing prescription charge system. However, they recommended an expanded formulary (covering more drugs); and, rather than abolish the professional fee, they called for an expanded fee that would go beyond dispensing to counselling services. They also recommended that senior citizens receive formulary drugs free of charge.[54]

What this suggests is that the pharmacy business sees its own interests as basically compatible with state-funded drug insurance schemes. Most important, they see free prescription drugs for the largest consumers, the elderly, as compatible with business enterprise. It is possible that this position is in part motivated by a concern for the welfare of the elderly. The deterrent effect of elderly people having to pay a dispensing fee for prescriptions is well documented. It is also likely that full payment from the government for prescriptions for the elderly would simplify their business and be the easiest way to ensure greater sales.

This is not to say that increases in the dispensing fee are not a burden, especially to the high proportion of the elderly who are disadvantaged. The maximum fee that can be charged the Saskatchewan customer by the pharmacist has doubled (from $2.00 to $4.00) since the plan was introduced in 1975. But the greater proportion of the total maximum dispensing fee — which has more than doubled (from $2.00 to $5.30) since the plan began — comes directly from the government. (The government *subsidizes* the difference between the fee charged the customer and the total fee.) From the point of view of the pharmacy business, why not simplify paper work, expedite the filling of prescriptions; and in the case of the highest users, the elderly, simply bill the government for the works.

A system that ensures co-payment for the prescribing of drug products can appear to be in the best interests of the consumer until the rationality of the drug products themselves comes into question. The rationality of the mood-modifiers is particularly questionable. Certainly the use of a formulary in Saskatchewan, as in many Third World countries, can act as an important quality control on proliferating drug products. However, in the case of the mood-modifying drugs that the elderly are more likely to receive, the control is particularly weak.

The prescription drug regulatory system in Canada has come under growing criticism as public awareness of the risks of drug products grows.[55] Before 1951 the safety of a drug did not even have to be proved before it was put on the Canadian market. The control system was tightened *after* the thalidomide disaster. After 1963 drugs marketed in Canada finally had to be proved effective. It may seem astonishing that before that they did not, but this only goes to show the power of the "free market" ideology that persists even in a period of publicly funded health care. And all is still not well regarding regulations:

> ... while drugs are now required to be safe and effective before being marketed, they are not required to be any better than other drugs currently on the market for the same problem.[56]

This leads, in the name of public regulation, to the proliferation of CNS drugs like the benzodiazepine tranquillizers (and to other widely prescribed drugs like the anti-inflammatory drugs which were the most prescribed drugs in Saskatchewan in 1984 — 5), both of which the elderly are more likely to get.

Even with a formulary in existence in Saskatchewan, the overwhelming effect of an escalating multinational pharmaceutical market remains. There are now around thirty thousand products on the market, based on only about one thousand active ingredients. When the Drug Plan began in 1975, it listed four times the number of drugs recommended by the WHO in its list of essential drugs.[57] Yet the medical and pharmacy professions usually want even more products listed in the Saskatchewan formulary.

And more products continue to be added — fifty-two in 1983, for example. Fortunately the formulary also provides the opportunity for deleting drug products. The fact that thirty-seven drug products were removed from the Saskatchewan formulary in 1983 is both an indication of this public health potential and further proof that many drugs are still experimental when they are introduced on the market. And while it is better to have a secondary control like the formulary, after products are deleted they are still available on the market for a doctor to prescribe outside the Drug Plan.

The withdrawal of some products after they have been on the market for several years shows that because of the initial regulatory standards, loop holes, and the pressure to market more and more drugs, adverse side-effects may not be known until the drug becomes widely used. Because the elderly are extra sensitive to drugs, because so many elderly people are socially isolated; and because organ deterioration or failure due to drugs is not likely to be noted on a death certificate (especially by the prescribing doctor), detrimental drug effects for the elderly, in particular, may go unnoticed. Nor are they likely to be studied systematically.

IV THE DE-MEDICALIZATION OF DEVELOPMENT

The results of the SADAC study discussed earlier proved unquestionably that elderly women face greater risks from mood-modifiers than other segments of the population. Like the more limited studies done before, this research found that the elderly women receiving these drugs were more likely to be disadvantaged.

It is well known that more women than men tend to be below "the poverty line." Sixty-two per cent of women between 65 and 69, compared to 47 per cent of men in that age group were living in poverty in the late 1960s.[58] The figure for women over 70 was 70 per cent, and for men over 70 it was up to 66 per cent. If anything, the situation of elderly women and men is even worse today.

Not only mood-modifiers but poverty is widespread among Saskatchewan's elderly. Two-thirds of the single pensioners, a majority of whom are women, received both the Guaranteed Income Supplement (GIS) and the Old Age Security (OAS) payment during 1979. Single pensioners receiving these supplements and senior citizens benefits were still below the revised Statistics Canada poverty level.[59]

These statistics show that women face both the problem of poverty and of mood-modifiers earlier than men; but that as both sexes get older the differences decrease. These problems of elderly women must be placed squarely in the context of the failure of Canadian and global society to distribute opportunities equally. And they must be related to the socio-economic and political conditions that spawn this inequality. But we must also recognize that as both sexes age their inequality is reduced by a common despair and powerlessness.

In recent years there has been heightened attention to this unequal status of women and their special role in social and economic development. Similarities between the conditions of women in industrial and Third World countries are increasingly being pointed out. As was said at a Canadian conference on women and pharmaceutics,

> The oppression of women within Third World societies combines with poverty to create a particularly vicious cycle of deprivation and ill-health for women. The low status of women has a direct and devastating effect on their health. And we first-world women are familiar with the broad terms of this oppression, because it parallels our own.[60]

It is worth exploring this parallel in view of the above discussion of the particular risks faced by elderly women from mood-modifiers. In Canada, as in poorer countries,

> When women's economic position and low status within society is combined with poverty the effect on women's health in particular can be absolutely devastating.[61]

And these health problems, rooted in stratification and poverty, are usually dealt with medically rather than socially.

Still in Third World countries, unlike the developed countries, these problems tend to be most devastating for child-bearing women and children. In such countries poverty and discrimination tend to interrelate with underdevelopment and related population pressures. In more industrialized countries like Canada, the birthrate has fallen and the population is aging very quickly. Here it is women at the end, not the beginning, of their lives who are more seriously hit by the vicious cycle of poverty, low status, and poor-health — a similar structure but a different outcome.

There are, of course, other important parallels between Canada and Third World countries that pertain to women's health. Many parallels are due to the medicalization of underdevelopment by the global structure of the drug industry.[62] For example, fewer than one hundred companies control two-thirds of the pharmaceutical markets in the non-socialist world. A handful of companies dominate the markets that exist in therapeutic categories like psychotropics.

It is clearly in the industrial world, not the Third World, where pharmaceutical control is most firmly established. Though Canada is only the thirtieth-largest country in the world, we are the eleventh-largest pharmaceutical market, and the proliferation of psychotropics is greatly responsible for this. However, as in most Third World countries, in Canada the market is foreign-owned and controlled. This has remained the case in spite of the development of the government medicare program. In 1982 there were no Canadian-owned drug companies among the five hundred largest companies.

Third World countries, like Bangladesh, have struggled to free themselves of such foreign control and to tackle women's health problems from a broad developmental rather than a narrow pharmaceutical approach. Those of us in industrial countries with aging populations being targeted by American and West European drug firms have much to learn from these advances. With the growing influence of the United States in Canadian domestic and foreign affairs in the mid-1980s, the multinational lobby from across the border is pressing for even greater control of the Canadian drug market. Their strategy has been to challenge compulsory licensing of generic products that has been in effect in Canada since 1969.[63] Though the generic industry controls only 15 per cent of the domestic market, the multinationals are on the offensive to increase their profits, which are now more than twice the average for the manufacturing sector.

A supposed benefit for Canada is more domestic activity in the industry. However, there are no guarantees and in Canada as in the Third World, so-called research and development is mostly an attempt to get more patented products based on known compounds onto the market. In fact, most of the more educated personnel in the industry in Canada, as elsewhere, are in marketing.

In Canada, as in the Third World, it will take a fundamental redirection of pharmaceutical control from the multinationals to nurture a "science for the people." A developmental perspective on health that stresses the abolition of poverty and the redistribution of opportunity and control will be necessary to accomplish this change.

At the same time it is very clear that the aging, increasingly impoverished population of the industrial world — particularly elderly women — is going to be a growing target for those who desire to continue expanding the pharmaceutical market. The implications of the two paths — both globally and locally — are becoming clearer to the broad alliance of women's consumers, and alternative-health groups, an alliance whose growth is essential if we are to make the transition to a more humane and just world.[64]

◄►

NOTES

1. S. Rosenblatt and R. Dodson, *Beyond Valium: The Brave New World of Psychochemistry* (New York: Putman, 1981), p.42.

2. T. Smith, and J. Gilbert, "Edmonton Drug Survey," *Alberta Medical Bulletin,* May 1973, pp.36 — 41.

3. J. Harding, N. Wolf, and G. Chan, *Central Nervous System Prescription Drugs and Elderly People: An Overview of Issues and a Saskatchewan Profile:* (Regina, Sask.: Saskatchewan Alcoholism Commission, 1981).

4. Some pharmacological researchers associated with Ontario's Addiction Research Foundation (ARF), which is associated with the WHO, are considering using sales figures to estimate a "defined daily dose" for various drugs. This method would average the rates of prescribing over the whole population of the country using doses for major indications. It would allow some aggregate comparisons of prescription rates per capita with many European countries and the United States, where studies using this method have already been done. Consumer and health groups, however, should work for some qualitative improvements in the monitoring; for example, indirect indicators of the proportion of drugs going to the elderly, to elderly women, etc., should be taken into account. Otherwise the system will not provde the necessary information about the groups in greatest danger from inappropriate and overprescribing of mood-modifying drugs.

5. R. Cooperstock and M. Sims, "Mood-Modifying Drugs Prescribed in a Canadian City," *American Journal of Public Health,* 61, no.5 (May 1971) p.1012.

6. *Ibid.*

7. *Ibid.,* p.1010.

8. J. Levine, "The Nature and Extent of Psychotropic Drug Usage in the United States." Statement before the Sub-Committee on Monopoly of the Select Committee on Small Business, U.S. Senate, 1969.

9. M.B. Balter, J. Levine, and D.I. Manheimer, "Cross-National Study of the Extent of Anti-Anxiety/Sedative Drug Use," *New England Journal of Medicine,* 290, no. 14 (April 4, 1974) pp.769 — 74.

10. L. Guse, G. Morier, and J. Ludwig, Winnipeg *Survey of Prescription Drug (Mood-Altering) Use Among Women,* Technical Report, mimeo. October 30, 1976. Winnipeg has been particularly central in research on pharmaceutics in Canada. A government of Manitoba Commission on the manufacture and distribution of pharmaceutics encouraged the publishing of Alan Klass' book *There's Gold in Them Thar Pills* by Penguin in 1975. Winnipeg was the location of a major conference in 1982 on Women and Development, which focused on pharmaceutics. It was also the prairie office of the now defunct Non-Medical Use of Drugs Directorate, which helped fund the Winnipeg study.

11. *Ibid.,* p.4.

12. *Ibid.,* p.10 — 11.

13. *Ibid.,* p.8 — 9.

14. *Ibid.,* P.13.

15. *Ibid.,* p.17.

16. *Ibid.,* p.19.

17. *Ibid.*

18. *Ibid.,* p.20. Contradictory findings on the role of marital status were found in the Saskatchewan research discussed below.

19. R. Cooperstock, *The Epidemiology of Psychotropic Drug Use in Canada Today.* Paper prepared for workshop on Sociopharmacology, World Congress on Mental Health, Vancouver, Canada, 21 — 6 Aug., 1977, p.7.

20. D. Gutmann, *A Study of Legal Drug Use by Older Americans* (Washington: National Institute on Drug Abuse, 1977), p.10.

21. *Ibid.,* p.11.

22. *Ibid.,* p.12.

23. *Ibid.,* p.6.

24. *Ibid.,* p.12

25. *Ibid.*

26. R. Cooperstock, *Epidemiology of Psychotropic Drug Use,* p.5.

27. J. Harding, N. Wolf, N., and G. Chan, *A Socio-Demographic Profile of People Prescribed Mood-Modifiers in Saskatchewan* (Regina, Sask.: Saskatchewan Alcoholism Commission, 1978).

28. For a discussion of the significance of the semantic changes from "prescribing" to "utilization" see J. Harding, *A Comparison of a Final and Released Government Report on Prescribing to the Elderly in Saskatchewan,* Occa-

sional Paper Series No. 1 (Regina, Sask.: Prairie Justice Research, University of Regina, 1982).

29. Since the prescriptions for those aged sixty and over are part of the average for all ages, the difference between the elderly and younger ages is much greater than this comparison suggests.

30. See reference in note 28 above for discussion of why this research was never completed. For a discussion of the importance of such research see J. Harding, *Prescribing of Central Nervous System Drugs to School-age Children*, paper presented at Showcase 83, Regina, Sask., March 14 — 18, 1983.

31. Saskatchewan Health, Joint Committee on Drug Utilization, Report No. 3, *Utilization of Mood-Modifying Drugs in Saskatchewan: 1977, Part I* (Regina, Sask., 1977), p.1.

32. J. Harding, *Politics of Prescription Drug Research*. Occasional Paper Series No. 3 (Regina, Sask.: Prairie Justice Research, University of Regina, 1986)

33. Saskatchewan Department of Health, *Utilization of Mood-Modifying Drugs, Part I*, p.3.

34. Saskatchewan Health, Joint Committee on Drug Utilization, Report No. 4, *Utilization of Mood-Modifying Drugs in Saskatchewan: 1977, Part II* (Regina, Sask., 1979).

35. *Ibid.*, p.7.

36. *Ibid.*

37. Saskatchewan Health, Joint Committee on Drug Utilization, Report No. 6, *Use of Propoxyphene in Saskatchewan* (Regina, Sask., 1983).

38. Saskatchewan Health, Joint Committee on Drug Utilization, *Use of Benzodiazepines*, Report No. 7 (Regina, Sask., 1983).

39. ......, Report No. 9 *Triazolam Use in Saskatchewan* (Regina, Sask., 1984), p.3.

40. *Ibid.*

41. Ebba Hansen, *Use of Mood-Modifying Medicines Among Danish Men and Women*, paper presented at Medikamente fuer Frauen — Chemie fuer die Seele, Bremen, Nov. 4 — 6. 1985, p.3.

42. Saskatchewan Health, Joint Committee on Drug Utilization, Report No. 8, *Use of Mood-Modifying Drugs in Saskatchewan — Update (Regina, Sask., 1984), p.4.*

43. *Ibid.*, p.3.

44. Saskatchewan Health, Prescription Drug Plan, *Annual Report 1984-85* (Reginal, Sask., 1985), p.13.

45. Health and Welfare Canada and Statistics Canada, *The Health of Canadians — Report of the Canada Health Survey,* Statistics Canada Catalogue no. 82 — 538 (Ottawa, 1981).

46. R.G. Smart, and E.M. Adlaf, *Alcohol and Drug Use Among Ontario Adults*

in 1984 and Changes Since 1982 (Toronto: Addiction Research Foundation, 1984).

47. Statistics Canada, *Retail Trade,* March 1985, Catalogue no. 63 — 005, (Ottawa: Statistics Canada), Table 27.

48. "It was a Very Good Year" ("Business Barometer"), *Drug Merchandising* (Apr. 1983) pp.14 — 16.

49. H.J. Segal, "Financial: Information System Best Defense Against Problem," *Drug Merchandising,* May 1983, pp.8 — 10.

50. "It was a Very Good Year" ("Business Barometer"), *Drug Merchandising,* Apr. 1983.

51. W. Granger, "The Skyrocketing Costs of Drugs: A Review of the 19th Survey of Prescriptions," *Drug Merchandising* Jan. 1983, pp.17 — 21.

52. "20th Annual Prescription Survey. That $13.46 RX in B.C. is Just $9.26 in Quebec," *Drug Merchandising,* Dec. 1983, pp.18 — 20.

53. "Good Business to 1983 all but B.C." ("Business Barometer"), *Drug Merchandising,* May 1983, p.25.

54. Granger, *The Skyrocketing Costs of Drugs.*

55. Saskatchewan Pharmaceutical Association, *Newsletter,* 3, no. 3 (May 1983), p.2.

56. Health Action International, "Minutes," Toronto, Oct. 15, 1985, Appendix, p.4.

57. World Health Organization, Technical Report No. 615, *The Selection of Essential Drugs,* (Geneva, 1977).

58. *Poverty in Canada,* Report of the Special Senate Committee on Poverty, Ottawa, 1971.

59. Senior Citizens Provincial Council, *Poverty Among Seniors* (Regina, Sask., 1979).

60. V. Beardshaw, *Women, Health and Pharmaceutics: Some Issues of International Concern,* paper presented at Women and Development Conference, Manitoba Council for International Co-operation, Winnipeg, Oct. 15 — 16, 1982, 7.2.

61. *Ibid.,* p.4.

62. J. Harding, *Pharmaceutical Control,* Canadian Broadcasting Corporation Transcripts, Toronto, March 1983. (Available from CBC, P.O. Box 500, Station "A", Toronto, Ont. M5W 1E6).

63. ..... *Brief to the Commission of Inquiry on the Pharmaceutical Industry* on behalf of the Canadian Council for International Development, Ottawa, Nov. 2, 1984.

64. A. Gorz, *Paths to Paradise: On the Liberation From Work* (Boston: Southend Press, 1985).

II: Pharmaceuticals and Family Planning:
Women are the Targets

This part looks at some of the various drugs and devices used for family planning and their particular effects on the women who use them. In "Population Control and the Pharmaceutical Industry," Cary LaCheen documents exhaustively the influence of the drug industry in Third World family planning programs and its links with the international population-control establishment, and shows how contraceptive marketing techniques promote the ideology of population control. "Finger in the Dyke: The Fight to Keep Injectables out of India" by Vimal Balasubrahmanyan examines the effort to introduce injectable contraceptives on a massive scale into India's family planning programs and the efforts of women's and human rights groups to publicize the dangers of these drugs. In "From Birth Control to Population Control: Depo-Provera in Southeast Asia," Lynn Duggan explores the medical, social, and political issues surrounding the controversial injectable Depo-Provera. "The Rise and Fall of the IUD" by Ann Pappert gives a short history of the IUD and shows how serious health problems associated with its use have led to a sharp decline in its popularity in recent years.

POPULATION CONTROL AND THE PHARMACEUTICAL INDUSTRY

Cary LaCheen

CONTRACEPTIVES — THE DRUGS, DEVICES, AND PRACTICES that are used to prevent pregnancy — play a complex and unique role in modern history. While methods of preventing pregnancy and childbirth have been practised for hundreds, if not thousands, of years, with the use of potions, home-made vaginal sponges and pessaries, coitus interruptus, the rhythm method, abstinence, and abortion, the 1960s which saw the development of the birth control pill, modern IUDs, and injectable contraceptives, are generally considered to be the beginning of the modern contraceptive era.

In the West, the modern contraceptive era is associated with the "sexual revolution" and women's liberation, because contraceptives further separated sex from procreation and enabled women, for the first time, to plan their families with some certainty.

With the rise of the multinational global economy and the simultaneous acceptance of theories of global overpopulation in the 1950s and 1960s, modern contraceptives, produced by American and Western European companies, spread to the Third World. While at first glance contraceptives might appear to give women in developing countries more control over reproduction their effect has actually not been so beneficial.

Weak drug safety laws and a lack of basic health care for the majority in developing countries have meant that women in the

Third World have been exposed to untested and dangerous contraceptives as well as to contraceptives that cannot possibly be used safely. Moreover, contraceptives have been made available in the Third World, not to increase reproductive options for women, but as part of national population-reduction strategies. Thus, participation, and not free choice, is the goal of most programs and many programs have used coercive and high-pressure tactics to achieve this goal. Many population programs in developing countries were developed or encouraged by people outside of the Third World who view population control in developing countries as politically and economically beneficial to the United States and the rest of the developed world.

While the benefits of population control programs for women in developing countries are questionable, one clear beneficiary has been the contraceptive industry, which considers the Third World to be an important source of future growth. The industry's products have been introduced into these markets by governmental and non-governmental organizations (including the American government) that pay for distribution, fund much of the basic scientific research, and sometimes even fund market research and promotion of these products.

Fortunately for the contraceptive manufacturers, the goals and priorities of the population-control establishment are almost completely consistent with their own. Population-control programs and enthusiasts seek to maximize the number of contraceptives distributed. Programs therefore stress the number of new contraceptive "acceptors" who can be "motivated" to use contraceptives, and a lower priority is given to the delivery of medical care, the provision of information, and the client's freedom of choice. Program evaluators, who usually judge the success of population programs by the number of "births averted," not by the patient's satisfaction, value a contraceptive's effectiveness over its safety.

In several countries, population programs have used financial incentives to doctors, health workers, and patients to encourage the use of contraceptives, and health workers have been pushed to meet pre-established quotas of "acceptors" for each type of contraceptive. These policies encourage — and have resulted in — misinformation and coercion, not reproductive freedom.

Not surprisingly, the contraceptive industry has cultivated and taken steps to protect this important market, through lobbying, financial support of population-control groups, and other ties to the population-control establishment.

This article will examine the underlying assumptions of the population-control establishment, the priorities that shape contraceptive research and development, the financial and other ties between the population-control establishment and the contraceptive industry, and the degree to which the industry benefits from and is dependent upon population-control programs. It will also examine some of the strategies that have been used to increase the use of contraceptives in population programs, including a new breed of programs that eliminates the "extras" like health care, relies on extensive market research and product advertising, and more closely resembles private-sector marketing techniques than efforts to improve the health and well-being of people in the Third World.

OVERPOPULATION OR UNEQUAL DISTRIBUTION OF RESOURCES?

The political lines of the issue of world population control were redrawn in 1984, when the Reagan administration began to follow the demands of Right to Life groups and restrict the American role in population control programs. For many, this trend gives the programs the embattled image usually held by "liberal social programs" under attack from the right. But population-control programs are far from liberal. Much of the motivation for their creation was to contain growing Third World populations, which were seen as a threat to democracy and "stability."

Population-control programs are based on a number of basic assumptions about the causes of population growth and poverty in developing countries.[1] First, population-control enthusiasts assume that children are an economic burden to families in developing countries, as they are often seen to be in the West. They therefore conclude that women in developing countries want to limit their families and need only additional information and contraceptives to do so. But, as many have pointed out, children are usually an economic asset to the family in developing countries and make an important economic contribution to the family from an early age. Another important reason for having a large number of children in developing countries is that children often do not survive to adulthood. In the absence of government social security programs, many parents wish to have at least two living adult children to care for them in their own old age. In other words, having a large number of children in developing countries is often a rational choice made in self-interest, and persuading people to bear fewer children is doomed to failure until economic development lifts the majority above the margin of survival.

Secondly, most population-control enthusiasts also assume that population growth *causes* hunger and poverty in developing countries. They maintain that the current population growth rates will outstrip the world's capacity to provide food and other resources for everyone. Population growth is believed to impede economic development in less developed countries, since, it is argued, increases in the GNP will just be absorbed by the increasing population.

The fact is that these arguments over the *limits* of resources fail to address the real causes of poverty, primary among which is the *distribution* of resources. Unequal distribution of land and other resources and undemocratic governments that perpetuate often grotesque inequities between rich and poor are largely responsible for the fact that many in developing countries cannot meet their basic needs.

In the mid-1970s, 17 per cent of the landowners in South America controlled 90 per cent of the land. In Asia, one-fifth of the landowners controlled three-fifths of the arable land. In Latin America, over a third of the rural population owned only 1 per cent of the cropland, and in Africa, three-quarters of the population had access to less than 4 per cent of the land.[2] Contrary to widely held beliefs, India produces enough food to feed its poor. The problem is that many simply do not control the land on which food is produced and do not have the money to buy food. Thus, while agricultural production has increased in the country in recent years, the proportion of food eaten by the poor has actually declined.[3]

If overpopulation caused hunger and poverty, one would expect to see a global correlation between hunger and poverty and population density, but this is not the case. France is as densely populated as India, but obviously does not suffer from the same degree of poverty. The Netherlands is far more densely populated than Mexico, but Mexico has much higher rates of hunger and poverty.[4]

In any case, population controllers' theories don't stand up to the evidence: while the global population growth rate has declined since 1974, economic development and increased standards of living — the supposed goals of these population policies — have not advanced in the majority in developing countries. Even the 1984 World Population Plan of Action acknowledged that, in spite of declining population growth rates over the last ten years, many countries have experienced "a period of instability, increased unemployment, mounting external indebtedness, stagnation and even decline in economic growth" and that "the number of people living in absolute poverty has increased."[5]

Far from addressing the problems of hunger, poverty, and underdevelopment, the fundamental principle underlying much population policy is to keep the lid on these problems before they disrupt current political and economic structures and threaten the developed world. It is for this reason that the United States has directed so much population assistance to countries that are of strategic economic and political importance to American interests: in particular, India, Thailand, Indonesia, the Philippines, and Central American countries.[6] These countries have serious problems unrelated to population density, but rather than deal with these problems the United States attempts to ease the pressure while maintaining the political and economic status quo. Through population control, (as well as various types of economic and military aid), the United States has tried to protect its own interests and control the unrest that threatens its interests, rather than address the underlying causes of poverty and discontent in developing countries.

This has always been true in the population-control movement. In the 1940s, Hugh Moore, the founder of the Dixie Cup Corporation and one of the first to sound the alarm about the population "crisis," argued that overpopulation was a threat to world peace. In 1954, Moore distributed a pamphlet, *The Population Bomb,* which warned that:

> The population bomb threatens to create an explosion as disruptive and dangerous as the explosion of the atom, and with as much influence on prospects for progress or disaster, war or peace.[7]

This mentality persists to this day. Take the following passage from a recent brochure of Population Services International, an organization that distributes contraceptives in developed countries:

> Most experts agree that widespread and chronic famines will inevitably occur if present growth rates go unchecked. Apart from the suffering of those who die of starvation and disease, we can expect to see racial and class strife, large scale terrorism, economic upheaval, abrupt decline of raw materials production, psychological breakdown, and sporadic wars of survival. In this bleak event, the more democratic governments will doubtless be the first to crumble, and the net weight of harsh authoritarianism in the world (presumably on the pro-communist side) will sharply increase.
>
> It is plain that such a situation will confront the U.S. with dangerous military vortexes and booby traps of the Vietnam type. Beyond that, we shall face the loss of vital raw materials that keep our industrial economy going. Serious shortages and disruption of supply lines will cripple our production and push prices up. We also may face demands from desperate nations in Africa, Asia and Latin America to create the "new world economic order" through which they could effect an immediate redistribution of the Western World's wealth.[8]

From these faulty assumptions and self-serving motives, a whole complex of governments, intergovernmental organizations, non-governmental organizations, and private interests has developed to carry out population-control policies.

THE POPULATION CONTROL ESTABLISHMENT: WHO ARE THE BIG SPENDERS?

Who are the big spenders in the population-control field, and what are their links to the contraceptive industry? The United States government, through its Agency for International Development (AID), is by far the largest donor to population assistance, spending around $211 million in fiscal year 1983 — or close to one-half of all aid spent by developed countries. Between 1965 and 1982, AID spent $1.9 billion on population assistance.[9]

AID established its Office of Population in 1964, mostly as a result of pressure from those outside the agency, namely, members of Congress, State Department officials, and influential population-control enthusiasts outside the government, such as General William Draper, a New York investment banker who, at the urging of Hugh Moore, adopted the population crisis as his cause célèbre and was extremely influential in convincing the U.S. government of the population problem.[10] At first, AID's Office of Population was small and the agency did not earmark funds for population activities. But after a United Nations report on world hunger in 1966, Senate hearings,[11] and intense lobbying by General Draper and others, Congress earmarked $35 million for population activities in 1967, up from $9 million the previous year.[12] By 1973, the Office had a budget of $115 million — which has climbed fairly steadily ever since.[13]

In the early years, AID used its population money cautiously, spending it on research to study the population problem and providing "technical assistance" to countries that requested it, rather than on direct family planning services. In 1964, AID began to provide money for maternal and child health grants to academic institutions and to give grants to organizations like the International Planned Parenthood Federation (IPPF) for conferences.[14] In 1967, AID began to offer grants to population-control organizations for direct family planning activities[15] and began to purchase contraceptives for use in overseas family planning programs.[16] During the same year, AID made a 108,000 rupee loan to a subsidiary of G.D. Searle, one of the largest manufacturers of contraceptives, to help set up a plant in Pakistan to manufacture contraceptives (and other drugs).[17]

At present AID provides both direct assistance to foreign governments for family planning and financial support to a wide variety of private organizations in the field, such as the International Planned Parenthood Federation, the Population Council, the Pathfinder Fund, and many others.

Why does AID provide much of its funding through intermediary organizations, rather than supply it directly to foreign governments? There are several reasons. From the start, AID's Office of Population had to spend its money quickly to prove that it needed more. In 1968, the first year after the Office had been granted a large increase in its funding, the agency was not able to spend all of the $35 million that it had been allocated. Therefore it had to channel some of it through other organizations. This has continued, because AID can disseminate its funds more quickly through other organizations than it can on its own.[18]

Secondly, AID has always used intermediaries to do what it could not do on its own. In the very different political climate of the 1960s and early 1970s, AID was an ardent promoter of abortion in overseas population-assistance programs, until the 1973 Helms Amendment prohibited the use of AID funds for this activity. After 1973, AID used IPPF to channel money for abortion. The agency gave IPPF a number of vacuum aspirators, used to perform abortions, and claimed that they were to be used for training purposes only.[19]

More recently, it is possible that AID funds have been used for the purchase and distribution of Depo-Provera, an injectable contraceptive manufactured by the Upjohn company. Under American law, AID is not permitted to purchase the drug for overseas family planning programs, because it is not approved as a contraceptive in the United States.[20] But for many years, AID provided substantial financial support to the International Planned Parenthood Federation, which does purchase and distribute the drug in over fifty countries.[21] Whether AID money has been used for this purpose is not clear, since IPPF has made conflicting statements about the organization's policy on earmarking of funds. At times IPPF officials have claimed to separate money from different donors to avoid the problem of using American funds for activities that are against American law to support,[22] and at other times they have claimed to commingle all of their funds,[23] which suggests that AID money is used for all of the group's activities, including the purchase and distribution of Depo-Provera.

Finally, AID channels part of its money through other organizations to avoid some of the bureaucratic tangles that come with direct country-to-country assistance and to avoid the stigma that is attached to AID in some parts of the world. In testimony before the House Committee on Appropriations in 1975, Reimar Ravenholt, then head of AID's Office of Population, stated that

> There are many countries where we can move more quickly and efficiently on a bilateral basis than the multilateral agency is able to move. On the other hand, participation of the multilateral organiza-

tions, particularly the UN and the IPPF, have been indispensible for the rapid development of population programs during the past decade. Had we not multilateral activity as well as bilateral, there would be unfortunate polarization against the United States, particularly. Yet in some ways they are limited in how fast they can move. We need both instruments. It is analogous to the needs of a boxer. He needs both arms.[24]

Foreign Affairs, Ravenholt, reiterated this theme:

Population is a global problem that is as sensitive as it is acute in some countries. ... Multilateral-sponsored programs may be invited where no bilateral assistance would be acceptable.[25]

By channelling its money through private organizations, AID can act quickly and more discreetly, avoiding criticism and public scrutiny at home and abroad. In short, over a twenty-year period, AID has spent more than $2 billion on population control, much of it through private organizations, with almost no supervision or public accountability.

Recent events have given the public a very different impression of AID. In December of 1984, AID announced that it would no longer fund the International Planned Parenthood Federation, because the organization uses some of its funds for abortion,[26] and in 1985, AID delayed and then attempted to redirect[27] $10 million of funding promised to the United Nations Fund for Population Activities (UNFPA)[28] after a series of articles in the *Washington Post*[29] drew attention to coercive practices, including forced abortion and the killing of female babies in China's population-control program. UNFPA funds population assistance in China, but says that it does not fund such activities.[30] While public scrutiny of AID-funded programs is long overdue, the Reagan administration has chosen to pursue this role selectively, to further its anti-abortion policies in one case and its anti-communist policies in the other.

When coercive practices were exposed in other family planning programs that were clearly funded with American dollars, AID was not in much hurry to accept responsibility or modify its funding practices. In June 1984, Betsy Hartmann and Jane Hughes exposed coercive practices in Bangladesh's sterilization program funded by AID[31]. The program uses incentives, including money and new clothing, to encourage people to be sterilized. Under the Foreign Assistance Act, it is against the law for U.S. funds to be used for financial incentives to encourage people to be sterilized.[32] AID gets around the law by calling the incentive payments "compensation" for travel and lost time from work. But Hartmann and Hughes revealed persuasive evidence that people submit to the operation in order to get the incentives. AID policy also requires "voluntary, knowing assent," but a study by the World Bank, the Bangladesh government, and other organizations found that many patients had not been adequately informed about the operation beforehand. Instead of cutting off funds, AID made a number of excuses for the program. It went even further and in 1983 pressured the Bangladesh government to step up its birth control program by increasing thé role of the military and adding more incentives for sterilization and other methods of birth control.[33]

A number of other organizations are involved in population assistance. Governments of other developed countries, particularly Japan, the United Kingdom, West Germany, Norway, Sweden, and Canada all provide aid for international population assistance. But the aid of all of these countries combined does not come close to the amount spent each year by the United States.[34] Intergovernmental organizations are also a major source of international population assistance. The largest of these is the United Nations Fund for Population Activities, which began operating in 1969. UNFPA had an annual budget of $117 million in 1983. It receives money from donor governments and provides funds through other UN agencies (like UNICEF, UNESCO, ILO, and WHO) and directly to governments and non-governmental organizations.[35] The second-largest source of intergovernmental assistance is the World Bank, which spent an estimated $58.7 million on population-assistance activities in 1982.[36]

The International Planned Parenthood Federation (IPPF) is the largest non-governmental organization supporting population assistance. Founded in 1952 by Margaret Sanger, the crusader of the American birth control movement, IPPF is an association of private family planning organizations in 119 countries. IPPF gives funding to its member organizations and also provides them with contraceptives, medical equipment, and other supplies. More than 90 per cent of its funding comes from governments and the rest comes from private sources. IPPF receives contraceptives free of charge from AID for distribution on its programs. Its annual budget in 1984 was $57.8 million[37] — up from $42.6 million in 1975.[38] A number of smaller non-governmental organizations and private foundations are involved in population control; they include Family Planning International Assistance, Family Health International, Population Crisis Committee, the Pathfinder Fund, the Ford, Rockefeller, Hewlett, Jewett and other foundations, and many others. Their spending on population projects in 1983 ranged from $3.2 million (Population Crisis Committee)[39] to $18 million (the Population Council).[40]

Given the population-control establishment's underlying goal of national security, it is not surprising that several of these organizations have a fair share of retired State Department officials and prominent members of international lending institutions on their boards. For example, the board of the Population Crisis Committee (one of the few groups that receives no AID funds, so that it can lobby freely) contains Robert McNamara, William Westmoreland, and Philander Claxton Jr. (ex-head of the State Department's Office of Population).[41] Among the board members of the Population Council are McGeorge Bundy (former Special Assistant to the President for National Security Affairs and former political analyst for the Council on Foreign Relations, and W. David Hopper (Vice President of South Asia at the World Bank).[42]

What is less wellknown is that several organizations in the population field have ties, in the form of interlocking directorates and financial support, to the contraceptive industry.

Dr. William Hubbard, President of the Upjohn Company (which manufactures the injectable contraceptive Depo-Provera), also sits on the Board of Directors of Family Health International (FHI), an organization based in North Carolina that conducts research on new contraceptive products.[43] In January 1983, Dr. Malcolm Potts, President of FHI and past president of the International Planned Parenthood Federation, testified at a U.S. Board of Inquiry that Depo-Provera should be approved as a contraceptive in the United States.[44] Dr. Robert Zimbleman, a board member of Planned Parenthood Federation of America is also a scientist at the Upjohn Company.[45] Planned Parenthood's international arm, Family Planning International Assistance, supplies contraceptives and technical assistance to international population programs.

The Population Crisis Committee (PCC), one of the smaller

population organizations, was founded in 1965 by Hugh Moore and General William Draper. The Board of PCC is co-chaired by Robin Chandler Duke, wife of Angier Biddle Duke (the U.S. Chair of Protocol under President Kennedy), and former Chair of Planned Parenthood Federation of America and past President of the National Abortion Rights Action League. Concurrent with her position on the Board at PCC, Duke sits on the boards of a number of corporations, including American Home Products, one of the largest makers of oral contraceptives in the United States. In 1983, Duke and her family owned two thousand shares of American Home Products' stock.[46]

A number of population-assistance organizations receive financial support from the contraceptive industry. Since its founding, FHI has received contributions from Ortho Pharmaceutical Corporation, G.D. Searle, Syntex Corporation (all of which are American contraceptive manufacturers), Organon (a Dutch oral contraceptive manufacturer), Eisai Corporation (a Japanese contraceptive foam manufacturer), Norwich-Eaton Pharmaceuticals (an American spermicide maker), and other drug companies.[47] Planned Parenthood Federation of America and the Population Crisis Committee, since the mid-1960s, have received contributions of $2,500 to $3,500 a year from the Syntex Corporation, a manufacturer of oral contraceptives.[48] Other organizations, including the Pathfinder Fund, (a Boston-based organization founded by Dr. Charles Gamble, of the Proctor and Gamble families, which funds a variety of family planning projects), Population Action Council, Population Resource Center, Population Services International, and others have received annual contributions of similar amounts from Syntex.[49] Since many population-control organizations will not divulge the names of large contributors[50] and some contraceptive manufacturers are just as reluctant to reveal where they direct their contributions,[51] the full extent of their support by contraceptive manufacturers cannot be determined.

CONTRACEPTIVE RESEARCH: WHO BENEFITS? WHO FOOTS THE BILL?

Contraceptive technology, like other technology, does not fall from the sky but is developed at a particular time, by particular groups with specific goals and interests. In the case of contraceptives, the goals and priorities of the population-control establishment have been crucial in shaping their development. Thus, one of the most significant links between population-control programs and the contraceptive industry occurs in the initial stages of contraceptive development, long before the contraceptives reach the villages of Pakistan and Bangladesh.

As Betsy Hartmann has persuasively argued in *The Right to Live: Poverty, Power and Population Control,*[52] the interests and priorities of population-control organizations and women are not the same — and may be in direct opposition to one another. In their drive to lower the birth rate at all costs, population controllers tend to value contraceptive effectiveness over safety and to prefer long-lasting contraceptives because they don't require multiple visits to clinics or continuing promotion to keep women using them. Yet these contraceptives tend to pose the *greatest* health risks to users and are the *least* suitable for Third World women, who usually do not receive regular health care. These methods also tend to lend themselves more easily to coercion, for, once implanted or inserted, they require less participation from the user and cannot be easily discontinued if the users experience side-effects or wish to have more children. Of course, it is precisely this lack of control that makes them attractive to the population-control establishment.

Historically, the population-control establishment has always played a part in contraceptive research, and its priorities have always shaped the direction of contraceptive development. In 1951, Margaret Sanger, crusader of the American birth control movement and founder of the International Planned Parenthood Federation, raised $150,000 for Gregory Pincus, a researcher at the Worcester Foundation, for his initial research on the birth control pill, because she believed that a contraceptive pill would be a suitable method of birth control for poor women, who she believed were not suited to existing barrier methods.[53] In the late 1960s, AID provided additional funding to the Worcester Foundation to develop a once-a-month pill because agency officials believed that women in developing countries could not be counted on to take a daily pill.[54] The twenty-eight day birth control pill (in which twenty-one days of active pills are packaged with seven placebos, making it easier for women to remember to take them) was developed with funding from AID expressly for use in developing countries.[55]

The priorities of the population-control establishment have continued to dominate the direction of contraceptive research. In 1979, the lion's share of money spent by governments and non-profit organizations on contraceptive research went to basic research and training and the development of new contraceptives, while less than 10 per cent went to safety assessments.[56] Moreover, the bulk of public sector funds for contraceptive research was spent on "high-effectiveness — low-user control" methods of contraceptive: almost half of all funds was spent on subdermal implants, injectables, vaginal rings, IUDs, anti-pregnancy vaccines, sterilization, and even nasal sprays. In contrast, only 2 per cent of all funds was spent on barrier methods of birth control.[57]

No organization demonstrates this close relationship between population-control organizations and contraceptive development better than the Population Council. Founded in 1952 by John D. Rockefeller III, and funded by AID, the Ford and Rockefeller Foundations and others, the Population Council is a non-profit organization that conducts contraceptive research and designs and implements family planning programs — most of which are used to launch their new contraceptives — in developing countries. The Population Council develops contraceptives that are, in its own words, "specially suited to the needs of couples in developing countries,"[58] that "require less attention from the user than is the case with oral contraceptives," and "have the potential for one to several years' protection following application."[59] In the 1960s, the Council developed the Copper T IUD, concentrating on IUDs because they believed the IUD was more suitable for women in developing countries than the birth control pill, since it required no daily attention from the user.[60] More recently, the Council has developed Norplant, a long-acting hormonal contraceptive consisting of progestogen-filled tubes that are implanted under the skin and remain active for up to seven years.[61]

Since pharmaceutical companies use the high cost of research to justify their high profits, most people would be surprised to learn that it is not contraceptive manufacturers but the American government that pays for most contraceptive research. Of the $155 million spent for contraceptive research throughout the world in 1979, $89 million, or 58 per cent, was spent by the American government. Only about $14 million, or 9 per cent of the total, was spent by pharmaceutical companies. The remainder was spent by foreign governments and non-governmental organizations.[62]

The American government was not always the largest funder of contraceptive research. From the 1940s to the mid-1960s, the big spenders on contraceptive research were the pharmaceutical companies and private foundations, such as the Ford and Rockefeller foundations. In 1965, $12 million, or 32 per cent of the world-wide expenditures on contraceptive research, was spent by the pharmaceutical industry.[63]

The idea of population growth as a threat to world security became more and more acceptable through the 1960s and gradually persuaded the American government to assume a much greater role in funding contraceptive research. In the late 1960s, at the same time that Congress agreed to spend more money on population-control programs, it also authorized the creation of organizations like the Center for Population Research in the National Institutes of Health, to conduct contraceptive research. At around the same time, intergovernmental organizations, such as the UN Fund for Population Activities and the World Health Organization's Special Program for Research and Training in Human Reproduction, were established and eventually received funds from AID. In 1976, Greep Report, sponsored by the Ford Foundation[64] recommended that the U.S. government spend even more money on contraceptive research. And of course, the contraceptive manufacturers have pushed for a greater government role in contraceptive research, arguing that tough American drug approval laws, government patent policies, and pro-consumer product liability laws made it too expensive for the industry to develop new contraceptives. As recently as 1978, when the U.S. government was already spending $77 million, or 52 per cent of world-wide expenditures on contraceptive research,[65] Dr. Sheldon Segal (then head of the Population Council), Dr. Carl Djerassi (long-time scientist and consultant for the Syntex corporation), and Dr. William Hubbard (President of the Upjohn Company and Board Member of Family Health International) appeared before representative James Scheuer's Select Committee on Population, urging increased government expenditures for contraceptive research.[66] As a result, Congress granted additional money to the World Health Organization for contraceptive research.

Government subsidization of contraceptive research takes a number of forms. First, the government funds organizations like Family Health International, the Program for the Introduction and Adaptation of Contraceptive Technology, and the Population Council that conduct contraceptive research. The government also conducts its own contraceptive research at the National Institutes of Health's Center for Population Research. In 1982, for example, NIH conducted animal safety studies for new contraceptives, including Noristerat (made by Schering A.G.) and for contraceptives developed by Alza Pharmaceutical (owned by Ciba-Geigy) and Syntex Corporation. These studies were financed jointly by the government and the contraceptive makers.[67]

The government also supports research by academic institutions and other research centers on the development of contraceptives, the results of which can be used by the contraceptive industry in its own work. New "liberal" patent laws have made it easier for patents to be transferred from government-funded research to private industry, though such transfers are supposed to favour small firms and promote competition.[68]

Yet while American (and some non-American) taxpayers foot a large part of the bill for this research, they have no say in the emphasis of the research or the ends to which it is used. Nor, of course, do the Third World women for whom most of these technologies are developed. Like other aspects of AID's population-control assistance, its funding for contraceptive research and development reflects the priorities of the population-control establishment, benefits the contraceptive industry, and operates with little public accountability.

THE CONTRACEPTIVE INDUSTRY:
BIG BUSINESS AS USUAL

The American contraceptive industry comprises five major segments: oral contraceptives, IUDs, condoms, diaphragms, and spermicides. Other contraceptive products include douches (which are not effective for contraceptive use, although they are used for this purpose by some women), the morning-after pill (DES and other estrogens and progestins have been used for this purpose, but none is approved for this use in the United States), and injectable and other long-acting contraceptives (which are also not approved for contraceptive use in the United States). Other methods of birth control, such as the rhythm method, other kinds of fertility awareness, breast-feeding, coitus interruptus, abstinence, abortion, and sterilization are not produced or controlled by the contraceptive industry.

The American and much of the non-American contraceptive markets are dominated by large corporations. Production and distribution of contraceptives in the United States and many other parts of the world is driven by the goal of profit maximization and not a concern for reproductive health. Selling contraceptives to the largest number of people, despite health risks, cultural suitability, or the users' needs, is the primary goal of the contraceptive industry.

A few examples illustrate this point. For almost twenty years, the Upjohn Company has been trying to obtain American approval of Depo-Provera as a long-acting (three-month) injectable contraceptive.[69] Depo-Provera, a progestogen (a synthetic form of the female hormone progesterone) causes cancer in animal studies[70] and more recently has been associated with an increased risk of cervical cancer in women.[71] The drug also has a number of other side-effects, including heavy bleeding, headaches, weight gain, and a possible delay in the return of fertility.[72] Despite evidence of the drug's dangers, Upjohn continues to lobby for American approval. The company also makes the drug available in over eighty countries[73] where drug approval standards are not as stringent as those of the United States.

The Dalkon Shield, the now-discontinued intra-uterine device manufactured by the A.H. Robins Company, is another glaring example of the casualties of the for-profit contraceptive industry. In its quest for profits, Robins manufactured and sold the device without first subjecting it to rigorous safety tests and then made false claims about its safety and effectiveness. When evidence began to mount that the device was associated with pelvic inflammatory disease, septic abortion, infertility, and death, the company concealed this information from the medical community and consumers, and according to one former company attorney interviewed by a *Washington Post* reporter, Morton Mintz, top officials at Robins ordered documents to be destroyed and false statements to be made to the courts and the public.[74] Like Upjohn, Robins has taken advantage of the inequities between the West and the Third World to maximize its profits. In 1972, when the Shield's problems were already apparent in the United States and company officials probably knew that its days were numbered, the company made a large sale of unsterilized Shields, at a 48 per cent discount, to AID for use in overseas family planning programs in forty-two countries.[75] In all, AID purchased 697,000 Dalkon Shields for population programs.[76]

Contraceptives can be evaluated on the basis of several different criteria: safety to the user, effectiveness in preventing pregnancy, reversibility, convenience, cost, and suitability to the user's culture, to name a few. While these factors vary in importance for individuals, a few general trends are worth noting.

The first is that while contraceptives do not pose the same risks for everyone, the contraceptives that are the most effective and most convenient (because they are dissociated from the act of sex) also tend to be the most dangerous to the user. The contraceptives in this category are oral contraceptives (which increase the risk of high blood pressure, blood clots, heart attack, stroke, gallbladder disease, breast and cervical cancer, and a host of other less serious side-effects); IUDs (which are associated with an increased risk of pelvic infection, tubal pregnancy, and infertility); and injectable contraceptives (which are associated with menstrual disturbances, possible cardiovascular problems, and in the case of Depo-Provera, according to a study by the World Health Organization, an increased risk of cervical cancer. Since long-term cancer studies have not been completed for norethindrone acetate or subdermal implants their risks are largely unknown). On the other hand, condoms pose no known health risks, diaphragms are associated with an increased risk of urinary tract infections, and spermicides can cause local irritation.

The second trend is that the methods of contraception that are most effective and most convenient also tend to be the most difficult to discontinue. IUDs and long-acting implants must be removed by a medical professional, sterilization is usually irreversible (but can in some cases be reversed by additional surgery), and injectable contraceptives require the user to wait for three months or more for the drug to wear off. (One exception to this trend is oral contraceptives). This means that users often sacrifice flexibility and control for effectiveness and convenience.

Contraceptives can also be ranked by the extent to which they require multiple purchases and the extent to which their manufacture demands expensive research and materials to manufacture. While there are exceptions, it is clear that "high tech" contraceptives and contraceptives that require multiple purchases are more expensive to the user than one-time contraceptives and those made of inexpensive materials. Thus, the cost of using birth control pills, which are "high tech" and require multiple purchases, is much higher than the cost of using the cervical cap, a thimble-like rubber device (not available for general use in the United States), which fits over the cervic, needs to be replaced only once every few years, and is used with little or no spermicide. The diaphragm, which is used with more spermicide than the cervical cap but also needs to be replaced once every few years, is also a relatively inexpensive method of contraception. Condoms (which are "low tech" but require multiple purchases) and IUDs (which are "high-tech" but last for several months or years) fall somewhere in between.

Not surprisingly, the shape of the American contraceptive market roughly follows this pricing pattern: oral contraceptives (the most expensive contraceptive to use) are the most widely used (after steriliztion); diaphragms are used by a small percentage of women; and condoms, spermicides, and IUDs fall somewhere in between.[77]

The cost of initial and follow-up medical care, which varies with different contraceptives, also figures into the total cost of contraceptives to the consumer. With the exception of the birth control pill, the items that require multiple purchases and are therefore more expensive, tend to be barrier methods that do not require a doctor's prescription or medical supervision, and thus may still be cheaper than "high tech" long-lasting methods. Taking the cost of doctor visits into account, oral contraceptives, the most widely used pharmaceutical contraceptive, are still probably the most expensive contraceptive to use in the United States.

Just how large are the American and world-wide contraceptive markets? Although exact figures are not available, estimates place the American (retail) contraceptive market at almost $1 billion a year.[78] World-wide sales are probably at least twice this figure.[79] If one includes countries like China, which produce their own contraceptives, the market is even larger. To provide some basis for comparison, the total U.S. pharmaceutical market was $18 billion in 1980, and the world-wide market was $84 billion during the same year.[80]

In the United States (and probably elsewhere), the biggest money-maker in the contraceptive market is oral contraceptives (birth control pills). According to Arnold Snider, a market analyst for Kidder, Peabody and Company, oral and injectable contraceptives "have an incredible profit margin" and are "among the most profitable of all pharmaceuticals".[81] In 1983, the U.S. oral contraceptive market was $520 million,[82] and the world-wide market has been estimated at $700 million[83] to $1 billion.[84]

Condoms account for the second-largest contraceptive market, followed in order by spermicides, IUDs, injectables, and diaphragms. In most of these markets, sales are concentrated in the hands of a few big companies. In the oral contraceptive market, for example, Ortho Pharmaceutical (a Johnson and Johnson subsidiary) and Wyeth Laboratories (owned by American Home Products) held, in the early 1980s, between 70 and 80 per cent of the U.S. market.[85] Similarly, two companies — Young's Drug Products, a privately held company that makes Trojans, and Julius Schmid (owned by the London Rubber Company) controlled 80 to 90 per cent of the U.S. condom market in 1980.[86] In the world market, concentration is also strong. The London Rubber Company held 45 per cent of the world condom market in 1983.[87] Figures on the IUD market are unavailable, but the one thing is certain: the U.S. market is rapidly disappearing. Ortho Pharmaceutical removed the Lippes Loop from the American market in 1985, and more recently, G.D. Searle (acquired by Monsanto in 1985) removed the Copper 7 and Tatum T IUDs from the American market. Both companies' actions were prompted by the large number of lawsuits brought by women who claim they were injured by the devices.[88]

Who are the users of these contraceptives? Although U.S. consumers are still an important part of the world-wide contraceptive market, the growth area of the market lies not in the United States but in the Third World, where population control programs are often the initial or primary source of contraceptives. In 1982 the Congressional Office of Technology Assessment described this phenomenon:

> [A] large, expanding market for contraceptives no longer exists in the United States but does in LDC's [less developed countries], where large percentages of people are either in their reproductive years or about to enter them.[89]

Take the case of birth control pills. First introduced into the U.S. market in 1960, oral contraceptives rapidly gained a substantial chunk of the U.S. contraceptive market, and by 1965 an estimated 24 per cent of currently married women using contraceptives in the United States used the Pill — a larger percentage than those using any other form of contraception.[90]

During this period, the Pill manufacturers earned a substantial percentage of their sales from the pill. G.D. Searle made $47 million in sales, or 44 per cent of its total sales, from oral contraceptives in 1965.[91] For Syntex, oral contraceptives and other reproductive physiology products constituted the largest product category and the largest percentage of sales in 1967.[92]

By the early 1970s, studies had established a link between oral contraceptives and cardiovascular disease,[93] and a widely publicized Congressional hearing by Senator Gaylord Nelson publicized the risks of the Pill.[94] IUDs came to hold a larger share of the U.S. contraceptive market,[95] and the share of sales that Pill manufacturers obtained from the Pill began to wane. For G.D. Searle, the growth rate of the Pill had abated by 1968. The proportion of the company's sales derived from the Pill dropped from 44 per cent in 1965 to 17 per cent in 1970 and to between 6 and 8 per cent in the mid-1970s.[96] In 1971, Syntex told its shareholders that "oral contraceptives are declining in importance in the overall Syntex sales picture."[97] During the 1970s, as studies confirmed the dangers of higher-dose pills, Pill companies introduced new formulations with lower and lower doses of the same active ingredients. By 1981, the low-dose Pill market was the only part of the pill market experiencing any growth. Diaphragms and condoms started to make a surprising comeback.[98]

Fortunately for the oral contraceptive makers (and manufacturers of other contraceptives), several events conspired in the 1960s to change American policy towards population assistance in general, and contraceptives in particular. In 1967, just as Congress granted a huge increase in appropriations to AID's Office of Population, AID changed its policy and eliminated its long-standing ban on buying contraceptives for population-control programs. Four of the biggest manufacturers of birth control pills Searle, Syntex, Ortho, and Parke-Davis, all anxious to get in on the new action, began supplying pills to AID free of charge, until the government could appropriate the necessary money to purchase them.[99]

By 1972, AID had already spent $17 million on contraceptives, $10 million of which went to birth control pills.[100] Since the mid-1970s, AID has spent an average of $15 million a year on birth control pills for its program.[101] Some of these pills are given to the International Planned Parenthood Federation and the Pathfinder Fund, and some go directly to foreign governments and family planning agencies, In 1977, the U.S. government was *the* major supplier of contraceptives for international family planning programs, supplying seven out of every eight pill cycles distributed by international organizations.[102]

Although sales to AID and other population organizations make up only a small percentage of world contraceptive sales, these purchases make a big difference to some contraceptive manufacturers. One prime example is the Syntex Corporation, a company with American roots (now based in Panama). Between 1968 and early 1975, AID spent around $30 million on oral contraceptives — two-thirds of which went to Syntex.[103]

From 1972 until at least 1979, Syntex was AID's sole supplier of oral contraceptives[104] and continued to be a major supplier thereafter. During this period most, if not all, of the $15 million spent by AID annually on pills went to Syntex. Meanwhile, Syntex pill sales were stagnant, or growing slowly, as compared with other Syntex divisions.[105] During some years, like 1978, 1979, and 1983, Syntex sales to AID accounted for 25 to 30 per cent of Syntex's total oral contraceptive sales.[106]

Other oral contraceptive manufacturers have also benefited from the boom in population assistance. In the late 1960s, many oral contraceptive manufacturers informed their stockholders about the new markets to be found in overseas family planning programs. In 1968, American Home Products advised its stockholders that they were

> cooperating with family planning organizations throughout the world. In India, for example, the U.S. government, through the Agency for International Development, has assisted in a birth control program which generated a significant purchase of Ovral [an AHP birth control pill] for distribution by Indian authorities.[107]

G.D. Searle informed its stockholders in 1967 that Ovulen 28-day pills were being used overseas by AID, and lamented that

> it is unfortunate that less-developed nations have been slow in adopting these programs, yet theirs is the greater need for such assistance.[108]

Apparently Searle shared this "need" with the developing nations.

Condom manufacturers have also benefited from AID purchases. The American condom market is around $245 million a year[109] (a figure that includes retail sales and bulk sales to family planning programs). At present AID spends around $25 million dollars a year on condoms,[110] so that AID sales constitute about 8 per cent of the total American condom market. What this means for individual condom manufacturers is even more striking. In recent years, AID has purchased condoms from Ansell Industries and Circle Rubber Corporation. In fiscal year 1984, Ansell sold $23 million worth of condoms to AID. Circle Rubber sold $20 million in condoms to AID in fiscal year 1983 and $15 million in 1982.[111] Together, these companies hold less than 10 per cent of the market.[112] This means that condom sales to AID represents at least three quarters of these companies' total condom sales during years when AID makes a large purchase. According to one industry source, AID contracts represent 95 per cent of Ansell's business and the company would go out of business if it lost its AID contracts.[113]

From fiscal year 1982 to fiscal year 1984, AID purchased $6.7 million worth of IUDs for population control programs, all from Finishing Enterprises.[114] Since Finishing Enterprises is a private company, it is anyone's guess what effect this has on the company's total sales.

AID seems to be well aware of the important service that it provides to the contraceptive industry, and AID officials or Congress apparently see this as part of its mission. In its fiscal year 1985 appropriation request to Congress, AID stated:

> More than other components of the population program, family planning service projects support the private sector. Through these programs, AID purchases high quality U.S. manufactured family planning commodities and uses private organizations to transfer resources and know-how to the developing world.[115]

AID also provides an important service to the contraceptive industry by providing free contraceptives to developing countries and then phasing out this support, thereby encouraging countries to purchase contraceptives on their own.[116]

Contraceptive manufacturers and their representatives protect these markets by lobbying on the severity of the population "crisis" and the need for continued AID involvement in family planning. The Select Committee on Population, which held hearings from March to August of 1978, was one platform from which the contraceptive industry could express its views and ask for assistance on a number of issues. Dr. William Hubbard, President of the Upjohn Company, appeared twice before the committee, once to complain about the FDA's decision not to approve Depo-Provera as a contraceptive[117] and once to request increased government funding for contraceptive research.[118] Dr. Carl Djerassi, a long-time consultant to Syntex, appeared before the committee to request increased government funding for contraceptive research.[119] Richard Rogers, President of Syntex Laboratories, also appeared before the committee, asking for increased AID funding for contraceptive purchases and larger guaranteed AID contracts. Rogers also asked the American government to encourage developing countries to allow contraceptives (including birth control pills) to be sold in retail outlets without medical supervision, and he tried to discourage the government from transferring contraceptive technology to developing countries, arguing that such countries would never be able to produce contraceptives for AID as cheaply as Syntex.[120]

Representative James Scheuer (Democrat — New York), who chaired this committee, embraces many of the traditional arguments of the population establishment and was a member of the Commission on Population Growth and the American Future at the time of the hearings.[121] Moreover, he is also a well-known friend of the pharmaceutical industry. In recent years, Scheuer has received contributions from fourteen pharmaceutical companies and two industry trade associations. Among the contributors were the contraceptive manufacturers Bristol-Myers, Johnson and Johnson, Schering-Plough, and Upjohn.[122] Scheuer is liked by the pharmaceutical industry not just for his stance on population control, but because he favours weakening the American drug approval process (making it easier for companies to get new products on the market) and favours laws that would allow U.S. companies to export drugs not approved in this country.

Lobbying by the contraceptive industry is by no means a new phenomenon. In 1966, Dr. Jack Lippes, inventor of the Lippes Loop IUD and consultant to Ortho Pharmaceutical and the Population Council,[123] testified before the Senate on the population "crisis" and the need for increased funding for population activities,[124] as did Dr. John Rock, one of the original inventors of the birth control pill.[125] Dr. William Hubbard, Upjohn Company president, was a member of the advisory panel of the Congressional Office of Technology Assessment, which in 1982 released a report detailing the need for additional government funds for population programs and contraceptive research.[126] Notably, it is the companies that receive AID contacts, like Syntex, Ansell Incorporated, and Finishing Enterprises, that are most active in Congressional lobbying and in contributing to non-governmental population-control organizations.

AID is not the only buyer of contraceptives for overseas family planning organizations. In recent years, IPPF has supplied $7.5 million of contraceptives a year to family planning organizations overseas, including 17.5 million cycles of contraceptives, 34 million condoms, almost 700,000 IUDs, 530,000 doses of injectable contraceptives, and 10.5 million foaming tablets.[127] The Pathfinder Fund, in 1981, supplied 2.9 million condoms, one million cycles of contraceptives, 950,000 IUDs, 9,200 units of foam, and 600 diaphragms to family planning projects.[128] (Since IPPF and Pathfinder receive some contraceptives free of charge from AID, these figures represent purchases from AID and additional purchases by the organizations.) Family Planning International Assistance (the international arm of Planned Parenthood Federation of America) purchased $2.7 million worth of contraceptives, including $1.5 million in condoms, $694,000 in oral contraceptives, $398,000 in IUDs, $118,000 in foam and jelly, and $6,700 in diaphragms for family planning programs in 1983.[129] Since 1972, FPIA has spent $40 million on contraceptives for its programs.[130] Population Crisis Committee also purchases contraceptives for its programs and spent $69,000 on contraceptives in 1981.[131]

CONTRACEPTIVE SOCIAL MARKETING : MARKET RESEARCH TO SOLVE "SOCIAL PROBLEMS"

Contraceptive social marketing, one of the growing trends in the population-assistance field, reveals just how important population-assistance programs are in prying open new markets for the contraceptive industry. Aptly named, contraceptive social marketing (CSM) programs aim to create new markets for contraceptives in the Third World. They do this, according to one organization in the field, by using "the proven techniques used to sell soap, soft drinks and toothpaste in every corner of the globe ... to solve social problems."[132] In CSM programs, contraceptives, mostly donated by AID and the International Planned Parenthood Federation, are sold in developing countries at subsidized prices (from one-half to one-twentieth the usual retail price) through "already existing marketing channels," namely, local vendors and shopkeepers who are already operating in villages and rural areas throughout many developing countries. Though contraceptives are donated to the programs, they pass through the normal marketing chain, through wholesalers and retailers to consumers. Wholesalers and retailers make a profit (and thus are motivated to participate in the programs), and money made from the sale of the contraceptives to wholesalers is put back into the program. Contraceptive social marketing was first used in India in 1968, and by 1980 CSM projects had been used in at least twenty-seven developing countries. Birth control pills, condoms, and foaming spermicide tablets have all been used in CSM programs.[133]

A handful of organizations are involved in contraceptive social marketing programs. The Ford Foundation was one of the first, with its support of the first contraceptive social marketing project in India in 1968.[134] Population Services International (PSI), an organization based in Washington, D.C., came next with projects in Kenya, Columbia, and Sri Lanka in the early 1970s.[135] PSI is currently conducting projects (under AID contract) in Mexico and Bangladesh.[136] PSI receives money from AID, the Population Crisis Committee, IPPF, Scaife Trust, the Ford Foundation, and Syntex, the birth control pill manufacturer.[137] The Futures Group, a private market research firm, has now entered the CSM field with a hefty AID contract to design and oversee all CSM programs funded by AID.[138] Many CSM programs are run directly by governments in developing countries, which in turn receive financial support from the usual array of population funding sources.[139]

Another organization, Program for the Introduction and Adaptation of Contraceptive Technology (PIACT), an organization based in Seattle, while not strictly a CSM organization, is involved in similar activities. PIACT, according to the organization's materials, exists to "identify contraceptive product-related problems and provide a link between private industry and users of such products and between private industry and public sector family planning programs."[140] PIACT develops packaging and instructional materials for contraceptives for developing countries and provides loans and technical assistance to governments and local companies to help them set up their own contraceptive manufacturing plants. While this would appear to threaten the profits of American contraceptive makers, American companies have cooperated with PIACT, since the existence of such facilities, even if not owned by U.S. corporations, creates additional business for U.S. contraceptive manufacturers in the form of equipment, raw materials, and licensing agreements.[141] PIACT was founded in 1971 by Dr. Gordon Duncan, an endocrinologist who had worked for eleven years as a researcher at the Upjohn Company and later returned to Upjohn as the company's Research Director.[142]

Contraceptive Social Marketing Programs have gained acceptance by AID and other population-control organizations because they are "cost-effective": they distribute contraceptives to more people at a lower cost than other types of programs.[143] They do this by cutting out expensive services like health clinics, which have traditionally been the distribution point for contraceptives in family planning programs. Population Services International puts it in the following way:

> The shops through which we reach people who want contraceptives cost us nothing. They are already there, serving every neighbourhood. In contrast, clinics and health centers (aside from being relatively few in number) are very expensive to build and operate.[144]

Social marketing is seen as "indispensable" in rural areas

> [s]imply because medical and paramedical services are beyond the reach of hundreds of millions of couples who live in rural communities in Asia, Africa and Latin America.[145]

Since some social marketing programs distribute birth control pills, this means that pills are distributed in the programs to anyone who wants to buy them, without a prescription or medical examination. In many countries, this does not conflict with official government policy. In 1973, the International Planned Parenthood Federation recommended that developing countries make birth control pills available without a prescription,[146] and since then at least eight countries (including the Philippines, Pakistan, Bangladesh, Antigua, Chile, Fiji, Jamaica, and South Korea) have dropped the prescription requirement.[147]

But this does represent a significant departure from former family planning strategies that attempted to link family planning to improved maternal and child health and increased access to health services. Contraceptive social marketing programs explicitly target those who do *not* have access to health care. This means that women with high-risk conditions may be more likely to use the Pill, and follow-up medical attention may be more difficult to find in the event of unpleasant or dangerous side-effects. Ironically, Population Services International, which distributes birth control pills through CSM programs, claims that its goal is to "promote the good health of parents and children."[148]

Contraceptive social marketing programs have whittled away the distance between population-assistance programs and the contraceptive industry, and they serve the industry's needs much more completely and directly than other types of population programs. CSM programs do this by reaching new rural consumers who have not been reached by clinic-based family planning programs, which are located mostly in cities.[149] This is particularly beneficial to the pharmaceutical companies, because well over half the population in most developing countries live in such regions, and the high cost of moving products to rural areas has previously made these groups out of reach for family planning programs and normal retail contraceptive markets, which do exist on a small scale in some developing countries.[150] Social marketing programs specifically target these populations, and they do it at their own expense — the industry pays nothing (except through contributions to CSM organizations).

Contraceptive social marketing programs also benefit the industry because they use extensive promotional campaigns to advertise contraceptive products. Billboards, radio and television, movie advertisements, shop signs, stickers, calendars, mobiles, and other promotional tools have all been used to saturate the consciousness of those in developing countries and make the (specially chosen) brand names for pills, condoms, and foam into household words.[151] In some programs, paid sales representatives (blood brothers to the infamous detail men of the pharmaceutical industry) travel to retail outlets to persuade retailers to stock their products.[152] Local promoters are also hired to hawk products through loudspeakers at bazaars, marketplaces, and other local gatherings, and at times give out free samples of pills and condoms.[153]

Apparently, some of the programs have achieved their desired results. The program director for a CSM program in Bangladesh run by Population Services International boasted that "the radio has made the 'Maya' [brand of pills] jingle the most well-known and popular advertising jingle in Bangladesh, so much so that children are often heard humming our Maya pill jingle."[154] The Director also boasted that "Raja and Maya [condom and pill brands] have now become household words synonymous with condom and pill."[155] CSM advertising is completely free to the industry, since it is paid for by population-control programs (and their usual funders, including the American government).[156]

This promotion, while clearly benefiting manufacturers whose products are the subject of such promotion, benefits *all* contraceptive manufacturers, by creating an increasing awareness of contraceptives. Officials in CSM programs often boast about this "spinoff effect," saying that it benefits all contraceptive manufacturers by increasing demand.[157]

CSM programs not only conduct massive promotional campaigns, but also conduct extensive market research to determine appealing brand names, logos, and packaging design for products used in such programs. All of this research is also paid for by the population programs and AID, and not the industry. In some cases, population programs have spent as much on market research as a commercial firm would when launching a new product.[158] Much of the information collected through this market research is undoubtedly useful to other contraceptive manufacturers who may hope to enter the Third World market on their own some day.

CSM programs have also taken over some of the work of spreading contraceptive information and education to consumers. Given the orientation of the programs, it is no surprise that this information tends to be more promotional than educational in content. A CSM program run by PSI in Thailand, for example, includes an "Information, Education and Communication" program to inform potential acceptors about the Pill. In the program, women are informed about the "side-effects" of pregnancy and the "positive attributes" of the pill and family planning in general. According to program administrators:

> [w]omen are told that the hormonal changes and related effects during pregnancy are "the size of an elephant" while the changes and side effects of the pill are "the size of an ant."[159]

This statement, which is tilted strongly in favour of the pill and gives women little concrete information with which to make an informed choice, is barely distinguishable from industry promotion. PSI also developed a patient information sheet for the Pill for use in Pakistan that explained how to take the Pill, and what to do if a Pill is skipped — information needed to make sure the Pill is used effectively — but said nothing about side-effects.[160]

The contraceptive industry plays a much more direct part in the design and administration of CSM programs than in other population-control programs. One CSM project started in Tunisia in 1976, which distributed condoms and birth control pills, was sponsored and managed by the Syntex Corporation (makers of birth control pills) in conjunction with the Tunisian government.[161] This project ended prematurely when the Tunisian government became reluctant to allow the sales of condoms and birth control pills outside of pharmacies. This prompted the President of Syntex Laboratories, Richard Rogers, to testify before Congress that AID should encourage developing countries to drop "pharmacy only" requirements so as not to impede other CSM projects.[162]

Another project launched in Thailand in 1974 by the International Planned Parenthood Federation was run, according to the program director, "in close cooperation with the ... pharmaceutical companies."[163] The Futures Group acknowledges that "social marketing programs have played a major role in expanding private sector involvement in social programs."[164] In .the early 1970s, AID, the United Nations Fund for Population Activities, and other organizations considered setting up an international agency to "promote commercial or social marketing projects," but the UN was reluctant to work so closely with the contraceptive industry.[165]

At times, the line between the interests of the programs and those of the industry seem completely blurred. Some CSM officials act as if their primary responsibility is to facilitate greater industry involvement in population programs and to provide legitimacy to the industry's involvement. At a 1979 conference on commercial retail sales of contraceptives, sponsored by the PIACT and attended by representatives of the contraceptive industry, two PIACT officials noted that one of CSM's benefits to the industry was that the "quasi-official status" of the programs "may make it possible to supply assistance to the commercial sector through its government contracts."[166]

CSM programs appear to solve a basic problem faced by contraceptive manufacturers who want to create new markets in developing countries where the consumers have no purchasing power and live in rural areas that are expensive to reach. In CSM programs contraceptives are introduced into these markets at no cost to the industry, and though the prices to consumers (and profits to manufacturers) are low, consumers at least become accustomed to paying *something* for contraceptives, thus increasing the likelihood that they will become "real" consumers (paying "real" prices) should the contraceptive social marketing programs be phased out.

But the CSM "solution" will probably not succeed for the industry or the American government, which wants to find less expensive ways to administer population control programs.[167] "Self-sufficiency," the ability of such programs to pay for themselves, and the dream of CSM designers, has not yet been achieved in any CSM programs,[168] and it is doubtful that large numbers of consumers would make the transition from buying highly subsidized contraceptives to paying full retail prices, given the widespread poverty in many developing countries. AID officials are already discussing a new approach: conducting research to determine the size of the commercial "pure" retail contraceptive market in developing countries and then turning the research over to the contraceptive industry so they can use it and penetrate the Third World market on their own.[169]

INCENTIVES, COERCION, AND OTHER ABUSES

Several family planning programs have used a variety of questionable techniques to induce women to participate. These techniques range from subtle forms of pressure, like encouraging some contraceptives over others, to outright coercion through the use of the military to force people to submit to sterilization.

For example, in the late 1970s, a program of compulsory Depo-Provera distribution was implemented in Kamput, Thailand. According to a 1980 letter from a medical co-ordinator for the International Committee of the Red Cross,[170] interviews with married women in the area revealed that Depo-Provera was given to women "as a pre-requisite to marriage." More than half of the women interviewed who received Depo-Provera stated that they did not know the purpose of the injection, and only 15 per cent had been asked about their menstrual history or whether they were pregnant before being given the drug.

Financial incentives have been used in a number of family planning programs. In 1967, the Indian government set up a program of incentives for IUD insertion and sterilization (mostly male sterilization) in many of its states and on government-owned plantations. Some programs paid incentives to physicians performing the operation or to "field workers" or "motivators" who found new patients, and others paid them to those undergoing the procedure.[171] In the mid-1960s, programs similar to that of India were set up in Pakistan, Taiwan, Korea, Turkey, and the United Arab Republic. A survey of these programs conducted by the IPPF in 1969 found that some workers "in their anxiety to increase acceptances," failed to inform patients adequately about the operation and that motivators brought in unmarried, childless, and elderly men for the procedure in order to receive the incentive payments.[172] The study also found that women in Korea went from clinic to clinic, having IUDs inserted and then removed, in order to take advantage of the incentives. A few years later, during Indira Gandhi's 1975-7 Emergency Rule, the Indian government engaged in the largest and most well-known programs of forced family planning. Millions of men were rounded up by the military and forced to undergo sterilization.[173]

Other programs have also used financial incentives. In Egypt, a state-run family planning program begun in the mid-1970s provided financial incentives to doctors, social workers, and other health clinic staff for each new Pill or IUD acceptor they could recruit. They did not offer incentives for other methods of birth control.[174] Not surprisingly, program implementers encouraged IUDs and the Pill over other methods of contraception, and in some cases forced patients to accept the Pill if they had come to the clinic seeking other kinds of medical attention.[175] As recently as 1983, India used a system of incentive payments for men and women agreeing to be sterilized. Government figures reveal that the number of persons agreeing to obtain the operation increased dramatically after an increase in the amount of the incentive payments.[176]

In India, family planning programs have used coveted government jobs, subsidized housing, and higher education as rewards for sterilization.[177] In Indonesia, government programs have used community-based rewards to encourage contraceptive use. Under this system, a whole village is rewarded with government assistance for building roads or health clinics if it lowers its birth rate to a specified level.[178] These programs have been criticized for dividing communities and creating intense social pressure that virtually eliminates freedom of choice.[179]

Quotas, a more subtle compromise to patients' freedom of choice, have also been used in a number of family planning programs. Despite its stated policy of participating only in programs that permit "freedom of choice,"[180] AID, in the mid-1970s, ranked contraceptives according to effectiveness and urged family planning programs to promote only the most effective methods.[181] AID then pressured program administrators in the Philippines to push the most effective methods — the Pill and IUDs.[182] At the urging of AID, top program officials sent a memo to clinics directing them to

> discourage condom acceptors and encourage more IUDs and pills. The clinic is evaluated on the method accepted by clients. There will be no more supply of condoms. So convince your condom acceptors to switch to pills and IUDs[183]

Program administrators were forced to meet quotas of new contraceptive users and were even found competing with one another over the same clients so that each could add them to their quotas.[184]

A recent Annual Report of the Pathfinder Fund (which receives 90 per cent of its funding from AID) describes dozens of family planning projects in which "contraceptive acceptors" are "recruited" through "motivations programs." Most of these programs have predetermined quotas of new recruits for each contraceptive, and one wonders how much flexibility the programs allow for patients' preferences.[185]

In their drive to increase and maintain contraceptive users, family planning programs have restricted freedom of choice in other ways. In Brazil, an IPPF-affiliated program started in the 1960s cut the strings on IUDs after they were inserted so that the program would be "more effective"; i.e., removal would be more difficult. Despite criticism from a Brazilian medical organization, the program continued this practice for many years.[186]

Yet another way in which programs have limited freedom of choice is to restrict the flow of information to patients. PRO-FAMILIA, the Colombian IPPF affiliate, failed to mention any of the risks of contraceptives in its promotional literature used by its family planning clinics in the 1970s.[187] Family planning programs in Egypt and Kenya in the 1970s dispensed birth control pills with no mention of side-effects.[188]

Donald Warwick, who studied family planning programs in eight countries under a grant from the UNFPA (the agency later refused to endorse his work, which was critical of the programs)[189] argues that quotas, incentives, and an emphasis on numbers of new acceptors over patients' satisfaction and an improved quality of life are the result of the underlying assumptions of program designers. According to Warwick, many program designers assumed, on the basis of faulty questionnaires and flimsy methodology, that people in developing countries wanted contraceptives but simply could not get them. This error, he argues, was the result of other faulty assumptions, including the assumption that additional children were detrimental to the well-being of families in developing countries and the assumption that women (who were the interview subjects) have the power to make reproductive decisions in the family. When couples did not flock to the clinics and the program results were dismal, program designers and administrators became more hard-nosed, going to more extreme lengths to meet the original goals of the program.

In other words, financial incentives and other high-pressure techniques are the flip-side of the search for new "high tech" contraceptives. Both are attempts to find a solution to the problems of low participation and continuation in family planning programs without addressing the real reasons why patients are dissatisfied with or uninterested in birth control.

But these strong-arm tactics have failed even in their own terms. Men and women, pressured to use contraceptives that they do not want or that cause unpleasant side-effects will not continue to use them. Thus, it is no surprise that continuation rates for contraceptives in many developing countries have remained, in the words of George Zeidenstein, President of the Population Council, "extremely low."[190]

Even when programs count participants as "acceptors," to please administrators and meet predetermined quotas, the use of contraceptives is sometimes extremely sporadic. In one study in the Philippines, for example, pregnancy rates for so-called "users" of oral contraceptives were higher than for those using the rhythm method.[191]

While quotas, incentives, and other strong-arm tactics may have more to do with the underlying ideology of population control than the direct influence of the contraceptive manufacturers, the contraceptive industry does benefit from them, at least in the short run. Each new Pill or IUD acceptor is a new customer for the contraceptive industry, which needs to make up in volume what it loses in lowered mark-ups from bulk sales to population programs.

A Future For International Family Planning?

All this is not to suggest that there is no place for family planning in developing countries. Reproductive freedom, of which access to contraceptives is an important part, is essential for self-determination. But freedom of choice and support services such as health care and balanced information are also necessary if reproductive freedom is to exist. Reproductive freedom is also nore likely when people are able to exercise control over other areas of their lives, and live in countries where governments consider individual freedom to be consistent with their own goals. Of course, these other elements are precisely what tends to be missing in most countries that are given population assistance. Contraceptives, when used in these countries in population-control programs, have tended to limit, and not enhance, the reproductive self-determination of women and men.

A number of concrete changes would improve the situation and make such programs better able to meet individuals' needs. The abolishing of incentive payments and forms of reimbursement that act as financial incentives would be an important step towards eliminating coercion. Quotas should also be eliminated in all programs. Birth control pills should not be given out without a prescription and should be used only in conjunction with preliminary screening and follow-up medical examinations. Given the high risks associated with IUDs and Depo-Provera, neither method should be used in population programs. Corporations should not be allowed to take advantage of weaker drug safety laws abroad to boost their sales. All programs should be required to provide information on the benefits, risks, and effectiveness of contraceptives equivalent to that provided in the United States. Contraceptive marketing programs should be radically curtailed, at least in their present form. At the very least, birth control pills should not be used in CSM programs, and government funds should not be directed towards marketing research and advertising campaigns.

Changes must also be made in the direction of contraceptive research. Hormonal methods of birth control are dangerous and should be de-emphasized. The safety of contraceptives should not be neglected in favour of effectiveness, convenience, and the long-term use, and high technology should not be used as a substitute for a motivated patient.

Population programs should disentangle themselves from the generous arms of the contraceptive industry. Industry directors, scientists, or consultants should not be permitted on the boards of organizations that work in the population field, and the contraceptive industry should have no part in designing or running population programs.

Congress must also change the way it oversees AID. It should stop funding all programs that use sterilization and contraceptives in a coercive way, not those that perform (or provide information on) abortions.

Above all, AID and other funders of population programs must drastically rethink their analysis of the "population problem" and its relation to political and economic crises in the Third World. Population-control programs should not be used in the hope that they will solve the problems of hunger, poverty, or political unrest in the Third World, and they should not be used as a replacement for other necessary reforms. Those who claim to be concerned about population because they are concerned about the problems of poverty and underdevelopment in the Third World should concentrate their efforts on addressing the gross inequality between rich and poor in Third World countries, and the role of the United States in intensifying such inequalities. Family planning assistance, to the extent that it continues, should be used only in conjunction with other measures that improve the economic status and self-determination of Third World men and women. Until these basic assumptions and priorities of the population-control movement are changed, many of the other needed reforms are not likely to occur.

◄►

NOTES

1. Susan George, *How the Other Half Dies: The Real Reasons for World Hunger* (Harmondsworth, England: Penguin, 1983); Betsy Hartmann, *The Right to Live: Poverty, Power and Population Control* (San Francisco, Calif.: Institute for Food and Development Policy, 1986); and Mahmood Mamdani, *The Myth of Population Control: Family, Class and Class in an Indian Village* (New York: Monthly Review Press, 1973) all contain excellent discussions of these issues.

2. George, op.cit., p.35.

3. Michael T. Kauffman, "India is Trying to Cancel Food Gains to the Poor," *New York Times*, Oct. 23, 1981, quoted in Hartmann, *op. cit.*, p.7.

4. *Ibid.*, p.4.

5. United Nations, *Report on the International Conference on Population, Mexico City, August 6 — 14, 1984*, (New York), p.2.

6. Office of Technology Assessment, *World Population and Fertility Planning Technologies: The Next Twenty Years*, U.S. Government Printing Office, Washington, D.C., 1982, p.52.

7. Quoted from Laurence Lader, *Breeding Ourselves to Death*, (New York: Ballantyne Books, 1971), p.1.

8. "The World Population Crisis and Social Marketing: A New Approach," Informational Brochure, Population Services International, Washington D.C., pp.7 — 8.

9. John Hopkins University Population Information Program, *Population Reports*, "Sources of Population and Family Planning Assistance," Series J, no. 26, Jan. — Feb. 1983, p.626.

10. Phyllis Piotrow, *The World Population Crisis: The U.S. Response*, (New York: Prager, 1973), pp.127 — 8.

11. *Ibid.*

12. *Ibid.*, p.128.

13. Johns Hopkins University Population Information Program, *op. cit.*, p.623.

14. Piotrow, *op. cit.*, p.95.

15. *Ibid.*, p.137.

16. Agency for International Development, "Removal of Contraceptives from Ineligible Commodity List," Manual Circular 14543, May 11, 1967, quoted in Piotrow, *op. cit.*, p.136.

17. Statement of William F. Gaud, Administrator, Agency for International Development, before House Committee on Foreign Affairs, "Foreign Assistance Act of 1968," 90th Congress, vol. 11, parts 1 — 6, Feb. 29, 1968. p.59.

18. Piotrow, *op. cit.,* p.152.

19. Donald Warwick, *Bitter Pills: Population Policies and Their Implementation in Eight Developing Countries,* (Cambridge, England: Cambridge University Press, 1982), pp.66 — 7.

20. Statement of Sander Levin, Assistant Administrator, Agency for International Development, before House Select Committee on Population, "The Depo-Provera Debate," Aug. 10, 1978, 95th Congress, 2nd session, vol. 12 p.130.

21. Written testimony of Pramilla Senanayake, Medical Director, International Planned Parenthood Federation, before Depo-Provera Board of Inquiry, Jan. 10 — 14, 1983 (Food and Drug Administration Docket no. 78N — 0124).

22. James R. Dickenson, "International Group Loses U.S. Family Planning Funds," *Washington Post,* Dec. 13, 1984.

23. Statement of Jill Sheffield, Chairman, International Planned Parenthood Federation, before House Select Committee on Population, "Population and Development: Status and Trends of Family Planning Population Programs in Developing Countries," 95th Congress, 2nd session, May 3, 1978, vol. 3, no. 8, p.138.

24. Statement of Dr. Reimar T. Ravenholt, Director, Office of Population, Agency for International Development, before the House Committee on Appropriations, Subcommittee on Foreign Relations and Related Agencies, "Foreign Assistance and Related Appropriations, Part 1: Economic Assistance," 94th Congress, 1st session, vol. 15, part 3, June 24, 1975, pp.722 — 3.

25. Statement of Reimar T. Ravenholt, Director, Office of Population, Agency for International Development, before the Subcommittee on Foreign Operations and Related Agencies, House Committee on Foreign Affairs, "Foreign Assistance and Related Agencies Appropriations for 1977," Apr. 7, 1976, 94th Congress, 2nd session, p.931.

26. James Dickenson, "International Group Loses U.S. Family Planning Funds," *Washington Post,* December 13, 1984.

27 Ruth Marcus, "Judge Bars AID from Releasing Population Funds," *Washington Post,* Oct. 1, 1985.

28. Douglas Johnson, Legislative Director, National Right to Life Committee, Letter to the Editor, *Washington Post,* Feb. 22, 1985.

29. Michael Weisskopf, "Shanghai's Curse: Too Many Fight for too Little"; "Abortion Policy Tears at China's Society"; and "China's Birth Control Policy Drives Some to Kill Baby Girls," *Washington Post,* Jan. 6 — 8, 1985.

30. "Family Planning Fight," Editorial, *Washington Post,* May 15, 1985.

31. Betsy Hartmann and Jane Hughes, "And the Poor Get Sterilized," *The Nation,* June 30, 1984, pp.798 — 800.

32. Foreign Assistance Act, Section 104 (f), 1978, Policy Determination 3, quoted in "AID Policy Paper: Population Assistance," Agency for International Development, Washington, D.C., Sept. 1982, p.7.

33. Hartmann and Hughes, *op. cit.,* p.800.

34. *Population Reports, op. cit.,* Jan.-Feb. 1983, p.623.

35. *Ibid,* p.633.

36. *Ibid,* p.624.

37. International Planned Parenthood Federation, Information Brochure (London, 1984).

38. Johns Hopkins University Population Information Program, *Population Reports,* "A Guide to Sources of Family Planning Assistance," Series J, no. 15, Mar. 1977, p.267.

39. Population Crisis Committee/Draper Fund, Report of Activities, 1982 — 83 (Washington, D.C.), p.18.

40. Population Council, *Annual Report, 1983,* (New York), p.80.

41. Population Crisis Committee/Draper Fund, *Report of Activities, 1982 — 83* (Washington, D.C.).

42. Population Council, *Annual Report, 1983* (New York).

43. Family Health International, *Annual Report 1983* (Research Triangle Park, N.C.), p.6.

44. Written testimony of Dr. Malcolm Potts, President, Family Health International, before Depo-Provera Board of Inquiry, Jan. 10 — 14, 1983, submitted Dec. 9, 1982 (Food and Drug Administration Docket no. 78N — 0124).

45. Planned Parenthood Federation of America, "Serving Human Needs, Preserving Human Rights, Annual Report, 1983" (New York); and Jaques Cattell Press, eds., *Men and Women of Science: Physical and Biological Sciences,* 15th ed. (New York: R.R. Bowker, 1982).

46. *Quantus: Compendium of Directors, 1983* (Trenton, N.J.: P.C. Research Services).

47. Family Health International, *Annual Report, 1983,* p.16.

48. Personal communication, Frank Koch, Director, Community Affairs, Syntex Corporation, May 25, 1985.

49. *Ibid.*

50. For example, Planned Parenthod Federation of America would not release information on individual contributors (personal communication, Anita Lapof, Resources Department, Planned Parenthood Federation America, May 22, 1985). Nor would the Population Crisis Committee (personal

communication, Sharon Carbell, Population Crisis Committee, Apr. 22, 1985).

51. American Home Products would not provide information on its contributions (personal communication, Jack Wood, Government and Public Affairs, American Home Products, May 13, 1985).

52. *Hartmann, op. cit.*

53. Piotrow, *op. cit.,* p. 16.

54. *Ibid.,* p.175.

55. Johns Hopkins University Population Information Program, *Population Reports,* "Oral Contraceptives: 50 Million Users," Series A, Number 1, Apr. 1974, p.23.

56. *Office of Technology Assessment, op. cit.,* p. 107.

57. *Ibid.,* p.107.

58. Population Council, *Annual Report, 1983,* p.3.

59. *Ibid.,* p.10.

60. Population Council, *The Population Council, 1952 — 64: A Report* (New York), pp.41 — 4.

61. Population Council, *Annual Report 1983* p.10.

62. *Office of Technology Assessment, op. cit.,* p.108.

63. *Ibid.,* p.108.

64. Roy Orval Greep, "Reproduction and Human Welfare: A Challenge to Research: A Review of the Reproductive Sciences and Contraceptive Development" (New York: Ford Foundation, 1976).

65. *Office of Technology Assessment, op. cit.,* p.108.

66. Statements of Dr. Sheldon Segal, Senior Vice President, Population Council; Dr. William Hubbard, President, Upjohn Company; and Dr. Carl Djerassi, Professor, Department of Chemistry, Stanford University, before House Select Committee on Population, "Contraceptive Technology and Development," 95th Congress, 2nd session, Mar. 7, 1978, vol. 3, no. 4, 134 — 41, 141 — 9, 162 — 6, 169 — 214.

67. *Office of Technology Assessment, op. cit.,* p.113.

68. *Ibid.,* p.112.

69. Upjohn Company: Kalamazoo, Michigan, "Supplemental New Drug Application for Depo-Provera for Injection as a Contraceptive Agent in Humans," submitted to the Food and Drug Administration, Feb. 27, 1967.

70. "Long-term Depo-Provera Study in Dogs, Final Report," (unpublished), International Research and Development Corporation, Mattawan, Michigan, June 1976; "Long-term Depo-Provera Study in Dogs, Final Report," Dawson Corporation, Orlando, Florida, June 1982; "Long-term Depo-

Provera Study in Monkeys, Final Report,'' International Research and Development Corporation, Mattawan, Michigan, 1979. (All three studies have been submitted to Food and Drug Administration Docket no. 78N — 0124).

71. WHO Collaborative Study of Neoplasia and Steroid Contraceptives, ''Breast Cancer, Cervical Cancer, and Depot-Medroxyprogesterone Acetate,'' *Lancet,* Nov. 24, 1984, pp.1207 — 8.

72. P.C. Schwallie and N.R. Mohlberg, ''Medroxyprogesterone Acetate: An Injectable Contraceptive,'' New Drug Application 12-541/s-004. September 1977; E.T. Tyler *et. al,* ''Present Status of Injectable Contraceptives: Results of Seven Years Study, ''*Fertility and Sterility,* 21, no. 6 (1970), p.469; World Health Organization Task Force on Long Acting Systemic Agents for the Regulation of Fertility, ''Multinational Comparative Clinical Evaluation of Two Long-Acting Injectable Contraceptive Steroids: Norethisterone Oenanthate and Medroxyprogesterone Acetate: Bleeding Patterns and Side Effects,'' *Contraception,* 17, no. 5 (1978) p.395; P.C. Schwallie and J.R. Assenzo, ''Contraceptive Use-Efficacy Study Utilizing Medroxyprogesterone Acetate Administered as an Intramuscular Injection Once Every 90 Days,'' *Fertility and Sterility,* 24, no. 5 (1973) p.331; T. Pardthaisong *et al.,* ''Return of Fertility After Discontinuation of Depot Medroxyprogesterone Acetate and Intrauterine Devices in Northern Thailand,'' *Lancet,* Mar. 8, 1980, p.509; E.B. McDaniel and T. Pardthaisong, ''Depot-Medroxyprogesterone Acetate as a Contraceptive Agent: Return of Fertility After Discontunuation of Use,'' *Contraception,* 8, no. 5 (1973), p.407; E.B. McDaniel, ''Return of Fertility Following Discontinuation of Three Month Contraceptive Injections of DMPA Plus Routine Oral Estrogen Supplement: A Preliminary Report,'' *Fertility and Sterility,* 22, no. 12 (1971), p.802; P.C. Schwallie and J.R. Assenzo, ''The Effect of Depo-Medroxyprogesterone Acetate on Pituitary and Ovarian Function, and the Return to Fertility Following its Discontinuation: A Review,'' *Contraception,* 10, no. 2 (1974), p.1981; R.J. Seymour and L.C. Powell, ''Depo-Medroxyprogesterone Acetate as a Contraceptive,'' *Obstetrics and Gynecology,* 36 no. 4 (1970), p.589 — 96.

73. I.S. Fraser, ''A Comprehensive Review of Injectable Contraception With a Special Emphasis on Depot-Medroxyprogesterone Acetate,'' *Medical Journal of Australia,* Supplement, Jan. 24, 1981, p.4.

74. Morton Mintz, ''Defense Raises Doubts: Destruction of Documents Alleged,'' *Washington Post,* Apr. 11, 1985.

75. Barbara Ehrenreich, Mark Dowie, and Stephen Minkin, ''The Charge, Gynocide; The Accused, the U.S. Government,'' *Mother Jones,* Nov. 1979, p.28.

76. Morton Mintz, ''A Crime Against Women: A.H. Robins and the Dalkon Sheild,'' *Multinational Monitor,* 7, no. 1 (Jan. 15, 1986).

77. Jaqueline Darroch Forrest and Stanley K. Henshaw, ''What U.S. Women

Think and Do About Contraception," *Family Planning Perspectives,* 15, no. 4 (July/Aug. 1983), pp.157 — 66.

78. Personal communication, Fred Greenberg, Analyst, Goldman, Sachs and Company, New York, Dec. 1984.

79. *Ibid.*

80. "Transnational Corporations in the Pharmaceutical Industry of Developing Countries," United Nations Center on Transnational Corporations, United Nations, New York, 1984, p.4. Both U.S. and world-wide figures refer to consumption, not production.

81. Quoted in Marjorie Sun, "Depo-Provera Debate Revs up at FDA," *Science Magazine,* July 1982, pp.424 — 8.

82. American Home Products, *Annual Report 1983* (New York).

83 Sun, *Op. cit.,* p.428.

84. Personal communication, Fred Greenberg, Analyst, Goldman, Sachs and Company, New York, December 1984.

85. *Office of Technology Assessment, op. cit.,* p.116.

86. "Barrier Contraceptives: New Products, Packages, Promotions and Profits," *National Association of Retail Druggists Journal,* July 1980.

87. IMS *Pharmamarketletter,* Nov. 28, 1983.

88. Tamar Lewin, "Searle, Assailing Lawsuits, Halts U.S. Sales of Intrauterine Devices," *New York Times,* Feb. 1, 1986.

89. *Office of Technology Assessment, op. cit.,* p.114.

90. Charles F. Westoff, "Trends in Contraceptive Practice, 1965 — 73," *Family Planning Perspectives,* 8, no. 2, Mar./Apr. 1976, p.54.

91. G.D. Searle, *Annual Report, 1969* (Skokie, Il10).

92. Syntex Corporation, *Annual Report, 1969* (Panama).

93. Royal College of General Practitioners, *Oral Contraceptives and Health* (London: Pitman, 1974).

94. Senate Select Committee on Monopoly, "Competitive Problems in the Drug Industry: Oral Contraceptives," 91st Congress, 1st session, vol. 1 — 3. 1970.

95. Russel Thomsen, *An Atlas of Intrauterine Contraception* (Washington, D.C.; Hemisphere Publishing, 1982) p.4.

96. G.D. Searle, Annual Reports, 1968 — 76.

97. Syntex Corporation, *Annual Report, 1971.*

98. *Population Reports, op. cit.,* Jan. 1976, p.57.

99. "Putting a Break on Runaway Birth Rates," *Business Week,* Sept. 23, 1967, p.76.

100. Piotrow, *op. cit.*, p.183.

101. Syntex Corporation, *Annual Report, 1979;* and response to Freedom of Information Act request to the Agency for International Development, Jan. 29, 1985.

102. Johns Hopkins University Population Information Program, *Population Reports,* "Filling in Family Planning Gaps," Series J, Number 20, Sept. 1978, p.376.

103. *Population Reports, op. cit.,* Apr. 1974, p.23.

104. Syntex Corporation, *Annual Report, 1979;* response to Freedom of Information Act request to the Agency for International Development, Jan. 29, 1985.

105. Syntex Corporation, *Annual Report, 1977.*

106. These figures were calculated by dividing Syntex's oral contraceptive sales to AID for 1978, 1979, and 1983 by the company's total oral contraceptive sales for these years. Both sets of figures were obtained from the company's Annual Reports.

107. American Home Products, *Annual Report, 1968* (New York).

108. G.D. Searle, *Annual Report, 1967.*

109. This figure was calculated by adding the total U.S. retail condom market (an estimated $225 million a year in the early 1980s) to condom purchases by AID.

110. Response to Freedom of Information Act request to the Agency for International Development, Jan. 29, 1985.

111. *Ibid.*

112. *National Association of Retail Druggists Journal, op. cit.*

113. Personal communication, Casey Kutsazawa, Secretary Treasurer, Circle Rubber Company, May 7, 1985.

114. Response to Freedom of Information Act request to the Agency for International Development, Jan. 29, 1985.

115. Agency for International Development, "Congressional Presentation, Fiscal Year 1985: Annex Five, Centrally Funded Programs," p.69.

116. Statement of Richard Rogers, President, Syntex Laboratories, before House Select Committee on Population, "Research in Population and Development: Needs and Capacities," vol. 3, no. 8, May 2, 1978, p.32.

117. Statement of Dr. William Hubbard, President, Upjohn Company, before House Select Committee on Population, "The Depo-Provera Debate," 95th Congress, 2nd session, no. 12, Aug. 8, 1978, pp.26 — 31.

118. Statement of Dr. William Hubbard, President, Upjohn Company, before House Select Committee on Population, "Contraceptive Technology and

Development," 95th Congress, 2nd session, vol. 3, no. 4, Mar. 9, 1978, pp.134 — 41, 169 — 214.

119. Statement of Dr. Carl Djerassi, Professor, Stanford University, before House Select Committee on Population, "Contraceptive Technology and Development," 95th Congress, 2nd session, vol. 3, no. 4, Mar. 9, 1978, pp.141 — 9, 169 — 214.

120. Statement of Richard Rogers, President, Syntex Laboratories, before House Select Committee on Population, "Research in Population and Development: Needs and Capacities," 95th Congress, 2nd session, vol. 3, no. 8, May 2, 1978, pp.27 — 39.

121. Statement of Representative James Scheuer before House Select Committee on Population, "World Population: A Global Perspective," 95th Congress, 2nd session, vol. 1, no. 1, Feb. 7, 1978, p.1.

122. Representative James Scheuer, Candidate Index of Supporting Documents, 1977 — 84, Federal Election Commission, Washington, D.C.

123. Jaques Cattell Press, *op. cit.*

124. Testimony of Dr. Jack Lippes, before Senate Committee on Governmental Relations, Subcommittee on Foreign Aid Expenditures, "Population Crisis," 89th Congress, 1st session, Sept. 22, 1965, p.1916.

125. Testimony of Dr. John Rock before Senate Committee on Governmental Relations, Subcommittee on Foreign Relations Expenditures, "Population Crisis," June 29, 1965, p.638.

126. *Office of Technology Assessment, op. cit.*

127. International Pllanned Parenthood Federation, Information Brochure (London).

128. Pathfinder Fund, *Annual Report, 1981* (Boston, Mass.).

129. Family Planning International Assistance, *Annual Report, 1983* (New York), p.213.

130. *Ibid.*

131. Population Crisis Committee, "Return of Organizations Exempt from Income Tax", (Washington, D.C.) p.2.

132. SOMARC, The Futures Group, Information Brochure (Washington, D.C.).

133. Johns Hopkins University Population Information Program, *Population Reports,* "Social Marketing: Does it work?" Series J, no. 21, Jan. 1980.

134. *Ibid,* p.396.

135. *Ibid.*

136. "Financial Report, 1984," Population Services International, Washington, D.C.

137. "Successful Innovation in Family Planning Through Social Marketing," Informational Brochure, Population Services International.

138. SOMARC, The Futures Group, Information Brochure (Washington, D.C.); and personal communication, Donald Newman, Chief, Commodity and Program Support Division, Office of Population, Agency for International Development, Washington, D.C., Jan. 1986.

139. *Population Reports, op. cit.,* Jan. 1980, pp.425 — 30.

140. Program for the Introduction and Adaptation of Contraceptive Technology, Informational Brochure, (Seattle, Wash.).

141. Personal communication, Betsy Morrow, Director, Program for the Introduction and Adaptation of Contraceptive Technology, May 22, 1985.

142. Written statement of Dr. Gordon Duncan, Director, Population Studies Center, Battelle Memorial Institute, before House Select Committee on Population, vol. 3, no. 4, Mar. 8, 1978, p.68.

143. *Population Reports, op. cit.,* Jan. 1980, p.424.

144. Population Services International, Information Brochure, (Washington, D.C.).

145. *Ibid.*

146. Johns Hopkins University Population Information Program, *Population Reports,* "Contraceptive Distribution: Taking Supplies to Villages and Households," Series J, no. 5, July 1975, p.74.

147. *Ibid.* It is not clear how many of these countries dropped their prescription requirement for the Pill in response to the IPPF recommendation.

148. Population Services International, "Successful Innovation in Family Planning Through Social Marketing,"

149. *Population Reports, op. cit.,* July 1975, pp.71 — 2

150. *Population Reports, op. cit.,* Jan. 1980, p.396.

151. *Ibid,* pp.415 — 16.

152. *Ibid,* p.412.

153. *Ibid.*

154. S. Anwar Ali, Operations Director, FSPMP, Bangladesh, "Social Marketing of Contraceptives in Bangladesh: A General Review of Program Directions Incorporating Additional Product Expansion," in Manuel Ylanan and Cecilia C. Verzosa, eds., "Commercial Retail Sales of Contraceptives," PIACT Paper no. 6, Program for the Introduction and Adaptation of Contraceptive Technology, Seattle, Washington, p.6.

155. *Ibid.*

156. *Population Reports, op. cit.,* July 1980.

157. Manuel Ylanan and Cecilia C. Verzosa, "Commercial Retail Sales of Con-

traceptives,'' PIACT Paper Number 6, Program for the Introduction and Adaptation of Contraceptive Technology, Seattle, Washington, p.17.

158. *Population Reports, op. cit.,* July 1980, p.397.

159. Ylanan and Verzosa, *op. cit.,* p.12.

160. *Population Reports, op. cit.,* July 1975, p.73.

161. *Population Reports, op. cit.,* July 1980, p.426.

162. Statement of Richard Rogers, President, Syntex Laboratories, before House Select Committee on Pupulation, ''Research in Population and Development: Needs and Capacities'', vol. 3, no. 8, May 2, 1978, p.31.

163. Ylanan and Verzosa, *op. cit.,* p.11.

164. Informational Brochure, SOMARC, The Futures Group, Washington, D.C.

165. *Population Reports, op. cit.,* July 1980, p.396.

166. Ylanan and Verzosa, *op. cit.,* p.17.

167. Personal communication, Donald Newman, Chief, Commodity and Program Support Division, Office of Population, Agency for International Development, Feb. 15, 1985.

168. *Population Reports, op. cit.,* July 1980, p.417.

169. Personal communication, Donald Newman, Chief, Commodity and Program Support Division, Office of Population, Agency for International Development, Feb. 15, 1985.

170. Letter from Dr. N.J. Wilmott, Medical Coordinator, International Committee of the Red Cross, Kamput, Thailand, to Dr. M. Duboulon, Medical Coordinator, International Committee of the Red Cross, Bangkok, Thailand, Feb. 14, 1980.

171. International Planned Parenthood Federation, ''Incentive Payments,'' Working Paper no. 4, (London, 1969).

172. *Ibid.*

173. Warwich, *op. cit.,* pp.30, 140.

174. *Ibid,* p.11.

175. J. Waterbury, ''Manpower and Population Planning in the Arab Republic of Egypt, Part IV: Egypt's Governmental Program for Family Planning,'' American Universities Field Staff, Field Staff Reports, Northeast Africa Series, vol. 17, no. 5, 1972, cited in Warwick, *op. cit.,* p.151.

176. William Clareborne, ''India Begins Crash Program to Develop Injectable Contraceptive,'' *Washington Post,* July 10, 1983.

177. Statement of Representative James Scheuer before House Select Committee on Population, ''Research in Population and Development: Needs and Capacities,'' vol. 3, no. 8, May 3, 1978, p.130.

178. Statement of Dr. John P. Lewis, Professor of Economics, Princeton University, before House Select Committee on Population, "Research on Population and Development: Needs and Capacities," 95th Congress, 2nd session, vol. 3, no. 8, May 3, 1978, p.130.

179. Hartmann, *op. cit.*

180. "Agency for International Development Policy Paper: Population Assistance," Agency for International Development, Washington, D.C., Sep. 1982, p.5.

181. Warwick, *op. cit.,* p.138.

182. *Ibid.,* p.139.

183. *Ibid.*

184. *Ibid.,* pp.130 — 2.

185. Pathfinder Fund, *Annual Report, 1983* (Boston, Mass.).

186. Bonnie Mass, *Population Target: The Political Economy of Population Control in Latin America* (Toronto: Women's Press, 1976), p.220.

187. *Ibid.,* p.253.

188. Warwick, *op. cit.,* p.167.

189. *Ibid.*

190. George Zeidenstein, "The User Perspective: An Evolutionary Concept in Contraceptive Service Programs," *Studies in Family Planning,* 2, no. 1 (Jan. 1980) p.26.

191. Statement by Judith Bruce, Associate, International Programs, Population Council, before House Select Committee on Population, "Research in Population and Development: Needs and Capacities," vol. 3, no.8, May 2, 1978, p.19.

FINGER IN THE DIKE: THE FIGHT TO KEEP INJECTABLES OUT OF INDIA

Vimal Balasubrahmanyan

O N MARCH 31, 1985, members of Stree Shakti Sanghatana, an activist women's group in Hyderabad in the Indian State of Andhra Pradesh, learned from a hospital source that a "camp" to administer Net-Oen, an experimental injectable contraceptive, was to be inaugurated the next morning at Patancheru, a village about two hours by bus from Hyderabad. The camp was to be part of an ongoing trial of the drug being conducted all over India. Early the following day, four members of the group, along with this writer, left for Patancheru to appeal to the doctors in charge to cancel the camp. Our arguments were based on the fact that Net-Oen had not been licensed for contraceptive use in the United Kingdom or the United States, that its long-term effects are still unknown, that it has a number of side-effects, and that it is not a safe method to be introduced in India under the present state of the health services. This mission was not successful. After over an hour's discussion and argument, the group was not able to dissuade the doctors and eventually had to return home. But the Patancheru incident was a crucial one, a turning point that convinced activists worried about the introduction of a potentially hazardous new drug into India's family planning programs that we would have to take the bold step of appealing directly to the Supreme Court of India to halt further experimentation with Net-Oen.

Just what happened at Patancheru? In response to the arguments made by the Stree Shakti members, the camp doctors pointed out that Net-Oen had no "life-threatening" side-effects and claimed that, while Western women tended to complain easily about side-effects, Indian women can tolerate these quite comfortably. They argued that an injectable contraceptive was needed in India because the IUD, the Pill, and tubectomy had all proved to be problematic with their side-effects and complications. They also attacked the group's credibility, saying that we were lay people and therefore misinformed. One doctor said that everything has side-effects and that even walking on the road can be dangerous. Another suggested that we had been reading Arthur Hailey's *Strong Medicine* and had got carried away.

During the discussion with the doctors, the women who had been recruited for the experiment began to arrive. There was a festive atmosphere, as though a great *tamasha* (celebration) was in the offing, with the health centre staff assembled in readiness, waiting for the formal speeches and for the collector (a senior government official) to "inaugurate" the camp. The collector, in an apparent effort to dispel any notion that the recruits were being compelled to accept the injectable, suggested that both the Stree Shakti group and the doctors should present their respective viewpoints to the women, who would then be free to do as they chose.

We then informed the women gathered at the camp that the injectable is an experimental method and found that they were unaware of this. They also said that they had not been informed of any possible side-effects. We told them that the injectable was being given to poor Third World women and not to white Western women, or to literate women like us. On their part, the doctors assured the women that the injectable was safe and said nothing about possible side-effects. They stressed that the family planning program is based on the "cafeteria" principle, that it was for the women themselves to choose the method they preferred. This, however, conflicted with the evidence of the women, who said they had been brought there that day with the specific purpose of receiving the injectable. All except five of the thirty women who had been brought to the camp walked out after hearing both sides.

Later, at the Patancheru bus stop, we spoke with some of the paramedics from the camp, who said things they had not felt free to say in the presence of the senior doctors. They had not distributed the local-language pamphlets containing information on side-effects to the women volunteers, nor had they explained to the women that the injectable was an experimental method, because if they had done so, they said, "no one would have volunteered." It was their job to produce the volunteers for the day's program, and the only way they could do so was by concealing adverse information. They also said they took care to recruit women from villages other than their own, so that if any problem should arise with the method they would not have to face angry women from their own community.

We had also spoken to one woman brought to the camp, who was very young and had not yet had a child, and to another who was barely eighteen and had an eighteen month-old baby in her arms whom she was breast-feeding. Both these are serious contra-indications to the use of Net-Oen. Perhaps they might have been weeded out later by the doctors, but it was shocking that such fundamental screening had not been done at the time of selecting the "volunteers," who had been brought that day from great distances. What, then, were their chances of proper follow-up care? While these women were walking away, we noticed one of the health centre doctors angrily accosting the young girl with the baby. He asked her why she would not accept the assurances of the doctors regarding the injectable and warned her that it was the same health centre she would have to approach when she needed any other treatment.

The group left Patancheru feeling deeply concerned. The government and medical authorities clearly were not prepared to listen. Instead, we were accused of jeopardizing the entire family planning program and of denying women access to control which they themselves wanted. The overall attitude of those in charge was that family planning policy is a purely medical matter and that medical scientists alone are competent to know what is best for the country and for the women who are the targets of this policy.

INJECTABLES: THE CONTROVERSY

Injectable contraceptives are synthetic progestogens that have a contraceptive effect for sixty to ninety days at a time. The two most widely used injectables are Depo-Provera (made by Upjohn) and Neo-Oen (made by Schering A.G.) though a number of others are reportedly being developed. The majority of the almost two million women in the world receiving injectables use Depo-Provera. However, because of the controversy surrounding that drug, more attention is being given to Net-Oen in recent years by researchers and family planning organizations, in an effort to find an acceptable alternative to Depo-Provera.[1]

The campaign in India against Net-Oen is an example of a movement to prevent the widespread introduction of a drug into the country's family planning program. This effort is based largely on the knowledge that injectable contraceptives have been misused in other Third World countries and that injectables are a potential hazard in the hands of family planning personnel who are pressed to achieve "targets." Activists in India are determined to prevent the mistakes that have been known to occur in other countries. In January 1983, the deputy director-general of the Indian Council of Medical Research (ICMR) announced to the press that Net-Oen had been "successfully' tested on 2,600 women at fourteen centres in the country and that it would soon be introduced into the country's family planning program. Health activists were disturbed by this announcement, and a number of articles appeared in the media about the controversy over injectables in other countries. However, active campaigning against Net-Oen began only in late 1984, when it was learned that the government had issued a directive permitting the import of Net-Oen and had decided to introduce it as one of the "cafeteria" methods through government clinics.[2] In December 1984, four women's groups of Bombay, along with the Medico Friend Circle (an activist health group whose members include doctors), held a demonstration to protest against a closed-door meeting where the Family Planning Association of India (FPAI) and representatives of government medical bodies and drug companies were discussing the "guidelines" for introducing Net-Oen.

Early in 1985, the Medico Friend Circle and a coalition of activist groups called the All India Drug Action Network (AIDAN) decided to launch an intensive campaign against Net-Oen. Women's groups in Bombay decided to concentrate on Net-Oen as a theme for International Women's Day on March 8, and other groups wrote letters of protest to the Health Ministry, the Drug Controller, and ICMR, asking them not to introduce Net-Oen and to stop the trials. When these efforts yielded no results, and after the incident at Pathancheru, Stree Shakti, along with Saheli (a Delhi-based women's group), decided to file a petition in the Supreme Court of India arguing that it would be unsafe to allow the injectable into India, and that unethical experimentation with the drug was being done on Indian women without their informed consent (see appendix). The petition asked for a stay on the current Net-Oen trials, full publication of all information on the drug, and the setting up of an independent panel of scientists and doctors to explore the issues surrounding it. Other co-petitioners were five doctors of Hyderabad and this writer. The petition has been circulated among activist groups that have agreed to join in an all-India campaign.

In India, in recent years, a phenomenon called "public interest litigation" has come into being. Socially conscious individuals and groups have written to the High Courts or to the Supreme Court, bringing to their notice instances of exploitation and violation of fundamental rights of the deprived sections of society, often by government departments themselves. The judges have frequently treated such letters as writ petitions and issued show-cause notices to the respondents. In 1983, for example, a lawyer from a public interest law society petitioned the Kerala High Court protesting against the continued sale of certain drugs which the government itself had banned, on the ground that this was a threat to life and therefore violated Article 21 of the Constitution. The court responded by passing severe strictures on the government for its negligence and ordered remedial action.

NET-OEN: HISTORY AND HEALTH EFFECTS

Schering began clinical studies of Net-Oen in 1957. The first major field trials were conducted in Peru, and in 1967 the drug went on the market there under the brand name of Norigest. It was withdrawn in 1971 and field trials suspended after pituitary and breast nodules were found in experimental rats. However, it was decided that these findings were not relevant to humans, and the drug went back on the market. Today Net-Oen is marketed commercially as Norigest, and as Noristerat when supplied to donor agencies. Although it is known to be "available" in at least thirty-five countries, it is not definitely known in how many countries it is "approved" for contraceptive use.[3] Clinical trials with Net-Oen are going on in several Third World countries. However, it is significant that in none of the advanced countries, which have stringent safety standards and vocal health and consumer movements, is Net-Oen or Depo-Provera (the two major injectables) approved for routine long-term contraceptive use.[4] There is, however, considerable documented evidence that injectable contraceptives have been used in some advanced countries on coloured immigrants and other disadvantaged women.

Side Effects:

The most common side-effect is menstrual irregularity, which is also the most common reason for discontinuation. The irregularity occurs in several forms: unpredictable bleeding, spotting, frequent and heavy bleeding, and sometimes amenorrhea, or absence of bleeding. Besides being extremely disruptive of women's daily lives and work, all these conditions are totally unacceptable in the Indian cultural milieu, where menstruation is associated with being "unclean". More importantly, excessive bleeding is a serious problem in a country where anaemia in women is a major disease. ICMR's own study has shown evidence of liver damage, which again is a serious contraindication.[5] Among the side-effects which are known to occur but are generally dismissed as "unimportant" are dizziness, headaches, and weight gain.

Cancer Risk:

According to WHO, the cancer-causing effects of Net-Oen are not fully known. This is of course the main reason why the drug has not been approved for use by white women in the advanced countries. Studies are being conducted in India and other countries to assess the cancer risk. This means that women recruited for these trials are serving as guinea pigs to determine the long-term safety of Net-Oen. This practice recalls the 1950s, when the oral contraceptive pill was also extensively tested on poor Puerto Rican and Mexican women before it was declared safe for women in the advanced countries.

Return of Fertility:

WHO has said that, since return of fertility after discontinuation has not been clearly proven, women who do wish to have children later should be advised to use another method.[6] In India, where the infant mortality rate is high, the risk of possible infertility is unacceptable, especially among the poorer classes of women who are precisely the ones being recruited for the trial.

Effects on Offspring:

It is well documented that steroids are excreted in breast milk. In India, women are known to breast-feed for up to two years after delivery, and the effects of the hormone drug on breast-fed infants constitute a serious potential risk. WHO also gives a list of serious contraindications and recommends careful screening of potential acceptors.[7]

INJECTABLES IN AN INDIAN CONTEXT

It is often argued that women themselves want an injectable contraceptive because it is convenient and can be taken without the knowledge of husbands and families. Doctors in favour of injectables also argue that, since all contraceptives have side-effects, why oppose only the injectable? The answer to these arguments is that a women who decides to accept the risks and side-effects of a particular contraceptive must be able to make an informed choice and should be given full information on the possible risks associated with that method. This criterion is *not* being fulfilled in the Net-Oen trials in India, in which in many cases women are given inadequate counselling and follow-up care and are generally seen as mere specks in the columns of statistics which go to make up the family planning "performance" of a particular state, or nameless numbers adding up to this or that health worker's quota. It is, of course, true that other contraceptives, such as the Pill and the IUD, have side-effects. The answer is to make current methods safer through better research and medical care rather than to introduce one more hormonal drug with many more long-term question marks surrounding it.

But it is easy to see why the government is eager to introduce the injectable. Women can be reduced from active decision-makers to passive recipients, especially in a milieu where anything coming from a needle is equated with "good medicine." Women cannot "forget" the injectable as they can the Pill, nor throw it away if they cannot tolerate its side-effects. Nor can it be pulled out like an IUD when it causes infection and bleeding. The injectable ensures transfer of control from the hands of the user to the hands of the health worker who wields the syringe. The potential for abuse in a system where health personnel are pressured to achieve targets is tremendous.

Past abuses in promotion of the IUD and of sterilization have been well documented in India and are confirmed once again by ICMR's own study. The circular to medical colleagues selected for the Phase IV Net-Oen trials refers to a high discontinuation rate during Phase III. ICMR's own deduction is that the women discontinued because of the absence of counselling, a lack of educational material for participants, and the "very casual behaviour of clinical staff." When the disastrous IUD drive of the sixties was evaluated, the same reason for its rejection was revealed — lack of back-up medical care. No program promoting "invasive" contraceptive methods (like injectables, pills, or IUDs) is safe or acceptable without sympathetic medical care. But many women in India do not have access to even basic primary health care, safe obstetrics, or medical abortion, and they are hardly likely to get adequate counselling in a high-pressure contraceptive injectable program. The preconditions did *not* exist in the sixties for a safe IUD drive, and they do not exist today for a safe injectable drive. Yet the ICMR intends to repeat its past mistakes at the cost of the health of this country's women. A drug like Net-Oen, which could perhaps be carefully and safely administered in a situation where adequate medical care is available, should not be introduced into a country where this basic precondition of safety does not exist.

CONTRACEPTIVE RESEARCH:
WHO MAKES THE DECISIONS?

Ever since the first ICMR press release on Net-Oen, women's groups in India have encountered a shroud of secrecy in their efforts to get more information about the trials. ICMR documents quoted in the petition to the Supreme Court, for example, were procured with great difficulty from a highly specialized scientific journal[8] and from friendly hospital sources. The aim of such exclusive control by the medical authorities appears to be to prevent any informed public debate on the suitability of the contraceptive research policy and on the theory that "expert" knowledge can be understood by experts only. But many are beginning to question the rationale by which decisions regarding contraceptive research are made. According to press reports, ICMR is currently experimenting with the hormonal implant, prostaglandins, for abortion, and with the anti-pregnancy vaccine.[9] Clinical trials are going on with all these methods, and all of them, significantly, are female methods. Who are the women thus being experimented on? It is hard to believe that the women in these trials are aware that they are being used for experiments with drugs whose safety is not proved. Moreover, in the event that a failure of the method results in pregnancy, there is no assurance that the women will be compensated or that they will be granted abortion without difficulty.

Since 1977, when the coercive vasectomy campaign precipitated a political disaster for the ruling party, Indian population controllers have been aggressively directing all family planning programs at women, in total disregard for their health or rights. Women seeking abortion, for example, are being compelled to accept the Pill, IUD, or injectable. One of the doctors involved in the Stree Shakti group encountered a woman who had actually had three different IUDs, inserted on separate occasions, and as a result was suffering from heavy bleeding. It is time that serious and systematic research into male contraceptives be undertaken. Perhaps the authorities are confident that, despite these abuses, women, because they *are* women, will not use the ballot box to express their anger and frustration.

It is often argued that women are the ones oppressed by frequent pregnancies and are better motivated than men to seek contraception. However, women are rarely consulted when the directions in family planning policy and research are decided. In the advanced countries, there is currently a major shift back to barrier methods like the diaphragm, and in 1983 a simple and effective vaginal sponge that needs no medical fitting was introduced in the United Kingdom and the United States in response to this preference. Yet no effort has been made to introduce it into India or to promote other barrier methods. Activists in India are demanding the development of better barrier methods and a greater emphasis on meeting women's needs rather than the quotas, targets, and incentives which lie at the heart of family planning abuses. There needs to be as much emphasis on safe child-bearing, for example, as there is on birth control.

The Ethics of Experimentation

The whole issue of medical experimentation also needs to be debated publicly, and safeguards against abuse should be introduced. We know from press reports and sources within the medical research fraternity that in India, as in many other Third World countries, the concept of "informed consent" is non-existent in practical terms, though many paper guidelines pay lip-service to the idea.[10] Third World populations are ideal research material for field trials, especially since the norms for such research are extremely stringent in the advanced countries and the public there is far too vocal and well-informed to allow rampant trials of potentially dangerous drugs. The research establishment in India, however, collaborates wittingly or unwittingly with the drug multinationals in conducting human trials to obtain the data required by these firms. It is only the more literate, socially conscious groups that can protest and put an end to this unethical practice, since the subjects of these experiments are ignorant and unaware that they have any rights at all in the matter. We are often told by senior medical researchers that there can be no medical advance without human experimentation and that all trials on human beings are only for "their own good." Then why not recruit articulate, well-informed, literate volunteers from the middle and upper classes, who can give truly informed consent, who will be vocal in demanding back-up medical care, and who will reject a drug or device if its side-effects are intolerable? For starters, perhaps the researchers ought to recruit volunteers from among their own medical community.

INJECTABLES IN INDIA: SOME HISTORY

Although the injectables issue has come into prominence only since 1983, India's experience with them goes back to the 1970s. Depo-Provera was tested in the late seventies, but the trials were abandoned and the report never published.[11] In a study supported by WHO that was conducted from 1977 to 1980 to determine the reasons for continuation or discontinuation of the Pill, IUD, and injectable at clinics in the Chandigarh area of Punjab, the injectable offered was Depo-Provera.[12] A "balance presentation" of the three methods was given to women seeking contraception, but it was not mentioned to them that the injectable was an experimental method. Out of a total 360 acceptors, only 34 chose the injectable, 25 or whom discontinued mainly because of erratic and excessive bleeding. Discontinuation of all methods was largely because of inadequate counselling and lack of sympathetic, supportive care. Some of the women who discontinued the injectable did so because their husbands were dissatisfied with the method, since erratic bleeding meant denial of sexual relations. One women was quoted as saying that she feared that denying sex to her husband would cause marital problems, and so she discontinued the method. This suggests that the argument that the injectable can be used without the knowledge of husbands is of doubtful validity. Also, since many Indian women observe segregation during menstruation, especially when religious ceremonies are performed, it is difficult to see how they can reconcile this taboo with erratic and unpredictable bleeding patterns.

ICMR's subsequent decision to select Net-Oen for trials is almost certainly because of the unsavoury global controversy over Depo-Provera. One medical scientist informed me that she was a member of the committee involved in planning the Depo-Provera trials and had strongly opposed the use of Indian women as guinea pigs when there was already so much controversy over the drug. She herself took one experimental shot of the drug and experienced severe menstrual irregularity for almost a year. Not surprisingly, she was not included in the new committee which decided on the Net-Oen trials.

It is difficult to pinpoint exactly when women's groups in India became conscious of the need to monitor family planning programs and the contraceptive research policy that use women as targets. In April 1981, the Feminist Resource Centre of Bombay organized a workshop entitled "Women, Health and Reproduction," where, probably for the first time, concern was expressed at the way in which the Pill, injectables, IUDs, and other devices were being tried out on Indian women. It was agreed that action should be taken by the women's movement, but no immediate program was mapped out. The workshop, however, was an important landmark which signalled the beginning of an informal consciousness-raising on the issue of women and family planning. One of the earliest articles warning against the impending introduction of injectables into India was by this writer in *Mainstream* (November 28, 1981), entitled "After the Pill: A Shot in the Arm for the Unwary?" ICMR had just then recommended mass distribution of the Pill by village-level health workers, and the article suggested that injectables could not be far behind, a prediction that turned out to be true. The *Mainstream* article contained interviews with two Calcutta doctors, one for and the other against the injectable. One, a senior woman gynaecologist, expressed strong reservation and said that all hormonal methods need careful medical monitoring and that if mass use of the injectable were introduced in India the chances were high that women with contraindications would receive the drug. The second doctor was an injectables enthusiast and was himself involved in the ICMR pilot study of Net-Oen. He belonged to the "benefits outweigh risks" school of thought, and described the injectable as a boon to poor Indian women who are the helpless objects of their husbands' lust.

Soon after the ICMR press release in January 1983 on the "successful" trial of Net-Oen, the Centre for Education and Documentation in Bombay produced a detailed paper entitled "Injectables: Immaculate Contraception?" Also during 1983-4 many articles appeared in the media, mainly on the controversy over Depo-Provera in other countries. The March 1983 issue of the *MFC Bulletin* printed a lead article on Depo-Provera and an editorial condemning the injectable as "Wrong Choice, Wrong Solution." However, as Padma Prakash points out in her article on injectables in the May 1985 issue of the *MFC Bulletin,* the debate in India over injectables remained largely academic until late 1984, when it was learned that the government intended to issue licences for manufacturing Net-Oen and to introduce the injectable into government family planning clinics. Since then there have been charges that the drug company, German Remedies has been persuading general practitioners to put their signatures on forms "requesting" a supply of a certain number of doses of Net-Oen and that these forms are to be presented to the government as "evidence" that there is a large and unmet "demand" for the drug.

DEPO REARS ITS HEAD AGAIN

In May 1984, an organization called the Indian Association of Fertility and Sterility urged the Health Ministry to allow without delay the use of injectable contraceptives in India to solve the country's pressing population "problem." At a press conference Dr. C.L. Jhaveri, chairman of the association, spoke in special praise of Depo-Provera, which, he said, was being used in eighty countries. Earlier, the Federation of Obstetricians and Gynaecologists had also issued a call for an early introduction of injectables to curb population growth. In the September 1984 issue of *Science Age,* Dr. M.C. Watsa, a consultant to the Family Planning Association of India, strongly argued the case for injectables, particularly Depo-Provera. Subsequently, Dr. Jhaveri filed a case in the Bombay High Court against the Drug Controller of India for refusing to give him a licence to import the drug from Belgium, where the Upjohn company has a plant. He has a family planning clinic in Bombay and had applied for a licence to import a limited quality of Depo-Provera for "examination, testing, and analysis," arguing that since the government had not formally banned the drug, it had no right to refuse an import licence under the present regulations. The Women's Centre of Bombay and the Medico Friend Circle applied for permission to intervene in the case, which the court has granted. The case is still pending.

In their argument before the Bombay High Court, the activists have asserted that Dr. Jhaveri plans to use the drug for family planning, and not for testing and analysis as claimed. As Ammu Abraham of the Women's Centre points out, if Jhaveri is allowed to import the drug, any general practitioner in India can do likewise, and under present conditions in India its use on women for population control cannot be prevented.[13] The Drug Controller's failure to issue a proper notification has left scope for ambiguity and litigation. It reveals how weak the laws are which regulate the entry of drugs and their possible use on unsuspecting subjects in a country where the concept of informed consent exists only on paper. Even the use of Net-Oen and other contraceptives such as implants, prostaglandins, IUDs, and vaginal rings in clinical research shows how easy it is to bring into the country, through WHO channels, products that have not been formally assessed and approved by the government.

The efforts to "rehabilitate" Depo-Provera show that many establishment doctors who feel that drastic population control is necessary are in favour of injectables. But what about the doctors in government service? Do they support the introduction of injectables also? For one thing, the fact that WHO and ICMR have declared that injectables are "safe" is accepted unquestioningly by most government doctors without considering the social situation within which the drug is to be used and the past record of the family planning program. Not a thought is given to the nexus between the medical establishment, the drug industry, and the world population-control establishment. For example, none of the doctors at Patancheru, except the two senior women doctors who were in overall charge of the trial, had even seen the ICMR report describing its pilot study. Usually pro-injectable doctors cite the "success" of the injectable in Thailand as a reason for encouraging its introduction into India. Very likely the missionary image of Dr. Ed McDaniel, who is a vocal spokesman for injectables in Thailand, and the genuine concern he shows for the poor in his community health project, help to sell the injectable concept. No wonder, then, that tours of Thailand are arranged for India doctors and family planning personnel, to make sure that they come back as ardent converts to injectables.[14]

There is tremendous pressure on government doctors to achieve family planning targets, and drastic methods are considered by the doctors themselves to be the only way in which these targets can be achieved. Besides, those who dare to question contraception policy are sure to get their fingers burned. In 1983, the Hyderabad branch of the Indian Women Scientists Association (IWSA), many of whose members are government doctors and scientists, wrote to the then health minister urging him not to carry out his proposed policy of mass distribution of the Pill, as it was fraught with health hazards in the Indian situation, where the health-care network is deficient. ICMR authorities were very annoyed, and IWSA members were suitably chastised for voicing such views. After such a commendable effort to express its social consciousness, IWSA, which had adopted such a bold position on the mass Pill policy, understandably was silent over the issue of injectables for quite some time. However, after the Patancheru incident, ICMR luminaries were keen to have a dialogue with the women's groups and journalists opposing the injectable and asked IWSA to organize a meeting. On March 8, 1986 — International Women's Day — a discussion was held in Hyderabad on the feasibility, acceptability and safety of mass hormonal contraception programs in India. The key ICMR scientists involved in the current Net-Oen trials developed cold feet and chose not to attend! The consensus at the meeting was that mass hormonal programs are not justified in the present Indian set-up and that all Net-Oen trials should be stopped immediately.

INJECTABLES — BOON TO WOMEN?

No description of the Net-Oen campaign would be complete without a mention of the debate on whether, by opposing injectables, activists in India are unjustly denying poor Indian women an option which they themselves want. There is the now famous interview in *Spare Rib* (March 1982) with an Indian woman doctor, Hari John, who said that she herself had used Depo-Provera and that she had offered it to women at her community health project at Deenabandhupuram. Her argument is that Third World women have the right to choose a contraceptive method they can use without the knowledge of patriarchal families. In the present debate in India, the family planning establishment presents itself as the saviour of women who desperately need freedom from unwanted pregnancy, while the activists are condemned as unfairly and misguidedly abrogating the rights of poor women to decide for themselves. But the injectable in the hands of sympathetic and concerned health workers is quite different from the injectable in the hands of target-oriented family planning personnel. Countless studies by social scientists have shown that, over the years, the poor in India have come to view the very health system with suspicion because of family planning excesses and abuses. People have been known to reject even immunization or the obstetric services of trained midwives, for fear of being sterilized without their knowledge. For example, in November 1985 a polio immunization drive launched in the slums of Hyderabad was rejected by the people, who were afraid it was a ruse by the government to sterilize their children!

Because of the known abuses of existing contraceptive methods (including laparascopic sterilization camps, where unacceptably high mortality and morbidity rates have been reported since 1983 because of negligence and the pressure to achieve targets), the government must improve the health-care delivery system before any more invasive methods are introduced. The government's failure to ensure safe provision of the IUD, the Pill, and sterilization is driving women to ask for the injectable. The fault lies not in the IUD, the Pill, or tubectomy, but in the health system which delivers these methods. The "failure" of these methods is therefore not a logical justification for introducing the injectable.

Then there is the question of the relevance of animal studies. Beagle dog studies with Net-Oen have shown that the drug may be inhibiting carbohydrate metabolism, and this could cause diabetes. One case of endometrial cancer was reported in the monkey studies, but the WHO Toxicological Review Panel has decided that the findings of the animal studies are not applicable to humans.[15] Activists in India are asking: if basic toxicological data from animal studies now stand invalidated, on what basis are human studies being conducted? It is also felt that the position taken by the United States Food and Drug Administration's Board of Inquiry on Depo-Provera can also be valid to Net-Oen, since all the injectable progestogens are basically brothers under the skin. The FDA has said that the animal studies showing the development of cancer in beagles and monkeys *cannot* be dismissed as irrelevant to the human without conclusive evidence to the contrary.[16]

One of the problems in the Net-Oen campaign in India is the impossibility of locating women and interviewing them about their experiences with the drug — how they were approached, how much information they were given, what medical care they received, whether they were offered any incentives, and so on. Mona Daswani, an activist from Bombay who is a biochemist by training, read a paper on Net-Oen at a feminist conference on reproductive technologies in West Germany in April 1984. She reported that, even though she managed to find doctors to get information on how contraceptive research is carried out, she was not able to meet a single woman recruited for the Net-Oen trial in Bombay. To press further would have endangered the doctors' jobs and dried up the already limited sources of information. Another activist recalls how she stumbled by chance on some information when a nurse, who had approached the Centre for help with a domestic crisis, mentioned that a few women who had been recruited for a Net-Oen trial had been made to drop out after they exhibited some uterine disturbances.

Another problem is that the Net-Oen issue has the image of being a *women's* issue and a family planning issue, rather than a campaign against a potentially dangerous drug. If one looks back at the campaign against the use of EP drugs for pregnancy testing in 1982 and compares it with the present Net-Oen campaign, the differences are many. In the EP drugs çampaign, even government doctors were willing to speak out. It was seen as a drug issue and a health issue, and its parallel with the thalidomide disaster fired the imagination of both media and the public so effectively that, within two months of the campaign launch, the Drug Controller bowed to public opinion and issued a ban order. (It is another matter that the drug companies obtained a stay order from the courts; but public opinion is still largely on the side of the activists.)

WHOSE BENEFIT? WHOSE RISK?

The reason that the Net-Oen campaign has not succeeded in a similar way is probably because there is a great deal of ambivalence in India over the question of family planning and population control. The literate middle class has been brainwashed into believing that population growth is the country's most serious problem. It is quite common to see letters to editors advocating compulsion and coercion to "save" the country from disaster. The indignation over coercion expressed in 1977 has largely subsided. Birth control as a human right has been submerged under an ideology of family planning as a "patriotic duty" essential to the "national interest." The feeling among the middle-class public is that the illiterate and the "ignorant" need contraception desperately and that the "benefits" do indeed outweigh the risks. The question they fail to ask is: whose benefit, whose risk? Because of this, unlike campaigns against other harmful and irrational drugs like, say, antidiarrheals, clioquinol, and anti-arthritic drugs, educating the public on the Net-Oen issue involves a longer discussion on the politics of population control ideology. It is very difficult to persuade people who are convinced of the urgency of population control that the issue is more complex.

Among the various aspects taken up by the Net-Oen campaign in India, one which is yet to receive serious attention is the possibility that injectable contraceptives may reduce resistance to infection. This can be a very potent argument against giving injectables to women who are already malnourished. The 1985 Magsaysay award winner, Dr. Zafrullah Chowhury of Bangladesh, has been quoted as saying that this has very grave implications for Third World women.[17] He himself stopped offering Depo-Provera at his People's Health Centre when women experienced heavy bleeding, and since then this possibility of immuno-suppression has strengthened his opposition to injectables in Bangladesh.

In India, it is surprising that the human rights activists who have been vocal on a whole range of issues related to civil liberties and violation of fundamental rights have so far not paid much attention to the issue of drug dumping and unethical experimentation. The People's Union of Civil Liberties did protest in May 1984, when six women died as a result of negligence at laparascopy camps in Rajasthan, and it is to be hoped that such activists may be persuaded to join the Net-Oen campaign as well, which is also a protest against violation of human rights. So far it appears that the women's groups have not really tried very hard to bring into the

Net-Oen campaign all those progressives who are potential supporters and sympathizers.

How will the campaign against Net-Oen affect future campaigns against dangerous drugs? What will be its impact on future drug trials? Will the debate over informed consent succeed in arousing public indignation? Will the movement help in getting the drug laws tightened? Will the Supreme Court appoint a commission, with citizen representatives, to go into these and other questions, like people's control over the scientific and medical decisions which affect their lives? These are some of the issues that we in India hope will be debated publicly in the wake of the campaign against Net-Oen.

APPENDIX

OPENING STATEMENT OF NET-OEN PETITION

The ICMR is conducting Phase IV of a clinical trial with Net-Oen, started in August 1984 through 45 primary health centres attached to 15 medical colleges all over the country. A total of 2,250 women are to be covered by this experiment. Earlier, Phase III had covered 1,553 subjects in 1983, while the initial 1981-82 pilot study by the ICMR had enrolled 2,600 women. This experiment with a hormonal contraceptive drug on several thousand Indian women is unethical and unsafe and should be stopped immediately.

The experiment is being conducted without the informed consent of the women recruited for the trial. The drug has not been approved for general contraceptive use in either the UK or USA. The WHO Scientific group has concluded that there are no adequate data from studies in women to assess whether progestogens used as contraceptives have any effect on the risk of neoplasia.[18] It is not conclusively proved that the drug is *not* cancer producing. The drug's immediate side-effects are unpleasant in the countries where it is being tried out, and has been a major reason for discontinuation by Indian women recruited for the ICMR trials.[19] These recruits come from among the most deprived, illiterate sections of society. Women seeking abortion are also recruited for the trial at government centres, their participation being spelt out as a condition for getting medical termination of pregnancy. This attack on human rights must stop.

We believe that every individual is entitled to knowledge of, and access to, safe birth control. The women who are receiving the injectable in the current trial are not given a chance to make an informed choice. Nor is their consent to participate in the trial informed consent as spelt out in the guidelines laid out by WHO's Helsinki Declaration of 1964, later revised at the World Medical Assembly, Tokyo, 1975. We have the evidence of our own eyes and ears to vouch for this.... We believe that by experimenting on Indian women with the injectable contraceptive, the ICMR is only serving the interests of the West German drug firm, Schering A.G., which is a subsidiary agency of German Remedies which manufactures a number of hormonal products. The promotion of Net-Oen is part of the larger pernicious practice of Western multinationals which are dumping in Third World countries products which are banned or heavily restricted for use by their own governments.

◄►

NOTES

1. War on Want, *Norethisterone Oenanthate: The Other Injectable Contraceptive,* (London, 1984), p.1.

2. Padma Prakash, "Campaign Against Long-Acting Contraceptives," *Socialist Health Review,* Mar. 1985, p.170.

3. War on Want, op. cit., p.1.

4. Britain licensed Depo for long-term contraceptive use, after much debate, in 1984. However, the drug has been allowed only as a last-resort method for women for whom no other contraceptive is possible or acceptable. Women are to be informed of potential side-effects and long-term health risks before they accept the drug. *(Newsletter of the International Contraception, Abortion and Sterilisation Campaign,* London, July 1984, p.8.) I may mention here a conversation I had with Dr. Kumariah Balasubramaniam,

Pharmaceuticals Adviser, CARICOM, during an Asian seminar on "Pharmaceuticals and the Poor" at Madras in December 1985, in which he expressed the view that if the UK's Committee on Safety of Medicines, after examining all the available scientific evidence regarding a drug which has been used by women for over twenty years, has arrived at the decision that the injectable should be allowed only for those women who cannot use any other method, then it is unethical to continue clinical trials with the drug. He felt that what is true for Depo-Provera is applicable to other injectable progestogens as well.

5. WHO *Bulletin*, op. cit., p.207. Conditions where special medical care is required include abnormal liver function or recent history of liver disease, history or evidence of cardiovascular disease, and diabetes.

6. *Ibid.*

7. WHO, *Injectable Hormonal Contraceptives: Technical and Safety Aspects,* Offset Publication No. 65, pp.23-6.

8. The journal referred to is *Contraception,* July 1983. According to Padma Prakash in her article, "Dangerous Drugs" *(Bombay Sunday Observer,* Apr. 14, 1985), the only paper available from ICMR for study and perusal appears to be one section of the most recent twenty-four-month study, on which is based the government's decision to introduce Net-Oen in the family planning program and to allow it to be imported. This paper has not been published in India nor disseminated widely, as it ought to have been, among doctors, women's groups, or health activists before the decision to approve the drug. One report of the study has been published in the prestigious foreign journal *Contraception*, which is unlikely to be available to doctors and non-research hospitals, though they are the potential distributors of the drug. In any case, two-year studies do not reveal long-term effects.

9. See also Kusha, "Contraceptive Research in India: Testing on Women," *Socialist Health Review,* Mar. 1985, pp.166-70.

10. The ICMR Bulletin, Sept. 1980, published detailed guidelines for ethical experimentation on human beings. However, many medical scientists admit that these norms are rarely followed.

11. Padma Prakash, "Retreat on Depo Provera?" *Economic and Political Weekly,* Dec. 8, 1984, p.2072.

12. D.N. Kakar, *Women and Family Planning* (New Delhi: Stering Publishers, 1984).

13. Ammu Abraham, "Campaign against long-active contraceptives," *Women's Centre Newsletter,* Mar. 1985, p.1.

14. M.C. Watsa, "The Case for an Injectable Contraceptive," *Science Age,* Sept. 1984, p.9.

15. WHO *Bulletin,* p.202.

16. Quoted by Padma Prakash, "Retreat on Depo-Provera?", *op. cit.*

17. Maya Jayasekara, "Depo-Provera: What are we going to do about it?", *Voice of Women*, Sri Lanka, Mar. 1981, p.22. I may add that Dr. Zafrullah Chowdhury stressed this point again in a conversation with me during the Madras seminar "Pharmaceuticals and the Poor" in December 1985. Earlier, Steve Minkin referred to the possibility that Depo-Provera may lower resistance to infection in "Depo-Provera: A Critical Analysis" *Women and Health*, No. 2, Summer 1980.

18. "Facts about Injectable Contraceptives: Memorandum from a WHO meeting," WHO *Bulletin*, 60, no. 2 (1982), pp.149-210, p.205.

19. According to Padma Prakash ("Injectable Contraceptives," *Medico Friend Circle Bulletin*, May 1985, p.2), there have been two major Net-Oen studies in India, both co-ordinated by WHO. The first was a two-year multinational comparative trial of a 90-day regimen of Depo-Provera and two regimens of Net-Oen at 60-day and 84-day intervals. Over three thousand women participated in the trials between 1977 and 1980. (*Contraception*, July 1983.) The other multi-centre trial was conducted by the ICMR at sixteen Human Reproduction Research Centres in India, comparing a 200-mg injection of Net-Oen at 60-day and 90-day intervals. Over two thousand women participated in the first phase, which ended in October 1983. (Undated mimeo of ICMR paper.) In the 1977 WHO trial, the drop-out rate ranged from 59 per cent to 89 per cent, and in the Indian trial it was about 50 per cent. (For more detailed information from ICMR documents, see Sujit K. Das and Pijus Kanti Sarka, "Case for Injectable Contraceptives," *Economic and Political Weekly*, Oct. 5, 1985, pp.1713-14).

FROM BIRTH CONTROL TO POPULATION CONTROL: DEPO-PROVERA IN SOUTHEAST ASIA

Lynn Duggan

DEPO-PROVERA, WIDELY distributed to Asian women by an American multinational corporation, is a useful tool for understanding the difference between birth control and population control. A woman's ability to decide when and whether to conceive children is clearly a critical element in being able to choose the kind of life she wants to live. Population control, on the other hand, seeks to lower fertility rates without changing other aspects of the status quo, such as women's access to education and employment. It relies on the top-down distribution of contraceptives and directives regarding their use and is an instrument for policy makers who fear the demands for social, economic, and political justice that "too many" poor people may make. The promotion of Depo-Provera demonstrates how multinational interests have transformed birth control into population control.

Depo-Provera, commonly referred to as "Depo," is an injectable contraceptive for use by women. Manufactured by the Upjohn Corporation of Kalamazoo, Michigan, from the synthetic hormone progesterone, Depo-Provera suppresses ovulation for periods of three months to a year. Family planning agencies consider it "more effective" than other forms of birth control and have promoted its use by over 10 million women in eighty countries. Southeast Asian women were among the first to receive it.

The attraction of Depo lies in its long-lasting effects, with which a client cannot interefere once she has received the shot. Advocates of population control, who frequently view Third World women as too ignorant or too irresponsible to take daily birth control pills or use barrier methods of contraception, regard Depo as an ideal contraceptive precisely because it transfers control over women's reproductive cycles to "experts."

Under a Food and Drug Administration ruling in effect since 1972, Depo may not be promoted for use as a contraceptive in the United States. (The Food and Drug Administration has licensed it for other purposes, however, and a physician may prescribe it for contraception if a woman gives her informed consent to its use). Nonetheless, the U.S. Agency for International Development (AID) — itself prohibited from distributing drugs banned in the United States — advocates the use of Depo-Provera in family planning programs in the Third World. In striking contrast, the Swedish International Development Agency refuses to supply Depo to countries requesting it, although the drug has been approved for limited use in Sweden.

The FDA ban, upheld by a Board of Inquiry in 1984 in response to an appeal from Upjohn, is based on 1971 and 1978 findings that beagles and rhesus monkeys developed breast and endometrial cancers when they were injected with Depo. Other effects of the drug on the test animals included increased risk of atherosclerosis and osteoporosis (bone deterioration), lowered life expectancy, and lowered resistance to infection. Some medical researchers believe Depo could cause permanent sterility, and the World Health Organization cautions women who have not had children to use other methods of birth control. The tests also indicated that people with liver problems, epilepsy, or diabetes should not take the drug. When a pregnant woman inadvertently receives an injection, her child is likely to develop abnormal sex organs, heart defects, and malformed bones. Upjohn has been accused of witholding evidence of most of these risks for several years during which it promoted Depo world-wide. It is not known what effect Depo has when it is passed to babies in breast milk, but it could interfere with infants' normal development and inhibit the transmission of immunities. Nevertheless, Upjohn advertises it for nursing mothers simply because, unlike birth control pills, Depo-Provera does not halt the flow of milk. Similarly, Upjohn's promotion to family planning administrators and physicians suggests that

Depo may be attractive to people in the Third World who expect miracles from injections as the result of their experience with antibiotics.

In addition to its effect on ovulation and its unknown long-term effects (inaptly termed "side-effects"), Depo affects health in readily apparent short-term ways. Its massive dose of hormones affects the whole body and potentially disrupts all aspects of health and normal body functions. Users commonly report depression, hair loss, headaches, weight gain or loss, menstrual spotting, heavy bleeding sometimes dangerous enough to require emergency medical intervention, amenorrhea (absence of menstruation), anaemia, skin changes, nausea, and loss of libido. The most common complaint among women who use Depo is that they lose interest in sex. This effect of the drug is so frequent and so strong that male sex offenders in the United States are sometimes offered early parole if they agree to receive Depo injections. Depression is another symptom which has a generalized impact on users' lives, particularly since it may alter perceptions and impair judgements in situations which are already precarious. These effects may take a year or more to wear off. The drug has been most widely promoted in Asia, but the doses in which it has been administered were designed for larger Western women. A 1980 study determined — fifteen years after Depo had been introduced in Asia — that half the conventional 150 mg dose would probably be effective for Asian women.

In addition to its own effects on a woman's health, Depo masks the true condition of her body. In the menstrual chaos that normally accompanies its use, the recipient loses one of the key indicators of developing health problems. There is no longer a standard for recognizing irregular bleeding, for example, a symptom which is universally regarded as a warning that something may be wrong in a woman's reproductive system. Depo users may easily mistake the signs of the onset of a debilitating disease or disorder as merely another effect of the drug and hence not seek medical attention.

The medical difficulties associated with Depo-Provera's use suggest that recipients should be closely monitored by medical personnel who are able to assess the drug's effect on individual users as well as screen high risk clients who should not receive it. In areas where health facilities are scarce, non-existent, or too expensive for the poor, such attention is not normally available. It is this consideration which led the Swedish Development Agency to refuse to supply Depo for use in Third World countries. Depo's backers, on the other hand, tout it as easily administered. Their reasoning is exemplified by a Thai public health official, who told the news agency, Depthnews Asia, that "Women in remote areas, including hilltribe women, do not have to go to a family planning clinic regularly because Depo-Provera has a longer lasting effect."

Thailand is in fact a revealing example of the way Depo has been tested and distributed in poor countries. In 1965, five years before the results of the beagle studies were known, a missionary doctor named Ed McDaniel who worked among hill tribes around Chiang Mai heard of the birth control shot and saw in it the answer to the tribes' contraceptive needs. He volunteered his parish hospital as an outpost and the tribal women as subjects for Upjohn's further research. Dr. McDaniel now has thirty-nine mobile family planning units pushing the injection in northern Thailand. A million Thai women have received the shot.

McDaniel justifies his promotion of this inadequately tested drug among the hill tribes as the best alternative to high maternal mortality and deaths from violent abortions by local midwives. Other promoters of the drug join him in arguing that the lifespans of Third World women are so short that they are likely to die of other causes before developing cancer and that the benefits of the injection thus outweigh its risks in some populations. This argument does not consider the option of providing other means of birth control or improving the primary health care system, seeming rather to use the status quo to justify a continuing failure to provide adequate health services.

At the same time, the research done in Chiang Mai by Upjohn and McDaniel has yielded few results of scientific value. In one study of the long-term risks of Depo-Provera, for example, they reported only that out of nine women the research team located who had developed breast or uterine cancer during 1974 — 8, none had used Depo. Another study found that twenty-two Thai women who had taken Depo continuously for eight to thirteen years did not show any cancerous lesions. On the basis of what is known about these thirty-one women, Upjohn claims that Depo does not cause cancer in humans.

In monkeys, however, endometrial cancer occurred at an age equivalent to human menopause. Surveillance of women for such cancers would take twenty to thirty years. In any case, notes Stephen Minkin, former UNICEF chief of nutrition in Bangladesh and author of several articles on the health effects of Depo-Provera, the diagnosis of endometrial cancer is often missed and requires special procedures. In 1980 he wrote, "In many African, Asian, and Latin American countries, where per capita expenditure on health services is less than a few dollars annually, an epidemic of endometrial cancer would never be discovered."

The Philippines is another country where "research" has been used to justify the widespread use of Depo as a contraceptive. The Philippine Food and Drug Administration authorizes the injection only for research purposes — but pharmacies and drug company sales representatives dispense it over the counter as a contraceptive. The actual research done in the Philippines, largely under the auspices of the UN Fund for Population Activities, International Planned Parenthood, and World Neighbors (a U.S.-based foundation), has focused on acceptance rates rather than health effects, producing results of dubious value. Family planning programs in the Philippines make no effort to develop scientifically comparable groups for study but welcome anyone who wishes to take Depo. When I asked whether Depo-Provera clients are informed of the American ban on the drug's use as a contraceptive, the staff of one IPPF-sponsored Philippine clinic answered, "Of course not." Similar reports have come from many other clinics in the Philippines and around the world, as have allegations that clients are not even warned about short-term effects.

In an interview, Malcolm Potts, director of the International Fertility Research Program (funded by U.S. AID) and former director of IPPF, took the stand that Depo must be given to millions of women over the course of decades before its risks can be assessed. Yet there has been little effort to monitor its effects on the approximately ten million women who have used it over the past fifteen years. Perhaps the lack of serious follow-up observation of the women who have already taken Depo reflects the attitude of Dr. Ruben Apelo, pioneer and proponent of Depo's use in the Philippines. Dr. Apelo told me that by the time a twenty-year study of Depo's long-term effects could be completed, new contraceptives would have taken Depo's place. Apelo wants the U.S. FDA to lift its ban on Depo so that AID can provide the injection free of charge — as it does other contraceptives. Thus far, Philippine agencies have received funds for Depo only as part of research grants.

The newest contraceptive on the horizon of marketability is Norplant, a timed-release implant of synthetic progesterone which lasts five to ten years and must be inserted and removed by medical personnel. Although animal tests are not complete, clinical trials have been initiated in eight countries. So far, Norplant — which releases a constant low level of hormones into the bloodstream — seems to have fewer side-effects than Depo's periodic massive shock to the body.

Whatever test results reveal about its safety, Norplant goes even further than Depo in taking direct control over her reproductive system away from the user. Like Depo, it is a two-sided coin. Its longer effectiveness could both free a woman from worry over unwanted pregnancies and give medical authorities veto power over her desire to conceive a child.

Injectable contraceptives have one advantage over other forms of contraception which their promoters do not frequently advertise: they are invisible. Husbands who fear their wives' infidelity or increased power often deny them access to contraception. Women in such circumstances, who risk beatings if their pills or IUD are found, may be able to conceal the fact that they are using Depo-Provera. Women without opportunities for divorce or safe abortion may judge the risks of Depo preferable to the burden of an additional child, but a real choice on this question requires full knowledge of what is involved.

Is Depo a viable solution to this kind of problem? Feminists living in industrialized nations debate the issue of whether Depo-Provera should be absolutely banned as a contraceptive. Some believe it should be available for use under ideal conditions with individual medical attention and informed choice, while others fear that even its limited authorization will lead to the kind of abuses its promoters have perpetrated and continue to perpetrate. Among the many issues raised in this context, however, one truth is self evident: Depo can benefit those receiving it only if they know what it will do to their own health and how it is being promoted to them. Drug companies and population control agencies are not providing this information.

As Judy Norsigian of the Boston Women's Health Book Collective has stressed in writing and speeches, women of this country have a responsibility toward those who do not know what Depo is and how it has been and is being used. In the end, the technology which allows control of reproduction confers power upon its users only when they have enough information to make truly informed choices. The promoters of Depo, who hide behind their contempt for women whom they see as "too ignorant" to understand whether they want to bear children and "too irresponsible" to use other forms of contraception, may in fact be frightened of the demands these women might make if they were allowed to make genuine choices in this and other areas of their lives. History has shown, after all, that women whose lives offer attractive opportunities have little difficulty remembering to use their chosen method of birth control.

◄►

This article was previously published in the *Southeast Asia Chronicle,* January 1985.

THE RISE AND FALL OF THE IUD

Ann Pappert

BY THE TIME G.D. SEARLE removed its Copper 7 IUD from the market early in 1986, it was the last major manufacturer of intrauterine devices. With the company's withdrawal from the market, this method of contraception is no longer available in the United States and its future elsewhere is uncertain. Although IUDs are still available in over eighty countries this could change. Searle has publicly said it is looking for purchasers for its foreign IUD business, and other manufacturers are also said to be looking for ways to withdraw from the market.

The withdrawal of the Copper 7 and, earlier, the Lippes Loop, once the standard by which all other IUDs were judged, along with the publicity surrounding the Dalkon Shield, has once again ignited the debate about the safety of these devices, a controversy that has raged since IUDs were first introduced at the turn of the century.

For many observers the demise of the IUD was inevitable; indeed the current dissatisfaction with IUDs is the third time in this century that the devices have been discredited.

The first modern-day IUDs were introduced in Germany in 1909 but quickly fell into disfavour after they were associated with infections. In the 1920s Ernst Grafenberg designed an IUD that was placed entirely within the uterus to lessen the risk of infection. But Grafenberg's ring also failed to win acceptance. By the 1940s most physicians believed IUDs were simply too dangerous to use; in some countries fitting a woman with an IUD was grounds for a malpractice charge.

By the 1960s, alarmed that the "problem of unchecked population growth is as urgently important as any facing mankind today," the New York-based Population Council, a private international agency, seized on the IUD as the one device with the potential for solving the impending population crisis in the developing nations. The goal of the council was to develop family planning programs for the Third World, and its principal tool was to be the IUD.

But first the council had to convince the medical community that IUDs could be made acceptable, no easy task. To promote the re-introduction of IUDs, the council convened a conference highlighted by glowing reports on IUDs from the handful of physicians who had continued their use over the years, notably Walter Oppenheimer of Israel and Atsumi Ishihama of Japan. The delegates were told "they could change the history of the world."

Participants were assured that two developments since the 1920s had made it possible to reconsider IUDs. The first was the creation of inert plastics that could permit the design of IUDs that could be inserted easily, and the second was the introduction of antibiotics that could cure any infections that occurred.

That infections would occur was taken for granted, but because in 1962 the goal was population control, infections were downplayed. Indeed, one conference participant, the esteemed gynaecologist Robert Willson told the conference, "If we look at this from an overall long-range view — these are things that I never said out loud before and I don't know how it is going to sound — perhaps the individual patient is expendable in the general scheme of things, particularly if the infection she acquires is sterilizing and not lethal."

"They hypnotized themselves into thinking that the ground rules had changed in 40 years, that those people who worried about infection were all idiots and we're into a new ballgame," Dr. Michael Burnhill, an American gynaecologist who developed an early IUD, has said.

Over the next decade the council spearheaded the re-introduction of IUDs, sponsoring other conferences and research and even funding several of the new designs. The rights to manufacture the new devices were quickly bought up by pharmaceutical companies eager to enter this new market.

Although the IUD was initially developed as a birth control method for the Third World, women in developed countries soon seized on the device because of its convenience and effectiveness. The IUD was intended primarily for married women in developing countries who already had their families, but in developed countries such as Canada the device appealed mainly to young, single women who had not yet had children. This was also the group most likely to experience problems with the IUD.

IUDs are designed to fit inside the uterine cavity. Although scientists are not exactly certain how the device works, it is believed that its presence acts as a constant irritant, causing the uterus to dislodge any fertilized egg that is implanted. Modern IUDs have tails that hang down outside the woman's vagina, primarily so that she can check to see if the device is still in place.

By 1968 the first signs began to emerge that, far from being the perfect method of birth control, the new generation of IUDs carried with them all of the problems of the past, and then some.

Early studies of these new IUDs downplayed the risk of infections, but a study by Nicholas Wright in 1968 showed an alarmingly high rate of pelvic inflammatory disease (PID) in women using IUDs. At the time, Wright's study was dismissed because his subjects were mostly poor black and hispanic women who would normally be expected to have high rates of pelvic inflammatory disease related to venereal disease. Before the 1970s physicians had rarely seen women with PID unless it was associated with venereal disease. But by the early seventies physicians began seeing large numbers of women with PID, and many of the women were using IUDs.

By the early seventies IUDs had really come into their own after numerous searching for a safer alternative. As well, A.H. Robins had begun marketing its Dalkon Shield as the first IUD specifically designed for women who had not yet had children. The company sold its product by the millions.

Even when the Dalkon Shield fell into disrepute in 1974 after it was linked to the deaths of several women, and the company removed it from the market, physicians still claimed that other IUDs presented no problem to the women who used them.

But by the summer of 1985, some ten years after the Dalkon

Shield was withdrawn from the market, the company faced four-teen thousand lawsuits from women seeking compensation for injuries related to the Shield, and new claims were pouring into the company at the rate of almost four hundred a month. Out-of-court settlements had already cost the company $378 million, and judgements in the few cases that had reached court had gone as high as $9 million.

Finally on August 21, 1985, in an attempt to gain the upper hand over the thousands of lawsuits pending, A.H. Robins sought the protection of the United States bankruptcy laws by means of a rarely used section of the law that allowed the company to file for so-called pre-emptive bankruptcy. Under this provision a company can postone payments of its outstanding debts until a court-ordered repayment schedule is drawn up and approved by the court. By doing this Robins, although financially healthy, hoped to put a cap on payments to Dalkon claimants by seeking a limit on liability. The immediate result of the bankruptcy petition was to freeze all pending claims against the company.

Indeed, one of the first requests from Robins was to ask the court to establish a deadline for the filing of any claims against the Shield. The court established April 30, 1986, as the final date by which any future claims against the device could be filed; any claims filed after the date would be invalid.

By the deadline, some 325,000 claims had been received by the court, more than six times the number anticipated. While the court, with the help of a committee of lawyers and bankruptcy specialists appointed by the court, sifts through the claims and designs a model for settlement, Robins has until September 30, 1986, to come up with a financial settlement acceptable to the court.

The Dalkon Shield had begun thought of as unique among IUDs in that its tail was made of thousands of fibres encased in a plastic sheath, while the tails of other IUDs were made of a single fibre. The tail of the Dalkon tended to act like a wick, drawing bacteria up into the uterus and causing infections. But by the mid-seventies scientists began to concede that the tails of all IUDs could cause infections.

The result has been a tragedy to women of enormous proportions. In the United States it is estimated that 250,000 women have become sterile from using IUDs. Some 200,000 women a year develop pelvic inflammatory disease, many related to the use of an IUD. And once an infection develops, it may re-occur years later, even after the device has been removed.

Studies over the past eighteen years now confirm that a woman using an IUD is nine times more likely to develop pelvic inflammatory disease, and twice as likely to become infertile as women using other methods of birth control. If a woman becomes pregnant while wearing an IUD, that pregnancy is seven to nine times more likely to be ectopic (tubal).

Armed with these statistics, opponents of the device want nothing less than a total recall of all IUDs. At the time the Copper 7 was removed from the market, Sybil Shainwald of the National Women's Health Network in the United States, an organization that has worked actively for a recall of the Dalkon Shield, said, "We're delighted the 7 has been taken off the market. IUDs are an unsafe birth control device and it's only a matter of time until all IUDs are gone. Not only shouldn't they be sold, but they should be removed from the bodies of women."

But proponents of the devices say that they're simply too valuable to be removed completely. "IUDs still have a definite role in birth control," says Dr. Marion Powell a Toronto gynaecologist and the Director of the Bay Centre for Birth Control. Dr. Powell is a former member of the Canadian Committee for Fertility Research, a group with close ties to the Population Council.

"There are many women who for some reason or another still need a wider source of choice than the Pill or the diaphragm. I would hate to see them withdrawn. I think we should be making a concentrated effort into making IUDs safer."

But with little, if any, research being done on making the remaining devices safer or designing new IUDs, and a growing list of problems and mounting lawsuits, the likelihood that IUDs will ever again reach their former popularity is slim. If current trend continues, by the next decade IUDs may be little more than a memory.

◄►

A version of this article was previously published in the Toronto *Globe and Mail,* March 21, 1986.

III: Taking Back Control

P*art III looks at some efforts to challenge the power of the multinational pharmaceutical companies and to return control of health to women themselves. In "Old Roles, New Roles: Women, Primary Health Care, and Pharmaceuticals in the Philippines," Milagros Querubin and Michael Tan describe innovative programs of primary health care in which women are the chief health care providers and which promote the use of the traditional folk remedies and herbs to counteract some of the ceaseless promotion of questionable, expensive drugs. In "The Strength of Links: International Women's Health Networks in the Eighties," Sari Tudiver examines the growing international network of women's and consumer groups that are involved in political action and advocacy around the issue of pharmaceuticals.*

Old Roles, New Roles: Women, Primary Health Care, and Pharmaceuticals in the Philippines

Milagros P. Querubin and Michael L. Tan

A S IN OTHER THIRD WORLD COUNTRIES, the health care system in the Philippines is top-heavy. This has created a paradoxical situation in which sophisticated, specialized medical facilities with the latest medical technology are available to an elite minority, while the majority of the people must rely on substandard, or even non-existent, health care. It was in response to this situation that various groups, mainly non-governmental, began to develop the concept of "community-based health programs" (CBHPs) in the early 1970s, with the idea that proper health care should be assured at the village level. By 1978, the World Health Organization (WHO) had begun to support the development of such programs in many parts of the Third World and was calling on national governments to foster what is now known as primary health care.

In the Philippines today, non-governmental organizations such as the Council for Primary Health Care, AKAP, the Rural Missionaries Health Team, and the National Ecumenical Health Concerns Committee, have been at the forefront in promoting primary health care, although the term CBHP is still preferred to distinguish some important differences in approach from the government's emphasis in CBHPs on organizing communities rather than simply providing health education or medical services. The approaches used in CBHPs therefore have a strong advocacy component, where health issues are linked to economic, political, and cultural factors. A good example of this approach has been the integration of issues such as women's health and the use of pharmaceuticals with primary health care. This article looks at some current research being conducted by AKAP, the Health Action Information Network, and other non-governmental groups to show the important links among these issues.

WOMEN HEALTH CARE PROVIDERS

When CBHPs were first being formed in the Philippines, health staffers found themselves confronted by the problem of drug supplies: if they were at all available, their high cost put them beyond reach of many Filipinos.

The use of medicinal plants was seen as one solution to this problem of drug supply, and health staffers scrambled for whatever materials were available to start a campaign to promote medicinal plants. Early in this campaign, the mostly city-bred physicians and nurses discovered that there was no real need to promote the plants since villagers had long been using them. Health professionals therefore found themselves becoming students, learning about the many medicinal plants and their diverse uses from the villagers.

We also learned that one did not have to go to herbalists for information on plants, that the best teachers were the housewives. In many rural areas, small backyard *boticas* (drugstores) exist, cultivated by women. As in many instances of folk knowledge in the Philippines, the use of medicinal plants and many other traditional healing skills are passed on from one generation of women to the next. Women are in fact the frontline health care workers. In our health programs, whenever men are interviewed regarding health problems in their families, a frequent answer is, "You'll have to ask my wife." Integral to the Filipino woman's roles (albeit stereotyped) as mother and wife is that of health care provider to the family.

Among traditional medical practitioners, the role of the *hilot* (midwife) is dominated by women and they, too, are found in large numbers as herbalists, bone-setters, and shamans[1]. Many of these female traditional medical practitioners, particularly midwives, have been integrated into primary health care programs as community health workers (CHWs).[2] However, other women, not necessarily traditional healers, are also elected by their communities to train with the primary health care projects. Today, an overwhelming majority of community health workers are women. In three poor urban communities where AKAP and UNICEF are implementing a primary health care project, *all* the CHWs are women.

These CHWs are taking on an increasingly important role in the health care system, providing vital preventive and curative services at the village level. The skills of these CHWs are not limited to maternal and child health, or to first aid. CHWs now participate in immunization campaigns, not just in the educational component but, more importantly, in the actual administration of the vaccines. Other CHWs have developed skills in laboratory diagnostics, doing sputum microscopy (for tuberculosis), standard blood examinations such as haemoglobin measurement and Wright's staining for malaria, fecalysis for intestinal parasites, and urinalysis.

Some of the first batches of CHWs are now health educators themselves and are reaching out even more effectively to other women villagers. We have become so confident about the CHWs that some of them help to instruct health skills workshops in other provinces or regions. In 1983, when a popular television show asked the chairperson of AKAP, Dr. Mita Pardo de Tavera, to speak on tuberculosis, her recognized field of expertise, she agreed on condition that a CHW be allowed to appear with her on the show. As planned, the CHW did much of the talking on the disease, explaining its prevention, diagnosis, and treatment by drugs.

Such challenges hurled at the medical establishment are important. Medicine in the Philippines has become mystified, controlled by an elite corps, which, incidentally, has been strongly dominated by men, a legacy from the Spanish and American colonial period. This situation is changing slowly: recent statistics, for example, show that women graduates from medical schools are now the majority. Other health professions have, traditionally, been dominated by women: nursing, dentistry, pharmacy, medical technology, midwifery, and physical and occupational therapy.[3] Despite the large numbers of women health professionals, the leadership in both governmental and non-governmental groups still remains largely in the hands of men. For instance, there has never been a woman health minister in the Philippine government, even under the new government, which is headed by a woman president, Corazon Aquino.

Another factor that contributes to problems in public health policy is the fact that most health professionals come from middle and upper-income families. Class-based elitism therefore remains strong among both male and female professionals. This elitism and the monopoly on medical knowledge are now being challenged with the emergence of primary health care and the CHW.

Drug Advertisements Aimed at Women

This development is all the more important when we consider the use of pharmaceuticals in the country. As in many other underdeveloped countries, the largely multinational drug industry in the Philippines has aggressively advertised its products as the only solutions to health problems. The marketing strategies are wellplanned, geared to specific income and age groups, and of course, to women.

The Health Action Information Network (HAIN), in a continuing study of the drug industry in the Philippines, has found numerous examples of the industry's marketing practices with women as their primary target.

The market for certain products of the drug industry, such as cosmetics, is mainly composed of women, and the advertising strategies reinforce sexist stereotypes, urging women to "keep beautiful" (and attractive to men) by patronizing particular products. The theme of "personal hygiene" is also heavily emphasized, as in the case of sanitary napkins. Significantly, PILIPINA, a women's group, has found in another study that even the advertisements for these "women's products" sometimes use a male voice; i.e., the men are still the authorities, ordering women to adhere faithfully to the traditions of "beauty" and "cleanliness."

In recent years, there has been the added theme of "youth," which, while oriented toward both sexes, is much more heavily emphasized for women. It is here that pharmaceuticals such as vitamins enter the picture. These products are advertised with lavish promises of perpetual rejuvenation. The drug companies also capitalize on the present back-to-nature fad, promoting "natural" vitamins, slimming teas, bee pollen, and similar products, all with alluring claims that they will enhance one's youth and vitality.

Since perpetual youth is clearly unattainable, especially for the many overworked women, other drug solutions are offered. Fatigued? Vitamins again, and tonics. Problems with menstrual pains? Winthrop Sterling now has two "versions" of its analgesic Midol, one labelled "PMS" for women to take even before menstruation starts, if they expect problems with dysmenorrhea.

Depressed? It all depends on the doctor — some prescribe tranquillizers while others dispense hormones. Myths about the menopause remain strong, and estrogen preparations such as Premarin are prescribed to rein in the cranky menopausal woman, with little effort to probe into the causes of the depression. Some of these are clearly related to the fear that the menopause marks a woman's loss of sexuality. But it is not just the menopausal woman who faces risks from irrational drug prescribing. In fact, young women at the height of their fertility are perceived as even greater threats, almost to the point of misogyny. The many studies projecting how many children each Filipino woman will have and their potentially disruptive effects on the latest five-year economic development plan are examples of such attitudes.

While activist groups in the Philippines are not opposed to family planning, they are vocal in exposing the manipulative methods used in population-control programs. Information on the advantages and disadvantages of the different contraceptive methods is inadequate, whether it comes in the form of advice from family planning promoters, or as inserts accompanying the products. While First World women are filing class-action suits against the makers of the Dalkon Shield and other intra-uterine devices, over 200,000 women in the Philippines who, since 1978, have been fitted with such devices, purchased mainly through international grants and loans, will probably never understand why they are beginning to get pelvic infections, or why they are unable to conceive even after the IUD has been removed.[4] At present, such controversial products as the injectable contraceptive Depo-Provera and the experimental Norplant are also being used in the country with the full blessings of the health ministry. In short, many aspects of the lives of women have become medicalized and the pharmaceutical industry has not hesitated to capitalize on this trend.

REINFORCING STEREOTYPES

Perhaps the most insidious aspect of the drug industry's promotion of "women's products" is the reinforcement of stereotypes. In a sense, practically any drug can be advertised for "women's problems." For instance, the multinational company G.D. Searle ran a comic strip in the newspapers for several months to promote its anti-motion sickness drug, Dramamine (dimenyhydrinate). Practically all these ads featured women, and in extremely sexist terms. In all instances, it is the woman who gets airsick, seasick, or carsick, her fearful face reinforcing the image of the timid woman who needs to be consoled by her boyfriend or husband and, of course, Dramamine. The advertisements took on ludicrous dimensions when one featured a housewife sweeping the yard and suddenly getting dizzy. Her neighbour comes to the rescue, advising her to take Dramamine. Searle would have us believe that now even housecleaning sickness can be remedied with drugs.

The drug industry has also recognized the importance of women as health care providers. Particularly in the last two years, with the Philippines struggling through its worst post-war economic and political crisis, drug companies have aggressively begun to promote over-the-counter drugs (OTCs) as more Filipinos resort to self-medication as a cost-saving measure. The key to the sales of these OTCs is, again women.

Advertisements for OTCs, whether directed at high or low-income groups, often use the theme of the wife or the mother as health provider. Many of these products are inessential or even dangerous. For example, in one television commercial, a mother is shown tutoring her child. The boy says, "I hope I get a hundred tomorrow." The doting mother then gives him Vi-Daylin, one of dozens of multi-vitamin preparations on the market. As expected, the camera pans in for the next scene: a happy child showing his mother his test paper, presumably with a perfect mark.

At present vitamins constitute the largest category of drugs imported into the Philippines. Most of the preparations are expensive, and the money spent could be put to better use to buy nutritionally balanced food. Moreover, the myths surrounding vitamins can be dangerous. Certain anti-tuberculosis products, particularly isoniazid, are sold in combination with vitamin B6, and physicians often fail to explain to mothers that the drug is being prescribed for tuberculosis. Therefore mothers sometimes think these products are vitamins, especially since some physicians tell them that the drug is "to strengthen the lungs." According to AKAP's Dr. Tavera, another factor is that the child does regain his appetite with isoniazid. Since "good appetite" is associated with the use of vitamins, the anti-tuberculosis drug is thought of as a vitamin.

Anabolic steroids, advertised among physicians as growth promoters, are also often mistaken for vitamins by mothers, and many physicians are not sufficiently aware of the adverse side-effects of these preparations. The Bureau of Food and Drugs requires that these drugs be dispensed only on prescription, but time and again, health and consumer groups have found they can be purchased over the counter.

Appetite stimulants such as Merck's Periactin and Sandoz's Mosegor are also problematic. Both companies produce these "appetite stimulants" in combination with vitamins, again misleading many mothers. The British group Social Audit has criticized the marketing of these "stimulants" as unsuitable to countries where hunger is widespread. Even if the products do stimulate the appetite, a highly questionable claim, there would still be nothing for the poor child to eat.

Cough and cold preparations form another category of inessential drugs whose promotion appeals to women's roles as mothers and wives. Some of these advertisements show women giving one of these cough or cold preparations to their husbands and children. In one television commercial, a child whimpers that he wants to go on a picnic the next day, knowing that his cough may keep him home. The answer: cough syrup. An overnight cure is depicted, the child gleefully joining the family for the picnic.

Despite their questionable value, cough and cold remedies are among the most popular drugs on the market. They are generally "shotgun preparations," containing irrational combinations of an analgesic or antipyretic, an antihistamine, and a cough suppressant — the more ingredients the better. Many cough remedies also use the irrational combination of a cough suppressant with an expectorant and are advertised as being effective "for all kinds of cough."

Parke-Davis produces Benadryl cough syrup, whose main ingredient is the antihistamine diphenhydramine. Like other antihistamines, Benadryl has a number of side-effects such as drowsiness and a drying of the mucous membranes. It is an over-the-counter drug, and the television commercials boast, again to mothers, that the drug is completely safe, "trusted by doctors" despite the fact that it is one of the most abused drugs today because of its availability and its relative low cost.

Women's desire for cleanliness is also exploited by the drug companies. Parke Davis has been running a series of "public service" columns in newspapers, explaining "what germ-conscious mothers" can do in cases of cholera, hepatitis, conjunctivitis, and other communicable diseases. The catch: Parke-Davis "germicidal" Neko soap is touted as one measure to deal with all these diseases.

Whether cough remedies, vitamins, or soap, drug companies have used women both as clients and as unpaid advertisers. Mothers trading their experiences with particular drugs at the neighbourhood corner store (which may also carry poster advertisements for over-the-counter preparations) are the best promotion for drugs, together with all the medical myths and fallacies on which the industry thrives.

Take the case of anti-diarrheals. Diarrhea is the third greatest cause of death among infants in the Philippines. The high mortality is usually due to dehydration. The industry thrives on this massive problem, with the market carrying hundreds of anti-diarrheal preparations. Some of these products have been described by experts as useless or of minimal value (as with kaolin-pectin preparations), while others that contain antibiotics such as chloromycetin can be dangerous.

In stark contrast, the promotion of oral rehydration preparations remains slow. These preparations can even be made at home, the most important ingredients being water, sugar, and salt to prevent dehydration. Doctors themselves are again ill-informed, mistakenly thinking that the oral rehydration solution is supposed to cure diarrhea; when it does not, the doctors consider it to be useless. Primary health care programs are promoting oral rehydration solutions among mothers, but these campaigns are weak compared to the drug companies' massive promotions of their anti-diarrheals as well as their own expensive oral rehydration solutions. (The government distributes oral rehydration salts without charge, but physicians continue to prescribe commercial preparations.)

The problems with pharmaceuticals in the Philippines are clearly the lack of political will to regulate the powerful drug industry's marketing practices, apathy on the part of health professionals, and the consumers' acquired misconception that drugs are cure-alls. Primary health care, particularly through the community-based approach, aims to promote alternatives to this situation, and in this effort, the community health worker can be a potent agent of change. CHWs have undertaken the task of promoting alternative medicines, including traditional medicinal plants. Instead of cough syrups, for instance, a CHW might suggest ginger tea, and entire communities have been mobilized for weekend "cook-outs" to prepare ginger powder. Another popular traditional remedy that is now produced by communities is banana powder, used for diarrhea. In fact, the powder is useful, not as an anti-diarrheal, but because it provides calories and some minerals, including potassium, one of the salts lost during diarrhea.

NEW ROLES FOR WOMEN IN HEALTH CARE

There is a need to curb the massive dependence on drugs that has developed in the Philippines and other Third World countries. Primary health workers explain that not all diseases can be cured by pills. Medicinal plants, particularly where they are processed and shared by the community, provide effective alternatives. Nevertheless, life-saving antibiotics cannot be replaced by herbals when it comes to communicable diseases, which cause nearly half of the total deaths in the country. Primary health care programs have to integrate alternatives including education on the rational use of the "Western" drugs, and the formation of drug co-operatives to reduce the cost of these products. To be able to introduce these changes, the CHWs must become leaders in the communities they serve. For women, then, primary health care creates added opportunities for them to take part in community development, as they organize and mobilize their fellow villagers for projects such as drug co-operatives, vaccinations, water supplies, and sewage facilities.

Some observers argue that Filipino women are in a better position than women in many other Third World countries, but the fact remains that three hundred years of Hispanic rule and half a century of American occupation have instilled a strange brand of sexism that continues to prevent women from participating more effectively in economic and social development. For instance, more Filipino women are joining the labour force, but they continue to occupy subordinate positions and are hired for work where "female virtues" such as docility and patience are required. At the same time, the working woman remains bound to domestic duties and Filipino schools still emphasize home economics courses to prepare future "home-makers," a somewhat secularized version of the Hispanic convent-school orientation.

These problems exist even in health programs. A recent AKAP survey revealed that some women CHWs have problems with their husbands because of their involvement in community health programs. The reason given was usually that the husband believed that the involvement would interfere with their wives' household work and her care of the children. But, paradoxically, husbands who supported their wives' participation in primary health care said that the health skills training had made them better wives and mothers. In a sense then, health programs need to grapple with the question whether the primary health care programs reinforce existing roles or whether they can help to transform the situation of women?

The CHWs themselves, for instance, felt that the constraints they faced in their work were related to their sex. Examples given: inability to travel at night, "weakness" expressed as aversion to blood or inability to lift patients, and being moody and gossipy. The "strengths" they cited were mixed: being more approachable, patient and industrious, having the time to deal with health problems because they were not employed outside the home, and being "motherly."

It is here that the CHW's leadership role is important, and where a change in the status of the CHW as a woman is needed. For example, the husband of an urban slum CHW said that his wife had been withdrawn and shy before entering the health program and had become assertive after the CHW training. Pol is not complaining; he feels that this change is valuable, especially because "in times like these, women must be strong."

This strength is acquired in many ways; and the acquisition of knowledge itself gives power. AKAP's community survey on the effectiveness of health workers as perceived by the CHW's neighbours and friends yielded several cases in which the CHW was able to save the life of a child suffering from diarrhea by using oral rehydration solution. Such simple but life-saving measures are vital in moving primary health care forward and helping to demystify medicine.

Education also involves consciousness-raising. So it is not surprising that CHWs lecturing on medicinal plants have become adept at explaining why drugs are so expensive or why some drugs banned in the First World are dumped in the Third World. The campaign to use medicinal plants is in a real sense a form of protest against the multinational companies, but without deceiving the public by telling them that the medicinal plants alone will solve all health problems.

Whether as mothers, wives, or community health workers, the women's vulnerability to the drug industry's marketing strategies needs to be counteracted through primary health care programs. Already, there are some alarming signs that CHWs may be adopting the over-prescribing habits of physicians and health professionals, because they think that is the "right" way of providing health care. Restoring self-respect and pride in indigenous skills is therefore as important as instilling new knowledge about Western medicine. For example, the use of rice gruel for diarrhea is an age-old practice in the Philippines and other Asian countries and in many ways it antedates the more recent oral rehydration solutions being promoted today. Rice gruel contains the water, sugar, and salt that prevent dehydration as well as providing calories.

The "motherliness" often cited as an asset for the CHW may be considered sexist by some. But it can also be transformed into a dynamic force in health care. One CHW herself explains: "We can spend time talking with the patient and the family. We listen, and this is important to the patient." This home-spun psychotherapy can be further developed and, in the process, primary health care will clearly prove that health and healing cannot be reduced to the mere use of drugs.

One thing has become clear in primary health care: demystification of medicine and drugs is an important part of the transformative process among women. One CHW's husband observes, "I can boast that my wife is now a doctor." Whether the drug industry again capitalizes on this or not is another matter, but primary health care programs can prevent this co-option process by arming women with the knowledge they need, using both their stereotyped and their transformed roles to combat the industry's manipulation of the public.

◄►

NOTES

1. A continuing study of traditional medicine in the Philippines by AKAP suggests that there are about forty thousand traditional midwives in the country, an average of one per village. Other traditional medical practitioners, using empirical and/or magico-religious methods, are estimated to number about two hundred thousand.

2. The Philippine government began its training of traditional midwives for maternal and child care as well as family planning in the 1950s.

3. A survey by the National Commission on the Role of Filipino Women (NCRFW), a government committee, showed that women's participation in the health professions increased for the period 1975 to 1983, not only in their traditional strongholds but also in medicine. Medical schools in the Philippines have generally required higher marks for women applicants, on the grounds that women tended to marry after their medical training and that their education would go to waste.

4. From 1978 to 1983, there were 247,367 acceptors for IUDs, according to the Commission on Population. There were also 23,253 acceptors for injectable contraceptives from 1978 to 1982. (National Economic and Development Authority, 1985 Philppine Statistical Yearbook, Table 9.18 p.445.)

THE STRENGTH OF LINKS: INTERNATIONAL WOMEN'S HEALTH NETWORKS IN THE EIGHTIES

Sari Tudiver

INTRODUCTION: NETWORKING IS A VERB

OVER 14,000 WOMEN attended the United Nations End of Decade for Women Conference in Nairobi, Kenya, in July 1985 and returned home with a clear message: an international women's movement is alive and well.[1] In a thousand workshops and cultural events, women marked the end of the official decade by taking stock of what still needs to be done, sharing information and strategies on a wide range of topics, and debating — at times even celebrating — our differences.

At the same time, official UN delegates struggled — successfully — to reach agreement on the *Forward Looking Strategies Document,* a 372-paragraph policy guide that spells out in some detail the matters to be addressed in achieving the unmet goals of the Decade for Women — equality, development, and peace.[2] The panorama of issues addressed in the document did not originate through the good will of the world's politicians. Rather, they were put on the agenda through the activities and lobbying efforts of women in thousands of women's organizations, self-help, and other groups throughout the world who have named what is wrong with our lives, organized new or better services, and demanded a voice in decisions affecting us and our families.

The scale of the conference offered the opportunity to observe how national and international women's networks have become key organizational forms of the past decade. Hugh numbers of organizations and individuals have joined together, formally or informally, across national boundaries "to network" — to exchange information and campaign against such practices as sex tourism and the traffic in women, violence against women, unfair labour laws, and poor working conditions; or to promote peace, political rights for women, research in women's studies, and alternative development strategies sensitive to women's needs.[3] "Networking" is now widely used as a verb, indicating the significance of the process to an international women's movement.

The health needs of women and our families are major targets for such organizing. Through newsletters and other means, women exchange information on a wide range of health issues; warn consumers about dangerous drugs and medical devices; lobby for better health legislation, and work towards developing good, alternative services, including preventive health education. It is through such initiatives that we seek to achieve greater understanding and control of our physical and mental health.

Women's health networks have been formed in India, Bangladesh, Kenya, Senegal, Morocco, the Philippines, the Netherlands, Canada, the United States, the United Kingdom, and many other countries. And the list keeps growing as networks extend across national boundaries.

The newly formed Latin American and Caribbean Women's Health Network, based in Santiago, Chile, links approximately 250 women's health groups throughout South and Central America and the Caribbean to others in Europe and North America. With support from ISIS International, which operates feminist publishing and documentation centres in Geneva and Rome, their bimonthly bulletins provide information on the activities of local groups, recalls of dangerous drugs, international campaigns, and educational resources.[4]

The Women's Global Network on Reproductive Rights (formerly International Contraception, Abortion and Sterilization Campaign) was started in 1978 by British and Dutch women. Now based in The Netherlands, the network maintains contacts with four hundred organizations and individuals in seventy-three countries and publishes a newsletter reporting on reproductive health. Women participating in the network share common goals: to ensure that all women have the right to decide if and when to have children; the right to safe, effective contraception and to safe, legal abortion; and freedom from coercion in reproductive matters. In July 1984, just before the United Nations World Population Conference, network organizers hosted a tribunal of which over four hundred women from sixty countries testified about the harsh effects that population policies, invasive contraceptive technology, and poor health services have on their daily lives.[5]

Health Action International (HAI), an informal network of consumer, development, women's health, and other public interest groups in over fifty countries was formed in 1981 to promote the safe, rational, and economic use of pharmaceuticals throughout the world. Through research, publications, and lobbying, the network has become an effective voice for consumers in international forums such as the World Health Organization. Tasks are divided among coordinating centres in The Hague and in Penang, Malaysia. The policies and research initiatives reflect strong participation by non-governmental organizations (NGOs) in Africa, Latin America, Asia, and the Pacific.[6] Working as part of the HAI network, the WEMOS Women's Group on Pharmaceuticals in The Netherlands is helping to co-ordinate the formation of an international network on women and pharmaceuticals.[7] They emphasize research, discussion, and active campaigning on the health problems that drugs pose for women, especially drugs used for fertility control and in pregnancy and childbirth. They have contact with several hundred women in different parts of the world.

During the past decade, many other groups have extended their contacts nationally and internationally. In 1980, the Boston Women's Health Collective from the United States joined with ISIS to publish an International Resource Guide on Women and Health, which contained information in Spanish, French, Italian, German, and English. In 1985, the Collective published a revised edition of its landmark work *Our Bodies, Our Selves* (first published in 1971) that included an examination of the politics of population control. A Spanish edition is widely used.

Regular contacts between groups of women in Canada and in Bangladesh have enriched the activities and strategies of both. Stories based on the lives of women in both countries were integrated into *Side Effects*, a play about women and pharmaceuticals written and produced by Canadian women, which toured Canada in 1985. This process has strengthened contacts among a broad cross section of Canadian women in different parts of the country and led to further exchanges with women in Bangladesh.[8]

Why have women's health networks proliferated in the 1980s? What have been some of the achievements of these organizational forms thus far? What are some of the problems that the participants and organizers face, particularly as networks expand? Are there significant differences in priorities and strategies between women in so-called First World and Third World countries? How do we assess the significance of these initiatives as part of broader movements seeking long-term social and political changes? The rest of this discussion will try to address these questions, drawing largely from my own experiences and those of other women involved in national and international networks.

WOMEN'S HEALTH NETWORKS: THE CONTEXT

While coalition building is as old as politics, the emergence of national and international women's health networks is relatively recent, based on the new wave of the women's movement that has developed rapidly since the late sixties in almost every country. These networks also have origins in the parallel upsurge of consumer and environmental groups formed in a number of countries to call attention to increasing health hazards posed by industrial pollution and various consumer products. There appears to be more overlap and exchange between these movements in the 1980s than in the previous decade. Together, they reflect significant popular action to grapple with deep-rooted problems within the international economic order.[9]

Throughout the world, women have formed thousands of local health groups to respond to crises in health care and to try to secure a better quality of life. These crises are well documented; by 1980, at the mid-point in the UN Decade for Women, the health status of a majority of the world's women was described as "deteriorating" in major UN reports.[10]

The UN reports offer official recognition of what many of the world's women know to be daily realities: too much work, resulting in fatigue and illness; inadequate nutrition, since we deny ourselves to feed and care for our families; poor public health measures, such as clean water and sanitation; inadequate medical services and limited access to essential drugs; unacceptably high rates of maternal and infant mortality. While such conditions are more marked among the poor and more prevalent in countries with low per capita incomes, large numbers of women in highly industrialized, wealthier countries are in poor physical and mental health as a result of occupational stress, abuse, and other forms of violence.

Institutionalized sexism is nearly universal. As patients, women tend to be treated differently from men, our complaints too often seen as trivial or psychological in origin.[11] Our bodies and particularly our reproductive systems are targeted by industry and health professionals as objects of research and product development. Indeed the vast array of oral contraceptives, inert and active intra-uterine devices, injectables, implants, vaginal rings, abortifacients, hormonal drugs and new reproductive technologies is staggering. Yet we are excluded from decision-making in most medical institutions and have no significant voice in determining research priorities and government health policies.

These conditions are part of an international economic order in which multinational corporations and national elites have a determining influence over government policies and spending to their own benefit and to the detriment of the needs identified by popular organizations. In such an order, agribusiness displaces subsistence farmers, many of whom are women, from their lands, and directs production towards export rather than towards improving the nutrition of the local population. Military spending takes priority over spending for basic social services, including health care. The pharmaceutical industry bases its decisions about research and the development of new drugs and devices on potential profits, not on demonstrated health needs. As a result, many Third World countries spend a disproportionate part of their health budgets on urban hospitals with specialized technologies and on an expensive array of non-essential drugs, rather than on primary health care and essential drugs for rural areas where the majority of the population live. In highly industrialized countries, the rising prices of drugs and medical technology have led to cutbacks in the range and quality of government health services and in regressive moves towards privatization of services in such countries as Canada and the UK.[12]

The medical model of curative medicine, with its military metaphors that "declare war" and "target" and "attack" diseases with an "arsenal" of new drugs and technologies remains dominant over preventive measures. And as most consumers have found, developments in high technology medicine have further isolated us from knowledge about our health care. Few health professionals take the time to help us become truly informed about our health needs and the options available to us. Only a small minority are willing to consider social and environmental circumstances as possible causes of ill health.

ACTION GROUPS AND NETWORKS — MOVING BEYOND ISOLATION

Organizing for better health care thus strikes a deeply responsive chord in most women. Almost everyone is a victim: all women can tell of instances in our own lives or those of our mothers, sisters, or friends where we suffered from medical neglect or incompetence, unpleasant or dangerous side-effects from drugs, over-medication, a lack of essential drugs, or too expensive medical care. Most women, even the highly educated, have at times felt patronized or demeaned by doctors, reduced to uncomfortable silence, and made to feel too ignorant to even know what to ask. Once women begin to move past the isolation of silence and speak with others, these experiences can become a catalyst to question why things are so and what can be done to change the situation. The need for all women to be provided with information and understanding about sexuality and reproductive health is a great leveller of class and ethnic-barriers and may lead to concerted political action.

Alternative Health Services and Training

Action comes not only from sharing experiences about poor medical services with other women but from building a common vision of what alternatives might be like — and then finding the means to work towards those goals. There is considerable diversity among women's health action groups, depending upon their membership and the particular problems they address. Some groups are professionally based, challenging sexist practices within medical institutions and the profession. The Venezuelan Alliance of Women Doctors was formed in 1977 to demand maternity rights, nurseries sponsored by the medical federation, courses on female health, and the right of married women to study for a master's degree. More recently, they have researched the use of indigenous plants for health needs specific to women.[13] The Union of Midwives in Senegal advances the interests of an exclusively female profession and seeks to ensure high standards of treatment for their clients.

New or alternative health services for women have been organized by health workers and community residents in many countries. In the six clinics that are part of the Bangladesh Women's Health Coalition, women receive comprehensive physical examinations, including detailed medical histories, sensitive counselling about birth control methods, and other health information.[14] Such clinics were begun as alternatives to government family planning centres or to private clinics, where women usually receive little personal attention or information and where contraceptives are administered without detailed screening and follow-up. In North America and Europe, women's health clinics provide similar services, often based on a self-help approach; some train women to do a number of gynaecological self examinations and sponsor groups where women explore health issues such as post-partum depression, drug and alcohol abuse, pre-menstrual syndrome, and alternatives to drug therapy. Some alternative services offer information that other doctors choose not to provide. In Morocco, women physicians and other health workers formed the Moroccan Association of Women and Health where women can go to ask about prescriptions they have received. Health workers try to demystify the widely prevalent attitude that "the best doctor is the one who prescribes the most drugs."[15] The association also lobbies for lower-cost drugs.

Many women have become involved in health action groups through primary health care projects funded by national voluntary associations, international NGOs or churches. Local women are trained as paramedics, midwives, or health educators to work in their communities. The best of these projects are those in which priorities are determined by local women who share information, develop new skills, and gain confidence working together and where outside experts are used effectively without jeopardizing local initiative and control.[16] In some cases, NGO field staff have helped local groups to identify abuses and gaps in health care systems and relay such information back to international organizations. Dianna Melrose's book, *Bitter Pills* (1982) published by Oxfam-UK is an excellent example of scrupulous documentation about pharmaceutical use in Third World countries gleaned from experiences with NGO projects and other research. It is an important source of information for consumer and health groups in many countries.

GETTING THE WORD OUT:
VICTIMS' ASSOCIATIONS AND INTERNATIONAL RECALLS

Global marketing has meant that many of the drugs produced by transnational corporations or their subsidiaries are available in scores of countries. National governments differ greatly in their legislation on standards of testing, acceptable promotion and marketing practices, and on controls over the import and export of drugs and devices. As a result, drugs that have never been approved or have been recalled in countries with more stringent regulations may continue to be sold elsewhere. Those available by prescription only in the United States may be widely available over the counter in Asian or Latin American countries. Drugs that are approved for specific conditions in Canada and come with detailed package inserts about possible contraindications may be promoted for many other medical conditions in India, with few or no warnings attached. And in most countries, physicians can prescribe a drug for a use not officially approved, if they feel the benefits outweigh the risks, without informing the patient they are doing so.[17]

Developing alternative sources of information to inform the public about such practices is a crucial step toward challenging the privileges of secrecy held by the pharmaceutical industry and governments. Governments accept manufacturers' data on drug safety in good faith, unless there are unusual circumstances to suggest otherwise. In most countries, consumers are not able to take part regularly in the drug regulatory process, whatever its form. There are no mechanisms for the public to scrutinize the information on how and why a drug was developed or alternative therapies already marketed and to evaluate the quality of the clinical research and other testing. Few regulatory agencies compile reports of adverse reactions nationally. Neither do they ask companies about their plans for promotion and marketing of a drug being approved. Such information is considered to be outside the scope of "scientific" evaluation. More to the point, it is an attack on trade secrets that may undermine a company's competitive advantage in world markets.

Studies have shown that doctors rely heavily on information provided by pharmaceutical companies in deciding what to prescribe.[18] While individual doctors may report cases of adverse reactions from particular drugs or devices to manufacturers and governments, they rarely take collective action through professional associations to challenge questionable actions of the industry. In fact, many doctors and their associations benefit from subsidies by the industry for research and other activities. Pharmacists are usually in the anomalous position of benefiting from the sale of drugs and having little power to influence either doctors or pharmaceutical companies. As a result, it has fallen to *consumers* to monitor and challenge the industry on unsafe practices and to lobby governments for legislation and monitoring procedures less partial to industry.

Women who are victims of dangerous reproductive drugs or devices have organized in order to obtain good medical care and accurate information about their conditions; to seek legal redress from manufacturers; and to raise public awareness about industry practices and gaps in government regulations. One such movement was initiated by the victims of the drug diethylstilbestrol (DES), marketed and widely prescribed in North America and Europe between 1941 and 1971 supposedly to prevent miscarriages. In the late seventies and early eighties, victims formed national DES Action groups in the United States, Canada, the Netherlands, and Australia to publicize the link between DES and certain rare forms of cancer in some daughters of women who took the drug and other reproductive problems experienced by daughters and sons. They researched, compiled, and distributed essential medical information necessary for monitoring and treating DES victims. As a result, medical researchers are now monitoring DES-exposed daughters, sons, and mothers and determining other health risks. These groups provide a network of individuals who have experienced similar traumas and can offer each other valuable support.

In 1984, DES Action/US initiated a project in collaboration with the national organizations in Canada and the Netherlands to identify DES-exposed individuals and concerned health professionals in other countries in order to educate them about the health risks and need for appropriate care.[19] Information was translated into Spanish for distribution to groups in Central and South America. By July 1985, these and other contacts confirmed that DES is still administered during pregnancy in at least thirty-five countries, including Kenya. It is also given as a morning-after pill, lactation suppressant, and growth stimulant for cattle and to control uterine bleeding resulting from the injectable contraceptive Depo-Provera.

The DES Action groups have formed DES Action International to pursue contacts with women's health groups and health ministries, particularly in countries where the drug is still used in pregnancy. The Latin American and Caribbean Women's Health Network and Health Action International help inform groups in other countries about the drug's hazards and support DES Action's call for a world-wide ban on the production of DES.

The DES story reveals the crucial role of consumer advocacy if women are to secure necessary information and greater control over their health. Aggressive marketing and false claims made by the drug manufacturers to doctors were never reviewed by appropriate government agencies or questioned by the doctors themselves. A major study, published in 1953, proved the drug to be ineffective in maintaining pregnancy. Yet it remained on the market and was widely prescribed in the United States and Canada for the next two decades. It was only through the persistent efforts of victims in several countries that information concerning the drug was revealed.

These experiences also teach us to be wary of industry's claims of safety based on limited animal testing and clinical trials. Adverse effects from DES only showed up in the next generation, suggesting that a much longer period of time should be devoted to animal testing before approving widespread use of hormonal drugs on women. The story of DES further reveals some of the problems facing the consumer in the pharmaceutical marketplace. Since it was sold under hundreds of different brand names and administered as pills, injections, and suppositories — even coated on vitamins — few women know whether they were given the drug, or if they do, what brand they took. Old medical records, where they exist at all, are hard to retrieve. In such cases, legal suits are usually complex and costly.

Other women are organizing to halt the marketing of high dose estrogen-progesterone (EP) drugs still used for pregnancy testing in many countries, despite the warning issued by the World Health Organization in 1976 that such use was associated with fetal abnormalities. In many countries EP drugs are sold over the counter, without warnings, and are also used, ineffectively, as abortifacients. An international campaign to publicize the drug's dangers is underway. Women from WEMOS in the Netherlands have coordinated a press campaign and translated information about EP drugs into a number of languages, including Swahili. Indian women organized to stop distribution of the drug in their country. Women from many countries are collaborating in these efforts.[20]

A blatant example of a contraceptive device proved defective in design and dangerous to women is the Dalkon Shield.[21] Marketed in approximately eighty countries, the device was officially removed from the market in the United States and Canada in 1974. In early 1986, victims, their lawyers, women's health groups, and consumer organizations were attempting to publicize widely the international recall of this intrauterine device and the American court decision that set April 30, 1986, as the final date for filing liability suits against the manufacturer, A.H. Robins. Robins had paid hundreds of millions of dollars in legal suits, and thousands of claims were still pending. In a clever legal manoeuvre, the company filed for bankruptcy, allowing it to establish a reserve fund against earnings to absorb the anticipated cost of legal suits. The April 30, 1986 date beyond which no woman anywhere in the world may sue the company allows it to limit its losses by denying women in Third World countries fair access to legal redress.

The American trials offered damning evidence against the company's senior employees Documents released showed that significant problems with the IUD's design had been identified *before* extensive marketing, but no modifications were made; reports from doctors citing problems with insertion and adverse reactions were ignored or dismissed; and information about pregnancy rates and ease of insertion used in promoting the Dalkon Shield were blatantly false. United States Federal Judge Miles Lord called the Dalkon Shield "an instrument of death, mutilation and disease" and accused top officials at Robins of putting profits above the health of women.[22]

Robins' attempt at recalling the product and publicizing the deadline internationally was feeble. Governments have not pressed the company on the matter. Those who do find out about the Dalkon Shield will most likely do so through the efforts of women in international health networks who have sent consumer bulletins to many parts of the world. Further legal action to have the deadline extended has been taken by women's health groups in Canada and Ireland.

Monitoring Reproductive Technologies

Experiences with DES, EP drugs, thalidomide, the Dalkon Shield, and other IUDs have made many women wary about embracing new high technology contraceptives or other reproductive technologies. A number of national coalitions have been formed to review what is known about depo medroxyprogesterone acetate (Depo-Provera), the three-month injectable contraceptive being marketed in over eighty countries, and to consider whether continued use of the drug is justified by available research. Women's health groups were actively involved in recent debates in the United States and England over whether to approve Depo-Provera for contraceptive use. Several years of review showed the difficulties of obtaining adequate assurances of safety and of interpreting the significance of malignant tumours in beagles and monkeys injected with large doses of the drug. It also highlighted the fact that epidemiological data on Depo-Provera were not comparable in quality to those on oral contraceptives, so that meaningful comparisons could not be made. Carefully designed, controlled studies of the drug are hard to find.[23]

The United States Food and Drug Administration opted for caution and in November 1984 rejected Upjohn's request for approval for the second time, arguing there was no evidence that Depo-Provera was *not* a carcinogen. This position was supported by the National Women's Health Network, the Health Research Group, and a number of independent scientists and consumer groups that had called for and testified at public hearings. In contrast, the British Committee on the Safety of Medicines recommended approval of Depo-Provera, but specified careful criteria for its use. These criteria were the direct result of recommendations made by British women's health groups.

The Canadian Coalition on Depo-Provera, which includes over eighty women's health, community and development organizations was formed in November 1985, when it was discovered that the federal government expected to approve Depo-Provera as an injectable contraceptive. The coalition called for public hearings and disclosure of information provided by Upjohn to the government and demanded that further data be compiled on women's experiences with the drug in Canada and internationally. The campaign has succeeded in informing many Canadians about the issue and temporarily stalling the approval process. The Minister of Health has promised some mechanism for "public input." At present the drug is administered to teenagers considered at "high risk" of becoming pregnant, to disabled women in certain institutions for hygienic reasons, and to others at a doctor's discretion.[24]

Depo-Provera has become something of a cause célèbre among women's health groups precisely because it illustrates a good deal about the politics of contraception. As women throughout the world are discovering, national regulatory bodies treat contraceptives with even less scrutiny than other categories of pharmaceuticals. Often, this reflects a government's desire to promote national population-control programs or to control reproduction among specific categories of women, such as indigenous, disabled, and immigrant women and those classified as "non-compliant." Increasingly, women are protesting our lack of control over decisions made about our reproductive health.

In India women's health coalitions have been formed in response to the testing and plans for approval of Net-Oen, a two-month injectable contraceptive manufactured by Schering and about which very little is known. Other groups are reviewing the new contraceptive "delivery systems" such as Norplant, a progestin that is released into a woman's bloodstream from six small silastic capsules implanted under the skin and which can provide up to five years' contraceptive protection. Initially developed by the Population Council, Norplant was licensed to Leiras Pharmaceuticals of Finland for manufacture and world-wide marketing. Clinical trials have been conducted in Finland, Thailand, Indonesia, Ecuador, Brazil, Chile, the Dominican Republic, and Jamaica, and Norplant is now approved for marketing in Finland and Sweden. Family planning programs in other countries are requesting it be registered for approval. Other new contraceptives include smaller IUDs that release progesterone and vaginal rings that release hormones into the vaginal walls.[25]

Other international women's health networks focus on what are termed the "new reproductive technologies" — *in vitro* fertilization, frozen embryos, artificial insemination, amniocentesis, and various methods of prenatal genetic screening. These results of new developments in biotechnology and genetics have considerable economic, political, medical, and ethical implications. The Feminist International Network on New Reproductive Technologies (FINNRET) includes women from North America, Europe, and a number of Third World countries who exchange information on existing technologies and explore issues concerning the control, promotion, and funding of such research. Through conferences and newsletters, the network provides a forum for the discussion of women's experiences as mothers, problems of infertility in different cultures, and how these new technologies can offer some women a better quality of life, if in fact they can. There is considerable debate going on about how women can significantly influence research and public policies in these areas.

Networks Aiding Networks:
Documentation and Support Services

Organizing an international campaign to ban a drug or holding transnational discussions on reproductive technologies are formidable projects, made possible in the 1980s largely because of other networks already in place. A number of organizations provide research, documentation, and other support services to action groups in different countries and have laid important groundwork for the formation of national and international women's health networks. Prominent among these is ISIS, feminist information and documentation centres in Geneva, Rome, and Santiago that gather data about women's organizations and their activities and put groups and individuals in different countries in touch with each other to share information and skills through exchange programs, conferences, and excellent publications. The American Friends Service Committee's Project on Women and Global Corporations, based in Philadelphia, also acts as a source of information and referral for women's groups in many countries seeking information about health, technology, and militarism. They maintain particularly close ties with women's networks in Asia and the Pacific.[26]

The International Organization of Consumers Unions (IOCU), with offices in The Hague and Penang, Malaysia, links consumer groups in over fifty countries and provides support through communications and research to HAI and other consumer networks such as the Pesticides Action Network (PAN) and the International Baby Food Action Network (IBFAN). In co-operation with HAI, IOCU has sponsored multi-country research on inappropriate marketing of anti-diarrheals and anabolic steriods, among others — drugs that women, as the targets of aggressive marketing campaigns in many countries, frequently purchase for their children. This and other high-calibre research are the result of successful collaboration among health professionals and consumers.

All these organizations serve as catalysts to bring women together from many different countries to share information and discuss strategies for action. The personal contacts made at international meetings are crucial to getting the word out about sources of information, new groups, and the latest research and legislation. More established organizations try to mobilize funds to ensure that groups with fewer resources, from a variety of countries, are represented at such meetings. Organizations such as IOCU that also hold consultative status at the United Nations are able to raise issues of concern to women's health groups in forums such as the World Health Organization. The American Friends Service Committee has broad contacts with international development agencies and churches and so can take issues beyond the women's health community.

It is in this context that one international coalition, the International Baby Food Action Network, has served as a useful model and training ground for other types of consumer action. Begun largely by American church activists, the seven-year boycott (1977 — 84) of the Swiss Nestle Company for unethical promotion of breast-milk substitutes in Third World countries involved international co-operation among consumers, health professionals, educators, researchers, and politicians.[27] The campaign used several strategies: a world-wide boycott of Nestle products and bringing the issue of infant feeding to the World Health Organisation to secure international recognition of the problem and action. Through documentation, lobbying, and the creation of widespread support, the network achieved a significant victory with the passage of the WHO Code on Breastmilk Substitutes in 1981. Many women active in international women's health networks — whether in the United States, Kenya, or Fiji — gained important experiences in political strategy and organization from this campaign.

ACHIEVEMENTS AND FUTURE DIRECTIONS

Women involved in local health groups, and in national and international networks have achieved a number of significant results through collective actions. Among these are the personal skills that women have gained by coming together to discuss common concerns, develop alternative services, or plan national campaigns. Increasing numbers of women have the confidence to approach — even confront — politicians, lawyers, doctors, and company officials to explain our concerns and state our demands. Having a supportive group of women who understand our fears and urge each other on is key to building such confidence. Hazel Brown from Trinidad and Tobago was active in the Nestle boycott and brought lobbying skills, creative tactics, and knowledge of the UN system to bear on other consumer and women's health issues. As she puts it:

> We never thought we'd win. At home we built on our successes and on what we had learnt — know your facts, mobilize professionals to help you when possible, support each other, go after the top man, be creative in your strategies for confronting people and asking for help … Our group called itself the Housewives' Association. What could be less threatening than that, eh? But in our group women come in docile and go out radical.[28]

International women's health and consumer networks provide highly effective mechanisms to compile and distribute information not readily available to women in most countries. The networks have become essential sources of information about the structure and practices of the pharmaceutical industry, drugs banned in one country but available in others, side-effects experienced by women taking contraceptives, methods of health education, counselling about sexuality, herbal medicines, lobbying strategies, and sources of funding. Such information is compiled in a number of ways. Individual women document their experiences with drugs and devices. Regular correspondents to newsletters report on health services and major issues in their countries. Researchers have undertaken special projects including fact-finding missions in Latin America and Africa to determine what drugs are on the shelves in rural and urban pharmacies and what sorts of promotional materials are used by the pharmaceutical industry and to interview health professionals, policy makers, and consumers. Films, slide and tape shows, information kits, action guides, and plays based on such information are produced and distributed widely.[29] Unpublished or hard-to-find studies critical of industry practices or of government regulations are identified through the networks. Individuals or groups with access to good medical libraries or to information secured through freedom-of-information laws in their countries pass on data to those needing specific information.

Despite limited financial resources, international networks have been able to get information out quickly, particularly about dangerous drugs and devices. Contact groups or individuals in each country ensure that other organizations are informed. They encourage local media to publicize an issue.

These alternative sources of information allow health workers to make more informed decisions about the care they provide. As consumers of such services, women learn what questions to ask and what products to be wary of. Those involved in advocacy and lobbying secure information about other national regulations or about international codes. For example, The National Women's Health Network in the United States has written a readable critique showing how inadequately the US Food and Drug Administration (FDA) determines the safety of drugs, and the implications for child-bearing women.[30] Since the American system is considered by many to be among the most stringent in the world, this can help other groups identify major gaps in their drug approval process. Similarly, women's health groups in Bangladesh are monitoring the impact of the 1982 National Drug Policy. They have also pointed to the fact that contraceptives were *not* included in the review of potentially dangerous drugs.[31] Exchanging critical reviews of how drug regulatory systems and policies affect women helps national and international groups formulate their demands more effectively.

Perhaps the most important is the value these networks place on women's experiences. Women's stories about side-effects from drugs and devices and inadequate medical care are told and recorded at meetings, conferences, and tribunals. Such stories are printed and circulated, and the pain acknowledged as deeply felt. These experiences rarely find their way into the published studies on numbers of "contraceptive acceptors," or the outcome of various clinical trials. They may be the women lost to follow-up, or dropped from a study because they complained of side-effects within the first three months, or part of the percentage of women who experienced "unusually" severe reactions to a drug. Yet the detail offered in their personal accounts is essential to a careful, scientific evaluation of the effects of a drug and to understanding the process of informed consent. For example, many disabled Canadian women were given Depo-Provera for years while they were living in institutions. They were not part of systematic research or follow-up medical evaluations.[32] The personal stories recounted in a 1981 report, such as the following, are therefore particularly significant:

I've heard so much bad stuff about Depo from other disabled women. A friend of mine had to have a hysterectomy because of Depo. Me, I started on it when I was eighteen. I was in this place for disabled kids. I had bad, bad periods so instead of some other solution, they came up with Depo-Provera. They didn't get my consent. I didn't sign a thing. I remember them telling a whole room of us disabled girls that "there were absolutely no side-effects." That's exactly what the doctor said. I remember it clearly. It was 1970. I don't know if we were guinea pigs or what or if they were testing it on us. The staff made me feel that everything would be a lot easier if we just went along with Depo. If I would have known the side-effects, I never would have gone on it, never, not in a million years.

I took Depo shots every three months for ten years. Doctors should've known that people who are always sitting down, like me, in wheelchairs should never take that kind of drug. It causes bad circulatory problems. I gained weight like crazy ... It caused irregular bleeding, but really problems with my whole reproductive system. It changes cervical cells. My lining to my uterus got very thick. It inhibits mucus and makes intercourse very, very difficult and painful. ... I got terrible headaches. I also think that although there is a history of blood pressure problems in my family, my blood pressure problems were aggravated by Depo. I had a blood pressure attack and I almost died.

I have very serious gynaecological problems now. I keep telling them that I think my problems are related to Depo. They don't seem to hear me. Maybe they are afraid of what I am saying. I have been in severe pain for over a year now. They think it may be a fibroid or cysts. Legalizing Depo, I say forget it. Just don't. It's a very dangerous drug.

Other disabled women who took the drug for as many as sixteen years have similar and other complaints, including severe depression. It is important to compile and circulate such stories internationally, given the absence of studies of women who have taken the drug continuously for this length of time.[33] Feminist epidemiologists and other researchers can work with victims to document and assess such qualitative data. Through women's health networks, we can lobby to have such documentation accepted as essential evidence in the evaluation of the safety of a new drug.

Women's health networks provide a much needed forum for women to discuss how best to use our personal experiences to achieve short-term goals and to develop longer-term strategies. In relatively successful campaigns such as DES, women's experiences become a way to catch the interest of the media, the public, government officials, and health professionals and to force them to acknowledge the problem. Such media exposure may add to the trauma of being a victim. As one DES daughter summarized her feelings:

> When I go to talk to those people, I can see them stare and squirm. They're thinking: she's had CANCER. But they also listen to what I have to say, so although it's hard being a "professional victim" I try and use it to my advantage. Sharing experiences with DES daughters here and in other countries and planning our actions helps me deal with my feelings and keep my sense of humour.[34]

Going beyond being a "professional victim" means developing visions of the kinds of services and organizational structures we would like to see in each of our countries and sharpening our understanding of how necessary political, economic, and social transformations may occur.

BUILDING ORGANIZATIONS

Women involved in international health networks bring with us many organizational skills, learned as we struggle to develop alternative health services for women and more democratic organizational forms in each of our countries. Developing regional or national women's health networks are difficult organizational tasks. Most networks have co-ordinating groups, which depend largely on volunteer labour. Co-ordinators must ensure that administrative tasks get done — that conferences and other meetings are organized, newsletters written and mailed, requests for information and support for campaigns responded to, and funding proposals written.

Most women's health networks are not incorporated as formal organizations but are loose coalitions of groups. They try to include within their membership very broad representation of women's health groups from various regions or countries and encourage wide participation at meetings or through newsletters. Trying to ensure a democratic process in setting priorities and in allocating tasks can be difficult and time-consuming at a local level.

"Working collectively across continents can be a mammoth task," as one British health activist put it. Major meetings are usually alternated among regions of the world, not only to shift the responsibilities of organizing such events but to permit women in a particular country to extend their own networks. For example, ISIS shares responsibilities and tasks, including publications, with women in Latin America and in this way has responded to an expressed need for information on women's health written in Spanish. In response to its rapid growth, the HAI network, which already divides co-ordinating tasks between the Netherlands and Malaysia, is instituting broad discussions among its membership concerning·future structure. Regular policy conferences, regional meetings, and representation on a co-ordinating body may be necessary as groups become too unwieldy for less formal structures.[35] These networks reject traditional concepts of aid and dependency and work from principles of collaboration, mutual exchange of resources, and support between First World and Third World participants.

For women involved in national and international women's health networks, the debates about structure and policies are complex. On the one hand, they must address concerns *internal* to an autonomous women's movement. International women's health networks are not immune to attitudes in the wider social order. Women of minority races and disabled women have raised concerns about racism or their minimal representation in such networks. This has often led to debate and a re-examination of policies and practices. Increasingly, special interest constituencies are forming their own networks nationally and internationally, for example, the Disabled Peoples International and DAWN, the Disabled Women's Network in Canada. It is as members of these larger groups that women may find a stronger voice and exchange information through women's health networks.

Conferences and newsletters provide opportunities for debating other problematic issues among women, such as differing cultural and religious attitudes towards abortion. Disabled women voice concerns that the new reproductive technologies, while holding out promise for some women with infertility problems, may be used to limit their choices and create further deep-seated prejudices against disablement. Women want the right to question unsafe, poorly tested birth control methods and have them removed from international markets, but, as Indian economist Gita Sen asks, "How do we distinguish ourselves in our campaigns from those persons against all forms of birth control and those trying to limit women's rights to safe abortion?"[36] Women exchange views on whether to accept particular government or foundation funds for their work and how to effect changes in policies and practices of male-dominated institutions. We strategize and fantasize about determining the priorities for funding contraceptive research and setting the criteria for what are considered ethical clinical trials. While consensus may not be achieved, women emerge with a clearer understanding of such issues that they can take back to their local communities.

On the other hand, debates about the structure and policies of international women's health networks must address questions about their *external* links to other networks and organizations, including some dominated by men. For example, the International Women's Network on Pharmaceuticals, co-ordinated through WEMOS, is compiling information about actions and research on women and drugs undertaken by groups throughout the world in order to develop more effective strategies for campaigns and the sharing of information. The network is part of Health Action International and influences policy priorities and research within the broader network. For example, its suggestion that the WHO develop an Essential List of Contraceptives similar to its List of Essential Drugs was presented by HAI and favourably received at a WHO Experts Meeting in 1985.[37] Since 1981, radical policy initiatives have been proposed by HAI participants — both women and men — such as an International Code of Pharmaceutical Marketing Practice, suggestions for an information clearing house and policies that would change the structure of the market, the nature of the industry, the training of health workers, and community attitudes that see every ill solved by a pill.[38] To bring these initiatives to fruition requires the collaboration of women consumers, health professionals, and researchers such as those identified through the women's network on pharmaceuticals. The evolving and sometimes delicate relations between these networks reflect a crucial alliance with a common goal: the rational use of pharmaceuticals on a world-wide scale.

FUTURE CHALLENGES

As women from different countries and different social classes meet to share our stories and debate these issues, we find we have certain things in common: the state and transnational corporations play invasive roles in our lives. National governments decide what contraceptive methods will be available and to whom: middle- and upper-class women may be urged to bear children, while poor or disabled women are the subjects of intense measures of population control. Some of us are over-medicated; others are under-medicated, victims of what has been termed "an international state of crisis ... which affects the development, production, distribution and use of pharmaceuticals."[39] On the other hand, some of us have greater access to basic resources and to information than others.

All over the world more and more people are sick as a result of the inappropriate use of medicines, from living near dangerous waste dumps or from drinking contaminated water, or as a result of where we or our partners work. Women of all social classes are experiencing more miscarriages, birth defects, and chronic illness. Men suffer damage to their reproductive systems and other illnesses. Children's health is endangered.[40] As we come to recognize how our personal lives are determined by such external forces, we experience anger, often a powerful catalyst to political action.

The interdependence of social and environmental issues on a global scale means that those working in the women's health movement must at times join forces with those working in networks and constituencies in the environmental, anti-nuclear, consumer movements, and with social justice activitists in the churches and in the international development community. This co-ordination is often difficult in terms of time and priorities, but it can prove an effective challenge to transnational corporations, as the activities of IBFAN have shown.[41]

International women's health networks are part of broad social movements that are becoming increasingly sophisticated in methods of challenging international capital and forcing governments to greater public accountability. The networks in these social movements tend to be loose coalitions, somewhat amorphous, able to respond with flexibility and creativity to crises. There are many challenges ahead. Groups must work together and mobilize further support without becoming inflexible and overly bureaucratized. Traditionally male-dominated organizations must deal honestly with the institutionalized sexism in their own backyards. The initiatives documented in this article suggest that there are many problems to be overcome and little money to help us attain our visions of a healthy, socially just, sexually equitable society. But there is considerable energy, commitment, mutual support, expertise, and political savvy to work with. And for most women, that's nothing new; it's the elements out of which we've always made history.

◄►

NOTES

1. The UN End of Decade for Women Non-Governmental Organization (NGO) Forum took place July 8 — 19, 1985, and the official UN Conference, July 15 — 23. The latter conference brought together about three thousand official delegates and media personnel. The previous Decade for Women conferences took place in Mexico City in 1975 and in Copenhagen in 1980.

2. The subthemes of the decade were health, employment and education. A consensus was not at all assured at the beginning of the conference since questions of procedure and substance were unresolved. The landmark Forward Looking Strategies Document is progressive and should be used as a lobbying tool by women's organizations throughout the world.

3. See for example, the range of groups and organizations listed in the newsletters and publications of the International Women's Tribune Centre, 777 United Nations Plaza, New York, N.Y. 10017. On networks for alternative development strategies, see Gita Sen with Caren Grown for Development Alternatives with Women for a New Era (DAWN), *Development, Crisis, and Alternative Visions: Third World Women's Perspectives,* Norway, June, 1985.

4. Bulletins and publications are available from ISIS International, Casilla 2067, Correo Central, Santiago, Chile; and Via Santa Maria dell 'Anima, 00186, Roma, Italia.

5. Information about the tribunal and other activities of the network are available from P.O. Box 4098, 1009 AB Amsterdam, Netherlands.

6. HAI News includes information on health policies and specific drugs in various countries, on useful resources, reports of seminars and conferences. This and other information is available from: The HAI Clearinghouse, IOCU, P.O. Box 1045, 10830 Penang, Malaysia.

7. WEMOS is an action and research group that launched a successful campaign to have Organon, the Dutch transnational pharmaceutical firm, withdraw anabolic steriods from being sold as appetite stimulants in Third World countries.

8. *Side Effects* was seen by over eight thousand people across Canada when it toured the country in the spring and fall of 1985. It was written and produced by members of the Great Canadian Theatre Company in Ottawa in collaboration with Women's Health Interaction, a Canadian women's health network linked to Health Action International. It received rave reviews. For more information about the play and other materials produced for community action, contact: Women's Health Interaction, c/o Inter Pares, 58 Arthur St. Ottawa, Ontario, Canada KIR 7B9.

9. See, for example, Nicholas Freudenberg, *Not in Our backyards* (New York: Monthly Review Press, 1984) for a discussion of some of these movements.

10. See Report of the World Conference of the United Nations Decade for Women, Copenhagen 1980, A/CONF/.94/35 and "Review and Appraisal: Health," presented to the World Conference to Review and Appraise the Achievements of the United Nations Decade for Women: Equality, Development and Peace (Nairobi, Kenya, July 1985) A/CONF.116/5.

11. See, for example, Ruth Cooperstock and Jessica Hill, *The Effects of Tranquillization: Benzodiazepine Use in Canada* (Ottawa: Health Promotion Directorate, Health and Welfare Canada, 1982) for a discussion of why women are prescribed more tranquillizers than men. See also P. Susan Penfold and Gillian Walker, *Women and the Psychiatric Paradox* (Montreal: Eden Press, 1983).

12. Further discussion of these factors is available in Dianna Melrose, *Bitter Pills* (Oxford, England: Public Affairs Unit, Oxfam-UK, 1982) and in Mike Muller, *The Health of Nations* (London: Faber and Faber, 1982).

13. Giovanna Merola, unpublished paper, Caracas, Venezuela, April 1985.

14. This information was provided by a Bangladesh physician at a workshop entitled "Quality Health Services" at the UN End of Decade for Women NGO Forum in Nairobi, Kenya, July 1985.

15. Information provided by a Moroccan physician at a workshop entitled "Women as Consumers" at the UN End of Decade for Women NGO Forum in Nairobi, Kenya, July 1985.

16. For useful discussions of project criteria and development policies in relation to women, see G. Sen, *op. cit;* Barbara Rogers, *The Domestication of Women: Discrimination in Developing Societies* (London: Tavistock, 1981); and Nicky May and Georgina Ashworth, *Of Conjuring and Caring: Women in Development* (London: Change International Reports, 1982).

17. Milton Silverman, *The Drugging of the Americas* (Berkeley, Calif.: University of California Press, 1976); Dianna Melrose, *op. cit.;* Virginia Beardshaw, *Prescription for Change,* (The Hague: IOCU, 1984); and Joel Lexchin, *The Real Pushers: A Critical Analysis of the Canadian Drug Industry* (Vancouver: New Star Press, 1984).

18. See the discussion in Lexchin, *op. cit.,* 1984.

19. "DES Action — Final Report to the Skaggs Foundation," 1985 (unpublished). See also the article in this volume by Ellen 't Hoen and Anita Direcks on DES.

20. For a more detailed discussion of this campaign see the article by Mira Shiva and Carla Marcelis in this volume.

21. A considerable amount of information is available on the Dalkon Shield. The most comprehensive treatment is Morton Mintz, *At Any Cost: Corporate Greed, Women and the Dalkon Shield* (New York: Pantheon Books, 1985).

22. The courtroom speeches of Judge Lord are quoted in full in Mintz, *op. cit,* pp.255 — 69. The specific quotation is on page 266.

23. See "Report of the Public Board of Inquiry on Depo-Provera," Judith Weisz, chairperson, 1984: and the film *The Ultimate Test Animal,* produced by Karen Brannan and Bill Turnley, Minneapolis, Minn., for a critical review of the major clinical trials of Depo-Provera in the United States.

24 Anne Pappert, "Disputed Drug May Be Approved as Contraceptive," the Toronto *Globe and Mail,* Nov. 22, 1985, p.1. Other information is available from the Canadian Coalition on Depo-Provera, c/o Winniepeg Women's Health Clinic, 404 Graham St., Winnipeg, Man.

25. *Long-Acting Progestins — Promise and Prospects,* Johns Hopkins University, Population Reports, Series K, No. 2, May 1983.

26. More information about the AFSC Project is available from AFSC Nationwide Women's Program, 1501 Cherry St. Philadelphia, Penn., U.S.A. 19102.

27. Mike Muller wrote *The Baby Killer* (London: War on Want, 1974), the original investigation into the promotion and sale of powdered baby milk in the Third World. Andy Chetley's book, *The Baby Killer Scandal,* (London: War on want, 1979) provided an important update of the boycott and company's responses. He has since written *The Politics of Baby Foods* (1985).

28. Hazel Brown, in the workshop "Women as Consumers" at the UN End of Decade for Women NGO Forum, Nairobi, Kenya, July 1985.

29. Numerous resources have been produced. For example, *Hard to Swallow,* a video film produced by Oxfam-UK in 1984; the video *A Healthy Business,* on the pharmaceutical industry in Asia; HAI *Problem Drugs,* 1986; other resources are listed regularly in HAI News.

30. "How the F.D.A. Determines the 'Safety' or Drugs — Just How Safe Is 'Safe'?" A Report released to the Congress of the United States by the National Women's Health Network, Washington, D.C. Prepared by Doris Haire, 1984.

31. Bangladesh's Drug Ordinance was passed in June 1982; it calls for the removal from the market of some seventeen hundred drugs that were considered harmful or non-essential. Despite many political obstacles, much progress has been made. See Andy Chetley, *Bangladesh: Finding the Right Prescription,* War On Want Briefing Paper, London, 1982, Dexter Tiranti, *Essential Drugs: The Bangladesh Example — Four Years On,* IOCU, New Internationalist, War on Want, Oxford, 1986.

32. See Zarfas, Fyre, Gorodyinsky, "The Utilization of Depo Provera in the Ontario Government Facilities for the Mentally Retarded." (Toronto: Ontario Ministry of Community and Social Services, 1981). This study was commissioned after three women who were taking Depo Provera died of breast cancer. The study could not draw clear causal links between the use of Depo and the deaths but was highly critical of the lack of monitoring of the health of the women to whom Depo was administered. Girls as young as eleven years old were given the drug for hygienic reasons.

33. Studies by the drug's manufacturer, Upjohn, refer to "woman-years of use"; upon closer scrutiny, such data reflect large numbers of women on the drug for relatively short periods of time. There are no controlled studies of women who have taken it for more than seven or eight years.

34. Personal communication from a Canadian DES daughter, 1985.

35. HAI internal documents, February 1986.

36. Gita Sen, in a workshop on Alternative Development Strategies, at the UN End of Decade for Women NGO Forum in Nairobi, Kenya, July 1985.

37. The Conference of Experts on The Rational Use of Drugs was held in Nairobi, Kenya, November 25 — 9, 1985, and included ninety-two participants from the health professions, industry, government, and consumers. The conference was significant since it included consumers as equal participants and acknowledged their role in "improving the relevance and quality of information for the public; sharing responsibility with governments and non-governmental organizations for the education of consumers on drug matters; maintaining vigilance and demanding compliance with established norms for drug advertising, and drawing the attention of the health authorities to suspected infringements; and supporting essential drugs programes." (Rational Use of Drugs: Cooperation Prevails at WHO Conference in Spirit of Nairobi, WHO Press Release WHO/32, Dec. 3, 1985). For a brief summary of the meeting see editorial, *Development Dialogue,* no. 2, 1985.

38. See "Summary Conclusions," the Dag Hammarskjold Seminar on Another Development in Pharmaceuticals, organized by the Dag Hammarskjold Foundation in Uppsala, Sweden, June 3 — 6, 1985. Published as a special issue of *Development Dialogue,* no. 2, 1985. The proceedings of this conference address a wide range of policy issues on the international regulation of pharmaceuticals. See also Charles Medawar. *Drugs and World Health* (The Hague: IOCU, 1984); and Health Action International, *An International Code of Pharmaceutical Marketing Practice,* Discussion Document, May 1982.

39. "Summary Conclusions," *Development Dialogue,* no. 2, 1985, p.130.

40. See for example, John Jackson, Phil Weller, and the Waterloo Public Interest Research Group, *Chemical Nightmare: The Unnecessary Legacy of Toxic Wastes,* (Toronto: Between The Lines Press, 1982); Harriet Rosenberg, "The Kitchen and the Multinational Corporation: An Analysis of the Links between the Household and Global Corporations," in Meg Luxton and Harriet Rosenberg: *Through the Kitchen Window: The Politics of Home and Family,* (Toronto: Garamond Press, 1986); Nancy Miller Chenier, *Reproductive Hazards At Work: Men, Women and the Fertility Gamble,* (Ottawa: Canadian Advisory Council on the Status of Women, 1982); and David Weir and Mark Schapiro, *Circle of Poison* (San Francisco: Institute for Food and Development Policy, 1981).

41. For a discussion of ways that such groups work together see Freudenberg, 1984, *op. cit.*

NOTES ON THE AUTHORS

VIMAL BALASUBRAHMANYAN is a freelance journalist who writes on health, women, and population issues for a variety of Indian newspapers and journals. She is the author of the booklet *Contraception as if Women Mattered: A Critique of Family Planning,* published by the Centre for Education and Documentation in Bombay.

ANITA DIRECKS is a founder of DES Action in the Netherlands. A Social Academy graduate, she developed a special interest in women's health issues through her DES activities and is now working to develop a feminist perspective on new reproductive technologies.

LYNN DUGGAN is a graduate student in economics at the University of Massachusetts in Amherst. She investigated the use of Depo-Provera in Southeast Asia during extensive field study in 1981.

ANN ROCHON FORD has worked extensively as an activist and writer in the women's health movement in Canada. She established DES Action in Toronto and is on the board of directors of DES Action/Canada. She currently works as Resource Co-ordinator of Women's Health Care Programs at Women's College Hospital in Toronto.

JIM HARDING was director of research for the Saskatchewan Alcohol and Drug Abuse Commission in Canada from 1977-9. Since then he has taught at the School of Human Justice at the University of Regina. He has published and lectured widely on such issues as the medicalization of socio-economic problems and the proliferation of pharmaceuticals. He welcomes inquiries regarding the research presented in his article, c/o School of Human Justice, University of Regina, Regina, Saskatchewan S4S 0A2 Canada.

ELLEN 'T HOEN is a co-founder of DES Action in the Netherlands and a Social Academy graduate. Besides DES, she has a general interest in women and pharmaceuticals, particularly drugs used in pregnancy and the consumption of hormones by women in Third World countries.

CARY LaCHEEN researched and wrote her article while working at the Institute for Policy Studies in Washington, D.C. She has also worked as a researcher at Public Citizen Health Research Group, a Washington-based organization that monitors the activities of the pharmaceutical industry, and the United States Food and Drug Administration. She is currently attending law school in New York City.

CARLA MARCELIS has been involved for a number of years in women's health and pharmaceutical issues in the Netherlands, both with WEMOS, a Third World solidarity group, and Health Action International. She recently moved to Canada, where she is active in Women's Health Interaction, a network concerned with women's health and development issues.

KATHLEEN McDONNELL is a writer, editor, and playwright who lives in Toronto. She is the author of *Not an Easy Choice: A Feminist Re-examines Abortion* and co-editor of *The Healthsharing Book,* both published by Women's Press in Toronto, Canada.

ANN PAPPERT is a journalist who has written extensively on women's health issues and other topics for a variety of Canadian newspapers and magazines.

MILAGROS P. QUERUBIN teaches community nutrition at the University of the Philippines, and is a research consultant with AKAP and the Health Action Information Network. AKAP which stands for *Alay Kapwa Kilusang Pang Kalusugan* (or Share a Friend Health Movement) is a community health organization in the Philippines.

MIRA SHIVA, M.D. is the co-ordinator of Low-Cost Drugs and Rational Therapeutics of the Voluntary Health Association of India, an organization composed of some 1,400 community health clinics across the country. She is also the co-ordinator of the All India Drug Action Network, which spearheaded the campaigns against EP drugs and injectable contraceptives in India.

MICHAEL L. TAN teaches anthropology at the University of the Philippines. He also heads the Health Action Information Network and is research director of AKAP.

SARI TUDIVER works as Project Officer for Women and Development with the Manitoba Council for International Cooperation, a coalition of thirty Canadian organizations which sponsors development projects overseas. She is active in a number of local, national, and international health networks, including Women's Health Interaction and Health Action International. She holds a doctorate in Anthropology from the University of Michigan.

◄►

Resources

The following list is by no means an exhaustive one, but can serve as a starting point for readers who wish further information on some of the issues dealt with in this anthology.

ORGANIZATIONS

WEMOS/HAI International Women's Network on Pharmaceuticals

P.O. Box 4098
1009 BA Amsterdam
The Netherlands
(020) 653115

Launched at a Health Action International (HAI) meeting in June, 1985, the network's aims are to provide women all over the world with unbiased information on drugs, to stimulate research on the drugs that women take and on non-drug alternatives, and to do political advocacy on pharmaceutical issues as they relate to women.

ISIS-Women's International Cross-Cultural Exchange

29 rue des Gares
C.P. 2471
1211 Geneva 2, Switzerland
(022) 336746

Isis-WICCE is a research and documentation centre which has produced a number of publications concerned with women, health care, and pharmaceuticals with an international perspective.

Latin American and Caribbean Women's Health Network

c/o Isis Internacional
Casilla 2067
Correo Central
Santiago, Chile
490271

This is a network of over four hundred groups in Latin America and the Caribbean concerned with women, health, and pharmaceuticals.

DES Action International

Contact addresses:
DES Action Australia
P.O. Box 282
Camberwell
Victoria 3124, Australia

DES Action Canada (Non-European francophone countries)
Snowdon P.O. Box 233
Montreal, Quebec H3X 3T4
Canada
(514) 482-3204

**DES Action The Netherlands
(Europe and Africa)**
*Maliesingel 46
3581 BM Utrecht
The Netherlands
(01131) 30-312331/340472*

**DES Action U.S.A. (Asia and
Latin America)**
*2845 - 24th St.
San Francisco, California 94110
U.S.A.
(415) 826-5060*

The international DES network
was formed at the United Nations
Decade for Women Conference in
Nairobi, Kenya, in July 1985 to
publicize the DES story in other
countries and to co-ordinate the
effort to obtain a world-wide ban
on DES.

Health Action Information Network (HAIN)

*49 Scout Madrinan
Quezon City,
Philippines*

A network of health organizations
which has been active in issues
pertaining to women and
pharmaceuticals in the
Philippines, and particularly in
promoting women's role in
primary health care programs.

Voluntary Health Association of India (VHAI)

*C-14 Community Centre
Safdarjung Development Area
New Delhi 110016,
India*

This organization has been
instrumental in the campaign to
have EP drugs taken off the
market in India.

National Women's Health Network

*224 Seventh St. S.E.
Washington, D.C. 20003
U.S.A.
(202) 543-9222*

The U.S. National Women's
Health Network is active in a wide
range of women's health issues,
among them Depo-Provera and
the Dalkon Shield IUD.

Women's Health Interaction

*58 Arthur St.
Ottawa, Ont. K1R 7B9
(613) 563-4801*

A Canadian women's health
network which focusses largely on
pharmaceutical issues, WHI
produced a play about women and
drugs, *Side Effects*, in 1984-85.
They also distribute a periodic
newsletter and an information kit,
*For Health or For Profit: The
Pharmaceutical Industry in the
Third World and in Canada*.

Women's Global Network on Reproductive Rights

*P.O. Box 4098
1009 AB Amsterdam
The Netherlands*

Among other things, this
international network is concerned with the uses and a-
buses of pharmaceuticals in
family planning.

PRINT RESOURCES

Who Needs Depo Provera?
by Marge Berer, 1984
Available from:
Community Rights Project
157 Waterloo Road
London SE1,
U.K.

A comprehensive booklet on Depo-Provera, intended as a guide for women considering taking the drug and as general information for those who want to know more about its history, adverse effects, and related concerns.

The Strategic Womb
by Betsy Hartmann, forthcoming from Harper and Row, New York, spring, 1987

This book is an analysis of the politics of population control in developing countries, and extensively explores the use of contraceptive drugs and devices in family planning programs.

The Effects of Tranquilization: Benzodiazepine Use in Canada
by Ruth Cooperstock and Jessica Hill, 1982
Available from:
Health Promotion Directorate
Health and Welfare Canada
Ottawa, Ont. K1A 1B4
Canada

This short book explores the phenomenon of the over-prescription of minor tranquilizers to women and includes data on drug use by elderly women.